FOPLAY2

D1378186

ARTHUR PONSONBY
The Politics of Life

Raymond A. Jones

'It was the politics of life which we spoke not the politics of parties'

Diary, 2 April 1903

CHRISTOPHER HELM
London

Christopher Helm (Publishers) Ltd, Imperial House,
21–25 North Street, Bromley BR1 1SD

ISBN 0–7470–1611–9

A CIP catalogue record for this book
is available from the British Library

Typeset by Opus, Oxford
Printed and bound in Great Britain by Biddles Ltd, Guildford, Surrey

Acknowledgements

Arthur Ponsonby's papers are used by permission of the copyright holder, Thomas, Lord Ponsonby of Shulbrede, from whom I have received unfailing encouragement and support. A double debt of gratitude must be expressed to Catherine Russell for her hospitality at Shulbrede Priory and for having undertaken the onerous task of reducing the Shulbrede Archives to order. Many librarians and archivists have facilitated the research upon which this book is based. In thanking Dr Angela Raspin, the archivist of the British Library of Economic and Political Science, who arranged the microfilm of Arthur Ponsonby's Diary, I thank them all.

Funding for my research was provided by the Social Sciences and Humanities Research Council of Canada and the office of the Dean of Arts, Carleton University. My wife, Margaret, has undertaken the preparation of the manuscript and has provided the support without which undertaking such an enterprise such as this would have been impossible.

CONTENTS

INTRODUCTION

Belief in the value of individual actions and the ability of individuals to shape events underlies this biography. Political biography is usually reserved for eminent people, Prime Ministers, Foreign Secretaries, and others who qualify as statesmen. However, other political figures who never achieved high office have made significant contributions to the political life of the nation. Such a person was Arthur Ponsonby, whose career in politics kept him on the backbenches except for two periods of minor office in the first two Labour governments and a longer period as opposition whip in the 'Citadel of inaction' in the early thirties. When measured by the standard of high office, it seems that his was a nondescript career of little importance. What makes Ponsonby significant is that he was one of A.J.P. Taylor's 'trouble-makers' whom Taylor credits with all change and advance in history.[1] While some would say that this is a typically large and perverse Taylorism, it is not without an element of truth when applied to the role played by Ponsonby and his fellow troublemakers in the search for a new international order.

The main theme of the biography is Ponsonby's internationalism. All his efforts were directed at removing force from international relations. Ponsonby's new international order was to be based on the moral authority of democracy. The means to this end was to be the democratic control of foreign policy which he advocated before 1914 and whose most visible expression today is to be found in the constitutional practice of the 'Ponsonby Rule'. The search for a new international order through democratic control was to take Ponsonby far from the corridors of power in the Foreign Office where he briefly served at the turn of the century. Pressure group politics in the Union of Democratic Control and the Peace Pledge Union were played out in dingy committee rooms and small backstreet halls the length and breadth of the country.

If the most important aspect of Ponsonby's career in politics was his internationalism, his life in politics is also notable for the unique record left behind in his papers of many of the leading figures of his time. He was a close observer of character and was in a position to record the strengths, weaknesses, foibles and eccentricities of many great contemporaries from

Edward VII's ginger beer laugh, Winston Churchill's musings on the trappings of power, and Ramsay MacDonald's suicidal despair to the eccentric mannerisms of Margot Asquith and Ottoline Morrell, and the unstable glitter of the Bright Young People, in whose antics his own daughter was to be tragically trapped.

The title of the book is drawn from an entry in Ponsonby's Diary referring to a conversation in 1902 with Charles Masterman when they were both about to enter political life. The politics of life seems particularly apt for a man whose ideas, it was said, were always in advance of the parties he served. Although a socialist by conviction, even before he entered parliament, he found a niche in Edwardian politics as a Liberal backbench critic of the balance of power politics of Grey's foreign policy. Rejecting the hysterical chauvinism of 1914, Ponsonby almost single-handedly, aided only by a tiny handful of radical friends, campaigned for a negotiated end to the war, and with them developed both a critique of the pre-war international system and the basis for a new international order – ideas that were to become highly influential in the new war aims debate at the end of the war.

If the war failed to resolve the international tensions that had led to its outbreak in 1914, it only too well succeeded in realigning the left in British politics. Ponsonby joined the Labour Party and, for a time, working with Ramsay MacDonald, together they made a valiant but unavailing attempt in 1924 to realign European politics. Their friendship derailed by the Zinoviev letter, Ponsonby drifted away from MacDonald embarking on his peace letter campaign in the country and, within the party, on disarmament by example, an early and often misunderstood first move towards unilateralism.

After the creation of the National Government, which in effect suspended the democratic process, Ponsonby's political life, now based in the Lords, centred on grassroots pacifism in a vain attempt to provide an alternative to rearmament and a new war. With the failure of appeasement and with the Nazi phenomenon providing impeccable credentials for a just war, the opponents of war were more isolated than ever. The Second World War gave power politics a new lease of life leading inevitably in the post-war era to the paradox of peace in a nuclear age. The search for a new international order continues unabated. Yet, progress has been made. Today, unbridled *raison d'état* which triggered war in 1914 would be unthinkable, and it is to that sea change that Ponsonby made his contribution to the politics of life.

1. Taylor (1969), p. 14.

CHAPTER ONE

Formative Years: 1871–1908

A Victorian Childhood

Arthur Augustus William Harry Ponsonby was born in the Norman Tower of Windsor Castle on 16 February 1871, the third son of General Sir Henry Ponsonby, Queen Victoria's principal private secretary, and his wife Mary Elizabeth. His paternal grandparents were Major-General Sir Frederick Cavendish Ponsonby, who served throughout the Peninsular campaign, and, miraculously, survived wounds from both sabre and lance on the field of Waterloo and his wife Emily, daughter of Henry, 3rd Earl Bathurst. His maternal grandparents were John Crocker Bulteel, MP and his wife Elizabeth, daughter of Charles, 2nd Earl Grey. A Ponsonby, a Bathurst, a Bulteel and a Grey. The Ponsonbys came from Cumberland, where they were established in the thirteenth century. An Irish branch of the family prospered and became the Earls of Bessborough. Sir Frederick Ponsonby was the son of the 3rd Earl of Bessborough, and, in Arthur's opinion, was the most distinguished member of the whole line. 'The Ponsonbys,' he wrote in his diary 'are very recognizable, generally fair, sometimes fat and rather awkward in movement. I have never heard of one who was a scholar, but very few of them have been fools. Wit is certainly their distinguishing mark, a peculiar apt, racy, humour, a twinkle and, sometimes, a thrust which is extremely amusing.' Characteristically, Arthur then concludes this little family portrait with the assertion that 'The present lot seem to have lost all the distinction of the last generation and are unforgivably dull.'

If Arthur held a low opinion of the Ponsonbys, his view of the Bathursts was even more severe. 'They were one of the dreariest families in the world. . . snobbish aristocrats, pretentious and punctilious, honest enough, but without a spark of originality which the Ponsonbys certainly had.' The Bulteels were largely unknown to Arthur, but he characterised them as 'a Devonshire county family, sporting, and quite unintellectual'. The Greys were certainly more distinguished and Ponsonby's favourite was his great-grandfather Charles, Earl Grey 'an advanced, almost revolution-

1

ary, aristocrat with a great love of domesticity – very charming and attractive, and wonderfully persistent, with a high sense of public duty'.

These quotations are taken from the retrospective part of Ponsonby's Diary written in 1911, when his political career as a radical had just been established, but long before his public notoriety as a socialist and pacifist. Even so, he concludes the passage 'I have never made any friends among my relations. I know very few of them and see them very rarely. Many of them regard me as an oddity some as a black sheep.'[1]

However mediocre Arthur's family antecedents may have appeared to him, they were, without a doubt, impeccably aristocratic. The family lived primarily at Windsor Castle, where their children were born, they knew no other home. Sir Henry had first lived in the Cloisters, and then moved into the Private Secretary's residence, the Norman Tower, on taking up his appointment in 1870. Alberta (Betty), the Ponsonbys' eldest child, was born in 1862, her sister, Magdalen (Maggie), in 1865, Arthur's brothers, John and Frederick (Fritz), in 1866 and 1867. There he grew up, surrounded by the trappings of monarchy. He was sent to a preparatory school at Farnborough, and then Eton was followed by Balliol College, Oxford. This conventional upper-class upbringing and education was taken in stride by Ponsonby. The qualities of mind and character that were eventually to produce the radical and pacifist were latent. There was no sign of the rebel passion of his mature years.

While Sir Henry Ponsonby is well remembered as Queen Victoria's secretary, the details of his life are chiefly known today because of Arthur's award-winning biography[2] completed and published during the Second World War, but in the memoir of his mother he writes: 'I am not mentioning my father, partly because I saw him very little and knew him therefore very little. He seemed always to be working.' This abrupt treatment reflected the strange environment of the Norman Tower. Sir Henry was the perfect embodiment of a private secretary, piloting the Queen through the political shoals of partisan politics with consummate skill and efficiency, but he had to be constantly available both at Windsor and also at Osborne, and in the summer at Balmoral. Locked despatch boxes were always beside his plate at breakfast, and the scratch of his quill pen was heard at night as the children went to bed. He took a quiet delight in family life, but was undemonstrative, given in trying times to morose silences. The special quality that Arthur inherited from his father was gentleness. Lord Stamfordham and Arthur Benson both considered Sir Henry a great gentleman, without conceit, always amiable 'the most perfectly and beautifully courteous man'.

Mary Ponsonby was a remarkable Victorian in her own right. She was very much more than simply the Queen's friend whose husband was her private secretary. Late in life, Arthur Ponsonby was led to write about

2

some people who had influenced him.[3] By far the largest essay is devoted to his mother. He was not at all sure of the propriety of the exercise, but felt compelled to write about his mother's 'overwhelming influence which permeated my thoughts and actions in trivial as much as in the great from my birth as I well know it will be to my death'.

As a small boy Arthur was shy, introverted and silent. 'I was very slow wondered at many things observed nothing. I was silent timid ready to do what I was told – but not the least original or spontaneous.' The family said he suffered from 'brain fog'. They were loquacious and amusing, arguments on all topics were normal and often heated. Naturally, Arthur, the youngest, failed to grasp the significance of the points under discussion, and developed a strong dislike for these situations, preferring an inner world of pretending. He hated lessons, but did not like getting things wrong, so got into the habit of pretending he could do things and know things of which he had very little idea.

If Windsor Castle was Arthur Ponsonby's home, so was it also Queen Victoria's, and Arthur grew up surrounded by the trappings of royalty. The Queen was an acknowledged institution. 'I could see her every day driving out with 2 grey horses and the outrider. In the winter evenings the lamplighter would tear round with his lantern and ladder to light up all the quadrangle lamps before she returned.' At Christmas and during the summer, the court went to Osborne. On hearing that Arthur admired Nelson, she gave him, one year, a print and Southey's Life, and, another year, a print of Wellington. There were rules for children – 'if you met the Queen or saw her outrider approaching you had to bolt for your life'. Maggie, walking with Sir William Harcourt, one day saw the white horse approach. 'You must run and hide,' she cried. 'Do you expect me to hide behind that?' he said pointing to a fir tree two feet high. The Queen was awe-inspiring and of extraordinary distinction, especially when compared to the rest of the royal family, who were, with the exception of the Empress Frederick, very ordinary and often stupid and ignorant.

When Arthur was eleven, he became a page of honour and attended a dozen drawing rooms, the Duke of Albany's wedding and the opening of Parliament in 1886. In red coat and white breeches, Arthur went to Buckingham Palace in a royal coach. Arthur's precise factual and unpretentious reporting of the people whom he recognised at the Drawing Room would have quite disappointed his colossal snob of a headmaster at Farnborough, had he been privileged to read it. Arthur simply regarded court functions as fun, especially as they involved getting a day off school.

I was never impressed by them nor was I the least proud of being a page. I took it quite naturally because my family with all their faults were never proud of their position and if anything looked down on rank and grandeur.

A GLORIOUS PAGE IN LABOUR'S HISTORY!

• SIXTY-EIGHT YEARS AGO CAME THE ONLY HUMAN LINK BETWEEN VICTORIA AND LABOUR!•

Arthur's governesses and tutors made little impression on his 'brain fog'. One governess produced the reaction of feigned illness and another used to lose her temper and roar at Arthur's stupidity. Arthur was quite musical, could play the violin after a fashion and sing. This, for a Victorian child, meant becoming a choir boy. His first choir was in a village above Windsor. Later he sang with the choir of St George's Chapel in Windsor Castle.

In 1882 Arthur was sent to Morton's preparatory school at Farnborough about six miles from Windsor. A fashionable school inhabited by Tecks, Cadogans and Hoods, Ponsonby later said it turned him into something of a prig. Contemporary evidence suggests a normal enough schoolboy life. Meals often were little more than sardines and weak tea, but he enjoyed his lessons, was reasonably proficient at Maths, played the fiddle

4

sufficiently well for school concerts, won prizes for drawing and had his teeth smashed by a cricket ball. His school reports all agree that Arthur's work was not very good.

'What I wish for him most is that he should become really interested in something, I do not much care what.'

This last report was written by Francis Warre Cornish, in whose House Arthur and his brother Fritz resided during their time at Eton.

Arthur was singularly fortunate in having Warre Cornish as his housemaster. Cornish, author of a number of scholarly works and a notable bibliophile, took a genuine interest in his boys. A small, older looking man than his years, who, Arthur thought, exactly resembled Holbein's portrait of Sir Thomas Godsabre, he had the curious habit, when particularly interested or seriously annoyed, of twisting his legs round one another. In his memoir of Cornish, Arthur records that his own laziness, apathy and indifference did not prevent Cornish from liking him and that this was the stimulant which made him 'wake up'.

As Captain of the house, he sat next to his housemaster at lunch, where Cornish would draw him out on the day's news, making impatient little noises if he felt Arthur had not read his paper intelligently. Mrs Cornish was a much more famous Eton personality than her husband. She is not mentioned in the memoir, but in a letter to his mother written in July 1889, the year in which he left Eton, Arthur reported that he had been out for an enormous water party with the Cornishes. 'Mrs C was in great form when we were rowing her home she said she thought being rowed along was the most delicious sensation "all the angles of life completely disappear".'

Arthur spent five and a half years at Eton, years that were enormously enjoyable. By Eton standards he had made his mark, House Captain and that ultimate Etonian accolade, election to Pop;

. . . getting into Pop was an immense surprise and of course an overwhelming honour. Nothing in after life can quite come up to it. Swaggering about with a cane in stick up collars childishly self conscious of the impression I was making seemed a great joy.

Arthur was Secretary of the Musical Society and President of his House Debating Society. These debates he later described as being the only spontaneously intellectual occupation that he found at Eton. Arthur was a dry bob, but not good enough to enjoy cricket. He was a much better player at fives and football. This pleasant round of sporting and social activities was only partially interrupted by academic work. The brain fog of earlier years remained and he only scraped through his examinations. In his last year many activities had to be curtailed in favour of academic work preparing for Oxford and, as Arthur was learning German, for Eton's

Prince Consort's Prize. He assured his mother that he had only one free hour after lockup in the whole week in which he was not working at either Smalls or German and he only played football three or four times a week, so that he already had two or three days without exercise.

During these years at Eton, the family had carefully to consider Arthur's future. Arthur's brothers followed their father into the Guards, and at first Arthur was also intended for the army, but his mother had many friends in the diplomatic service and this became his planned profession. Diplomacy is first mentioned in the spring of 1886, when Arthur and Fritz were on holiday in Heidelberg. So Arthur stayed at Eton through 1887 to 1889, going, in the summer of 1888, first to Heidelberg and then to Paris, in order to start the process of bringing his German and French up to the demanding standards required by the diplomatic service. Altogether Arthur went three times to Heidelberg, where he stayed with the historian, Professor Ihne. His German trip in the summer of 1889 was a much more ambitious undertaking than his earlier visits to Heidelberg. He spent his first three months with a Professor at Kiel. There he met many of the young officers of the nascent German fleet, who, although capable and fluent in English, were good about keeping to German when Arthur was about. He met Prince Henry of Prussia, turning up at the castle the first time in evening clothes, only to find them in casual dress, and the second time turning up casually dressed, only to find Prince Henry in uniform, medals and orders. 'A look of the deepest disapproval greeted me. I ought to have known the royal species better. I was made to feel very uncomfortable.'

Having failed his certificate examinations in the summer of 1889, Arthur was sent to the quiet rural scholarly atmosphere of Tathams' rectory at Abingdon to prepare for Smalls. Tatham renewed Arthur's confidence and, with the help of a tutor who knew how to make study interesting and meaningful, he made rapid progress. One day Jowett came over from Oxford, equipped for an overnight stay with a pocket Thucydides and a toothbrush, expressly to see what sort of a young man he had promised Mary Ponsonby he would admit to his college. Cherubic and chirping, he asked Tatham, of whom he had a high opinion, 'has he any knowledge?' The answer could hardly have been in the affirmative, but under Tatham's coaching he passed his exams.

I remember the result of the exam. We freshmen went up into a room where Jowett, Strachan-Davidson, Abbot in his chair and A.L. Smith were seated round a table. Brown (known as Harem Brown because of the decorations of his room) had been at Tathams with me he was a curious kindhearted ridiculously effeminate manikin. His name was read out as having failed. Then my name came and my rooms were assigned to me. They were beginning at the bottom of the list – which I did not realize at the time.

In October 1890, Arthur took up residence in Balliol. Tatham had worked out a programme of studies that involved taking in his first year a 'Smalls Extra Subject', a French or German book, and then at the end of the year, the 'Law Preliminary', which involved courses in Constitutional History and International Law, as well as further French or German. Then, after additional courses in Logic and Roman Law, he could take his degree in Law after three years. While Arthur no doubt had need of a programme of work, this was not the root cause of the problem that had prevented progress at Eton. All along his teachers had noticed Arthur's casual and indifferent attitude; hence the exhortations to 'put his shoulder to the wheel'. But it was not simply a question of transferring Arthur's attention from football to the study, for Arthur was affected by the debilitating belief that he was helpless in face of a predetermined universe. On the surface, Arthur appeared to be like any other undergraduate living a busy life, 'I find myself tearing about from one college to another and one don to another all the morning', but underneath this happy exterior, he was deeply troubled. Help came from three people; naturally his mother, the Master of Balliol and his cousin Charles Gore, at this time librarian at Pusey House. Mary Ponsonby wrote a number of what she termed 'interior letters' to her son at this time. The first of these letters was written in Arthur's second year at Balliol and in it Mary assured her son that his opinions and convictions could only be shaped by deliberation, care and intense truthfulness. Arthur, in thanking his mother for her letter, wrote 'It is the greatest comfort to me and I keep on reading it over and seeing more and more in it' and went on to explain that he had begun to write but had torn it up.

> I must wait till I see you. You see the subject is purely religious *not a doubt* but a sort of theory which has been gradually building up in my mind slowly and by degrees for more than 2 years and has been hammered out to the best of my ability.

Whatever Arthur's theory was, apparently he derived little comfort from it, for he was soon writing that he had got into a 'dismal state of mind' and found himself unable to do any work or even to have energy enough to get up at the proper time in the morning. 'I couldn't see where *myself* came in and I found myself pushed from side to side by circumstances.'

Charles Gore's solution to Arthur's problem was to show Arthur how to make real resolutions. Not to say by making them he had overcome this or that, but to say 'I dislike this and that and will not do them because not only do I think them wrong but they are thoroughly distasteful to me'. But, as Arthur explained matters to his mother, he was not at all sure whether this was due to his own efforts and resolution or was it the case

7

that it was always in him and his efforts were the result of it. Gore also offered Arthur some religious advice for combating the 'lower appetites', 'there is no failure except in ceasing to try', but this was not the problem, and, eventually, Arthur plucked up enough courage to talk to Jowett, whose advice was not to go and pray but to combat drifting by self assertion and endeavour.

This crisis, it should be emphasised, was a personal one for Arthur. It was, as Mary Ponsonby so aptly described it, 'an interior problem'. In all other respects, Arthur was an entirely normal undergraduate. He spent a great deal of time ragging and playing elaborate practical jokes – writing the Dean's name in paraffin on the grass and planting the quad with shrubs. His friends in these harmless nocturnal pursuits were Basil Blackwood, Hubert Howard and Claud Russell. He did not join the Union, but attended its debates, he reported home that he had heard Lord Ampthill address the Union on the subject of Russian nihilism, but offered no opinions himself. When Herbert Samuel invited one of the leaders of the London Dock strike to Balliol, Arthur was sufficiently outraged to express his disapproval by 'screwing in' Samuel, the docker and his 'socialist audience', with coffin screws through the door into the jamb. Arthur's main interests lay in the Oxford University Dramatic Society. Whatever reputation Arthur achieved at Oxford came from a Balliol production of *She Stoops to Conquer* in which Arthur played, to critical acclaim, the role of Tony Lumpkin. Arthur later took the production to Osborne House and, with the addition of several princesses, the play was put on for Queen Victoria. He also played the corpse in *The Frogs*, for which Hubert Parry, then professor of music at Oxford, composed the music, which set in motion the chain of circumstance that was to lead to his prolonged courtship and eventual marriage to Parry's daughter, Dorothea.

But this is to anticipate, for after having completed almost a year at Balliol, Arthur began to have second thoughts about his proposed career in diplomacy and, as he was taking courses for a Law degree, naturally enough thought of becoming a lawyer. He was told quite plainly that, in his mother's opinion, he would never succeed in the law, but that his special qualities – 'you understand people, you see the shade of a shade in what should be said or done or *not* said and *not* done, you are not the least egotistical or conceited and you have the gift of effecting what you wish by natural intelligence and keen interest' – were entirely suited to diplomacy. Arthur had been sent to Oxford to learn how to learn, not to learn languages, for that purpose he would have to leave Oxford and go abroad.

A further problem that began to loom large on the horizon at this time was the property qualification for the diplomatic service. Attachés were not paid any salary at all for two years and their parents were, in consequence, obliged to pledge £400 a year. A Royal Commission had begun to sit in 1890 and its recommendations were eagerly awaited, as it was hoped that the two branches of the service would be amalgamated and the property qualification, in consequence, would be abolished. The family could hardly afford such a sum and, while they awaited the Royal Commission's recommendations, it was decided that no immediate decisions would be taken and that Arthur would return to Oxford for a second year. Both Jowett and his tutor, A.L. Smith, were sufficiently impressed with Arthur to predict that, should he enter a proper degree programme, he would take First Class. Needless to say, with the proviso that Arthur would first really need to apply himself.

However, this was not to be, for, after completing his second year, Arthur left Oxford. Neither the Master nor A.L. Smith was pleased. 'I've seen Jowett, who, having said that he had received your letter and nothing more was to be said, stopped there and for half an hour I sat with him trying to make him talk but he wouldn't.' Jowett was sufficiently placated by an appeal from Mary Ponsonby to agree to tutor Arthur in political economy in the summer of 1892. The day began with breakfast with the Master alone and, afterwards, walking with him in the Quad for half an hour. After which Arthur worked in his room until one and then lunched in Hall. He was left to himself in the afternoon, but was again with Jowett for 7 o'clock dinner in Hall and they sat a long time after the wine, after which they walked in the Quad and then Arthur took his essay to him at 11 p.m.

One weekend that summer, Ponsonby was an interested spectator of one of the Master's famous weekend parties. The guests were Mr and Mrs Huxley, Lord and Lady Ribblesdale, Milner, Bowen, and the particular object of Arthur's attention, Margot Tennant. He was able to report back to the family that he was disappointed. 'She was very like Betty's imitation except that she didn't say nearly such good things as Betty makes her say. And there was too much of taking Jowett and Huxley by both hands and nearly kissing them.' Notwithstanding this poor impression, Margot retained her place at the centre of the social system Ponsonby sketched out in 1893 in a diagrammatic scheme that carries on its peripheries the Pope, the Queen, the Czar of Russia, Lobengula, the Archbishop of Canterbury and General Massingberd.

In the autumn of 1892, Arthur began his foreign language studies in earnest in German at Kiel and Berlin. In the early part of the winter of 1893, he went back to Oxford for an OUDS production of *She Stoops to Conquer*. His great friend at Oxford was Jack Talbot, with whom he had sung in the auxiliary choir at Eton, and who had been the moving spirit behind the OUDS production of *The Frogs*. On arrival at Oxford, the two friends went for a walk to exchange news and the meeting became famous as the origin of an expression which was afterwards adopted by both families.

> Shortly before we met an obscure Magdalen undergraduate called Bebb had thrown himself on the railway line and been run over by a train. Jack was present at the inquest the day before and could not get over the gruesomeness of the tragedy and the coroner's constant reference not to the body or the corpse but to 'the trunk'. 'Mr Bebb's trunk.' In our walk of over two hours we discussed nothing else. Jack had a wonderful way of recounting an episode and I was completely fascinated by the details and also by the rather curious fact that Bebb, whom I knew very slightly as a man of no particular account, had become a headline in the papers and a name on everyone's lips. So my impressions of Germany and all the gossip and news of Oxford were never mentioned before I had to catch my train back to London. Ever after 'Bebb's trunk' was the expression used when the main reason for the meeting of two people was extinguished by some entirely irrelevant subject of the moment. I believe there is a classic instance of it in the one and only meeting between Goethe and Heine when their talk was confined to the excellence of the plums on the road from Jena to Weimar.[4]

In the spring, he went on an extensive tour of Italy, taking in Assisi, Venice, Florence, Siena, and several other places. He then moved on to complete his French studies at Evreux. He returned to London to prepare for his diplomatic service examination.

Diptitch Scoones, the famous Garrick Street crammer, had become, by 1890, the essential ingredient in preparation for the Foreign Office and diplomatic service, for no less than 100 successful candidates had passed through his hands and the Foreign Office private secretary, who controlled the careers of young members of the service, was entirely in his confidence. The new examination that Arthur would have to face owed as much to Scoones' as to Lord Salisbury's dislike of constitutional history as 'unutterable trash'. Scoones was responsible for the exclusion of Ancient Greek from the new examination and for the primacy given to languages, for now it was necessary to offer French and German and also possible to offer as an optional language either Italian, Spanish, Portuguese or Russian.

Lady Ponsonby went to see Scoones in June 1893, but found that he was 'fresh gone' from Garrick Street. That immensely practical man did not wait for Lady Ponsonby to come again; the next morning prompt at 10 o'clock he appeared at the Ponsonbys' London home, Ambassador's Court, St James's Palace. The Ponsonbys had been undecided whether to let Arthur compete in the Foreign Office examination, for although the examination was exactly the same as for the diplomatic service, the competition was rather more severe. Arthur thought he should go in for the Foreign Office, but wiser councils prevailed, and, on Scoones' recommendation, Arthur's name was put down on the list for the next diplomatic service examination. Scoones wanted Arthur to come to Garrick Street in September, and, in the meantime, suggested that in his language studies he should concentrate on vocabularies of technical words in French and German, making lists for each subject. When he got to London, Arthur went to Scoones for six hours a day, concentrating upon geography and history. After 13 weeks of intense, concentrated and methodical work, he predictably failed, 8th out of 12. 'Just below the half, the keynote of my life', he confided to his diary. Fortunately, a second examination was called for February 1894, and so Arthur went back to Scoones in a very pessimistic frame of mind – 'All the prospect I have now is Scoones again . . . alone at St James's cramming perhaps for another failure.' Yet he still found it possible to see the humorous side of his predicament, continuing 'If failure has such a wholesome effect I shall become abnormally robust soon.' Rather than wait in London for the official envelope announcing the result of the February examination, Arthur went to Italy and was in Amalfi when he heard that he had been successful, passing first out of four candidates. Arthur's reaction was quite predictable, considering his previous inability in this particularly English form of torture – simple relief; excitement remained the province of his mother and sisters, Maggie and Betty. 'We shouted for joy.' Arthur wrote home, 'I should like to have been with you when the Blue envelope came. As what you think about it and the pleasure it is to you, is all I have thought of all along.'

The Diplomatic Service

The diplomatic service of which Arthur Ponsonby became a member in 1894 was small, exclusive, able and talented. The last point is often overlooked, but the top posts in the service were manned by eminent and distinguished men whose names were household words. As a career, it was an attractive proposition, but the glittering pinnacle of ambassadorial glory could only have been a distant dream for the new recruit. He had first to learn the ropes.

The two branches of the service, the Foreign Office and the diplomatic service, were kept distinct and separate from each other at this time. While the new common examination that Arthur had just passed qualified him for either branch, his competition had been for the diplomatic service and it was as an attaché that he started his career in diplomacy. All new attachés were required to spend six months in the Foreign Office before they went out to their first mission. The head of the Foreign Office was Sir Thomas Sanderson, known to his friends as 'Lamps' because of the

spectacular thickness of his eye glasses, but the most important person in
the Foreign Office to a new recruit was his head of department, Eric
Barrington, under whose supervision he would have to work. Both these
officials were known to the Ponsonbys and, before he left Naples to return
to London Arthur, addressed as 'My dear boy', received a postcard from
Barrington telling him that he was assigned to the Eastern Department.
Barrington's assistant was Charles Hopwood. In the second room were
Fairholme and Tyrrell. The third room was shared between the juniors,
R.D. Norton, Lord Granville and Charles Somers-Cocks. In this room,
the training for diplomacy consisted of copying out despatches, sorting
print and putting it in pouches for cabinet ministers, making multiple
copies of telegrams by pressing the copy made in copying ink on to an evil
smelling slab of lard, docketing papers and locking and unlocking
cupboards. Whatever Ponsonby may have thought about the Foreign
Office later in his career his immediate reactions were all positive 'the
work is by no means dull the company is very pleasant'.[5]

The routine of the day was lightened by after-lunch brewing – as
befitted the department dealing in part with the Near East – of Turkish
coffee. It was at one of these occasions that Arthur met for the first time
Charles Strachey, who was to become a life-long friend. Arthur was
persuaded by an Oxford friend to go and call on Lady Maud Parry, Hubert
Parry's wife, on the strength of his Oxford connection with the composer.
That was the beginning of it all, for he met Dolly. She accepted an
invitation to attend a small party to celebrate the Queen's birthday given
by the juniors of the Eastern Department and Arthur found himself
suddenly, painfully, and irrevocably head over heels in love. In love with a
girl who was far too young and immature to understand the havoc she had
wrought. So, in this pleasant way, Arthur passed his time before setting
out for Constantinople in December 1894.

The Ambassador at Constantinople in 1894 was Sir Philip Currie who
had previously served as permanent under-secretary in the Foreign Office.
He, too, was known to the Ponsonbys, so Arthur continued to move in a
self-contained, exclusive society, in spite of living in the Middle East. In
one of his first letters home, he described to Lady Ponsonby his first
impressions of Constantinople – 'camels, bazaars, hookahs and dirt'. The
Embassy building he described as rather like a large Pall Mall club and just
as if he were in London, he found himself being introduced to Cecil
Rhodes and Leander Starr Jameson, both of whom had news of Arthur's
brother Johnnie, stationed at that time at the Cape.

Ponsonby was the junior of eight diplomats and, as such, had to take
care of filing and registering papers and assist in the enormous task of
cyphering the flood of telegrams that arrived day and night from London.
Not everything was routine; he found himself translating an Italian piece

on the Armenian Question, and set to compose short despatches, so that, on the whole, he was well content, finding the work heavier than in London, but more interesting. Not that any of them were really overworked, and once the fortnightly diplomatic bag had been made up, he found himself with a good deal of free time. This was both an advantage, in that it gave him an opportunity to familiarise himself with the intricacies of Near Eastern politics which were at that time preoccupied with the Armenian Question, and, perhaps more pertinently, a disadvantage, given his seemingly built-in predisposition towards sloth. Both Norton and Granville, with whom he corresponded at this time, refer to Arthur's gloomy outlook; Norton was convinced that Arthur thought too much about happiness and expected too much from life, while Granville's advice was 'to give up having fits of the blues'. The trouble was Dolly; the further away the more the anguish. Fortunately, he found a sympathetic ear in Belle Herbert, the wife of the Secretary of Embassy Mungo Herbert, who was Lady Maud's brother.

The news of his father having suffered a paralytic stroke which deprived him of his speech made matters worse, for he felt deeply for his mother, wanted to comfort her, but duty kept him at Constantinople. He was eventually called home when his father's condition suddenly deteriorated. Sir Henry's positions at court were resigned and with them went the Norman Tower 'it is too horrible to think of'. He returned to Constantinople in May 1895, rather glad to be back at work, but still thinking of Dolly.

The Embassy was fully occupied at this time with the Armenian Question. One day in June, Arthur saw the Sultan close up for the first time: 'a little pale man in an old military greatcoat crouched on throne and carpet.'

Throughout the autumn of 1895 the Armenian massacres created an enormous amount of work in the Embassy in an atmosphere of constant talk of the Great Powers intervening and the fleet moving up to Constantinople. The Embassy remained at its summer home in Therapia, relatively isolated from the main centres of trouble, while at Pera where the Embassy was located Ponsonby heard that 2,000 Armenians were blockaded by the police in their church. After the Embassy returned to Pera in October, the excitement continued and rifles were stored in the Chancery.

News from home was equally bad. Lady Maud wrote a nice letter in which she asked Arthur to write no more. 'Really the restrictions that they have imposed upon me are almost more than I can stand. I daresay if they could control my breathing they would stop it.' Then came the inevitable and dreadful news of the death of Papa. Arthur went home immediately to attend the funeral at Whippingham on the Isle of Wight. He returned to

Constantinople in December. There the utter futility of the policy of the Great Powers was brought home forcefully to the Ambassador in the New Year when he took the occasion, when delivering an autograph letter to the Sultan from Queen Victoria, to lecture the old reprobate 'To which H.I.M. replied "You should always take warm milk in the morning when you have got a cold".'[6]

The continuation of the Armenian crisis, the growth of opposition to the Sultan, and a looming crisis between Turkey and Greece over Crete which escalated into war in April 1897 kept the Embassy under a great deal of pressure. However, in addition to all the work that surrounded these events, Ponsonby was preparing to make a journey to Beirut, Damascus and Jerusalem. He set out on 22 March and returned to Constantinople six weeks later on 3 May, describing the adventure as 'perhaps the most perfect thing I have done in my life'.[7]

Ponsonby travelled down to Beirut in a steamer and there engaged the services of a dragoman, who made all the arrangements for the main journey which was to be by horseback. Before turning south, Ponsonby took a side trip by train to Damascus where, accompanied by the consul, he did the normal sightseeing rounds. For the first part of his journey south, Ponsonby was accompanied by the Consul-General, Drummond Hay, who undertook to take him to see the Druses. At Muktara, he was received by Sit Bedra Jumblat in his castle. From there Ponsonby went on by himself, being received in Druse villages by guards of honour and flourishing trumpets. The roads were almost non-existent and the horse riding 'disagreeable', up and down precipitous faces of loose rock, before he finally came to Sidon. From here the ride along the coast to Tyre was much more pleasant. There he slept in a Franciscan monastery in a cell looking out over the sea – 'I believe St. Francis of Assisi slept with his head on a stone – at any rate I think the pillows were an attempt at imitating this – I ended by hurling mine in the middle of my cell and had a bad night.' Acre, Haifa and Mount Carmel were all taken in stride before arriving at Nazareth on 11 April. He went and saw the Church of the Annunciation with the altar down in a cave, but was more impressed by Mary's Fountain – 'as however improbable other relics may be undoubtedly there must always have been a spring of water here and to see the women with large black jars on their heads fetching [water]; it was most picturesque'.

Then his route took him to the Sea of Galilee and Tiberias before the climb up Tabor to see a stupendous view of the Plain of Esdraelon. He stayed in another monastery and as the monks were fasting, he asked his dragoman about dinner.

'The cook he gone, gone out to get a Robert.' Seeing I looked doubtful he continued 'You like Robert?' As I felt very hungry I was nervous that perhaps

Robert might not suit my taste – it turned out to be a rabbit and the best I have ever tasted.

On to Jennin, and then through Samaria to Nablus, where he arrived just in time to witness the Samaritan sacrifice on the top of Mount Gerizim.

Ponsonby had, quite naturally, engaged in constant religious discussions along the way with travellers, missionaries and clergymen, telling his mother that he, like his brother Johnnie, was always floored by 'but what does Ezekiel say' – 'of course you know I John 3.22'. He used the opportunity presented by this journey to try and formulate his ideas on religion. Before leaving Jerusalem, Ponsonby toured all the major historic and religious sites of the city. He fell in with Dr Bliss of the Palestine Exploration Fund, who took him down a shaft to see a street of Herodian Jerusalem and, not satisfied with that, insisted on Ponsonby going down the drain of the street (see page 16).

Having been more than two years in Constantinople, Ponsonby began to think about his next posting, which involved preparing the ground with an extremely touchy private secretary. In order to avoid Rio or Bogota, he wrote to Barrington suggesting either Cairo or Rome. Barrington was actually thinking of Copenhagen, which led Ponsonby to conclude that he would be better suited to Berlin, but the move was stalled for a time by the Ambassador, who told the Foreign Office that Ponsonby could not be spared because of the pressure of work in the Chancery. The Embassy was heavily involved in the peace negotiations between Greece and Turkey, and, for his part, Ponsonby found his Chancery work enjoyable. He registered the despatches and wrote small drafts of despatches on less important matters. Acting, now that the Embassy had moved to Therapia for the summer, took second place to rowing. Ponsonby had indulged himself to the extent of buying a caique, which certainly gave a false impression to the English community as to his financial resources and which also led naturally to moonlight expeditions and the inevitable thoughts of Dolly.

A man must have an absorbing work or an absorbing love to be happy – I have got neither and I don't see that I ever shall. I am left here too much to the morbid analysis of nothing. The work has grown less of late and hardly occupies one. At another post, this will be worse. It really can hardly be called a profession. I long for hard work with all its ups and downs. Not this drifting.[8]

Late in September, Ponsonby managed to get ten days leave in order to visit the Crimea. Going by steamer to Sevastopol by way of Kerch, he stayed with the Vice-Consul who had been up with him at Balliol. A quick visit to Balaklava was followed by a train excursion to the tartar town of Bakhchisaray. Whatever local colour he might have been able to absorb was ruined by the presence in the town of a voluble party of

Dr Bliss shows me the drains of Herodian Jerusalem

German tourists. Ponsonby's final two months in Constantinople passed all too quickly. He left Constantinople on 25 November 1897 comforted by a good report from his Ambassador which only partly served to ameliorate the discomfort of a bad journey home suffering from diarrhoea.

Back in London he found awaiting him a letter from Dolly. She had written a long '3-volume novel', not knowing he was coming home on leave. She feared its return and the contents were not to be divulged. While he waited in an agony of suspense, he imagined that she had accepted another suit and he was to be treated just as an old friend. The dreaded letter finally arrived on 12 December.

> I summoned up courage and read it slowly 4 sheets. I sobbed with crying then buried my head in the bottom of an armchair and then prayed after which I began to throw things about the room.

Finally, Arthur's courtship ran true and arrangements were made for a wedding, which took place on 12 April 1898 in St Mary Abbots Church, Kensington. Charles Gore officiated and Jack Talbot was best man. When the engagement was announced, one of the most interested was Queen Victoria. She buttonholed Fritz at Osborne,

> . . .asked what Dolly was like and whether she was very clever; what they had to live on and whether there was any chance of Arthur going to Berlin. She said that personally if she were Arthur she would not like to go to Berlin as the Germans were so unfriendly and that she had been told that they were not at all civil to English people there but that no doubt Arthur would be able to get on there and it would be more amusing for Dolly than Constantinople.[9]

Shortly after they returned to London from their honeymoon, they went to the Drawing Room and a day later saw Queen Victoria privately.

Although Arthur's brother Johnnie was correct in telling him that 'the game is to keep moving' in his profession, the move from Constantinople to Denmark was not necessarily a good move. The advantages were that they were close to home and the court connection gave them a special position at Copenhagen. The Parrys were particularly concerned that Arthur's profession would take their daughter completely away, so the Copenhagen appointment temporarily quietened Lady Maud's anxieties. At home, the court connection was now Arthur's brother Fritz who, in 1897, had been appointed assistant private secretary to Queen Victoria. Both the Prince and the Princess of Wales wanted to know how Arthur and Dolly liked Copenhagen and Fritz reported to Arthur that he had 'told them both that you liked Copenhagen immensely'. Fritz also reported that the court had heard through Lady Scott, the wife of the ambassador, of Arthur's wonderful acting in private theatricals; and Charlotte Knollys had spoken very highly of Arthur's ability, as Fane, the senior secretary, had 'told her that you were invaluable'. Altogether, then, it would appear that Arthur's career was set fair and that he would proceed smoothly forward through the middle ranks of the profession to an early appointment as head of a mission. The main disadvantage attached to the move was that Copenhagen was exactly the opposite to Constantinople. Instead of being exciting and filthy, it was dull and clean, a little miniature Chancery with no work. As diplomatic relations between the United Kingdom and Denmark revolved entirely around the court, the functions of the post were purely ceremonial. Arthur needed to work, he had to feel that what he was doing was useful and that he was making a contribution, doing something, however small, to make life meaningful.

This problem did not surface immediately and for the first few months at Copenhagen everything was what the newly-weds expected. They found a flat and busily set up house, giving dinner parties but particularly enjoying tea in the afternoon. They also found a good piano and Dolly's playing gave great pleasure all round. Arthur was working hard on his painting technique, and reported that he had been sketching in the beechwoods where he had completed a large study of trees on the big board given him by his mother. 'D. read out Felix Holt to me and we took Maggie's tea basket. Perfect undisturbed peace. I got the trunks fairly well, but got the foliage heavy and never know how to deal with it when it is bright against a dark part of the trunk.'

Arthur's reports on his colleagues 'Sir Charles Scott, an ugly little man but a gentleman and very amiable and kind,' 'The Johnstones are the regular Anglo-American diplomatic ménage, lots of money and very diplomatic,' are in keeping with this general air of optimism, but within six months a different note begins to sound as he began to fear that the diplomatic service would begin to mould him and that he would become, as he termed it, pâté de fois gras.

In August 1898, the Czar of Russia had proposed calling a Universal Peace Conference, with the object of securing general disarmament. When it was announced that the Conference would meet at The Hague, Ponsonby wrote home to the Foreign Office asking if he might be appointed Secretary of the British delegation. He received a very dusty answer from Barrington, who professed to know nothing of any peace conference and told Ponsonby that he need not bother to apply because the Office were considering posting him to Rio de Janeiro.

Rather overwhelmed with the hopelessness of my profession, to think, at the rate that Fane has gone, in 36 years I shall be allowed to do work which I am really capable of doing now. D doesn't like being abroad for always. I don't like having nothing to do and yet, when I ask 'May I be secretary on the Peace conference,' they answer 'No, but you may go to Rio de Janeiro.'[10]

After this rebuff, he plucked up courage to write to the famous theatrical actor/producer John Hare. Writing in the strictest confidence, he proposed to find out if his amateur talent as an actor could be sustained in the professional field. If Hare would give him a try out, he would come and spend his summer leave with Hare's touring company. The diplomatic service, he told Hare, he found, as time went on, hopelessly unsatisfactory, and he couldn't face the prospect of 'a career of almost uninterrupted leisure'. Hare's response was to say that he would do what he could and that he might even have an opening for Arthur in his London company at the Globe. This response made it impossible for Arthur to keep the matter from his family, and so he wrote, first to his sister Maggie, who could be expected to be sympathetic, and began to prepare his mother for the news by telling her that he was very tired at the absolute absence of work in Copenhagen. 'I think it is a horrible feeling one is doing nothing and has no prospect of doing anything. . . One thing is that if I hadn't been married I am sure I couldn't have stayed here six months.' If only, he told his mother, he could find a secretary who stood up for the profession, but they one and all abuse it. Now that he had finished his report on Commercial Education in Denmark, he was thinking of writing about charitable institutions for the destitute, but was held back by a feeling that the Foreign Office would never read such a paper. 'A lazy married man is such a horrible thing.'

Arthur's family were not at all sympathetic to the proposed try-out in the theatre. Maggie, who might have been expected to show the most support, thought that really the theatre was after all 'a lowering profession' and Fritz reminded Arthur of the financial sacrifices the family had made and which their mother was still making to get them started in professional careers. Diplomacy, really, was a gentleman's profession and his leisure time should be spent in improving himself by reading Spencer, Huxley and Mill. Fritz had heard from his minister Fane that Arthur was regarded as one of the rising men in the profession, wanted by all embassies. He blamed Arthur's discontent on Copenhagen. 'It is deadly' he conceded, but a move was possible and perhaps he would benefit from an exchange into the Foreign Office. Mary Ponsonby was content at first to remind her son that all the big men had gone through the small grind and then went on in her letter to discuss Arthur's second study of drawing and painting. If his work did not approach professional standards this did not matter – 'put all your work into the fire if you think it baaad but you will become twice yourself if you feel you *know* how beautiful those things are which perhaps you can never approach in your own work'.[11] When Dolly's follow up letter arrived at Gilmuire containing the unfortunate phrase 'we had no idea it would be such a bomb', Mary Ponsonby pointed out that two things went to make it a bomb for her. First, she would not have expected such a problem to emerge only nine months after the marriage, and, second, that as she had been the principal mover in choosing Arthur's career, she must have made a huge mistake.

So keenly did Mary Ponsonby feel for her son's predicament, that she put together a memorandum[12] intended at first for her own use, but which she eventually sent to Copenhagen. In it, she retrospectively weighed Arthur's choice of diplomacy in the light of his current discontent. After reviewing the alternatives they had originally considered, Mary Ponsonby concluded that all in all it had been a sound choice, and, if they disliked living abroad, an exchange into the Foreign Office would not lose all the advantages of his training and waste the money spent on equipping him for his work.

Discussions continued until his leave in the summer of 1899. Once in London, Arthur went to see John Hare and Arthur Pinero and talked the matter over with Hubert Parry. None was encouraging. Finally, Ben Greet offered him a clown's part and he decided that jumping about in tights at Brighton would hardly constitute a fair test of his capacity as an actor. So the idea of an acting career was quietly dropped and Arthur Brooke's (his intended stage name) life on the stage was over before it had begun. 'I am like a marble who wobbles in a groove and almost gets over the edge but gradually rolls smoothly on over the uneventful course.' An escape from Copenhagen would be, as his mother suggested, an exchange into the Foreign Office. What is significant about this proposed move is that the reasons advanced by Arthur were not on the surface political. The alternative to diplomacy was the a-political career of acting and the complaint against diplomacy was of its 'uninterrupted leisure'. Unfortunately, Arthur's first letter to his mother announcing his intention of leaving the profession is lost, but in her answer Mary Ponsonby disagreed with Arthur's comments about 'the young and rich noblemen who are to manage everything without knowing anything on the principle that the housemaid had better not know how to read and write as she would then clean the grates better'. Were these remarks just thrown into the arena or do they mark the stirrings of a political conscience? This is possible, but when Arthur wrote to Hare in July 1899 about his professional theatrical try-out, he told him that his enthusiasm had been worn down by opposition and he had come to the conclusion that to change his profession was too great a risk to take. The problem for Arthur was that he was caught up in the meshes of convention, and from Copenhagen there was no feasible alternative career, hence the unlikely choice of the theatre. Given sufficient income, there is no doubt that Arthur would have resigned and gone into Parliament, not because of radical convictions, but simply to get free from the continuous leisure of the diplomatic life. London would offer wider perspectives and new opportunities for a man who was clearly not so much a petulant and discontented wallflower as a man in search of a vocation.

The exchange into the Foreign Office was agreed fairly easily in the summer of 1899, but took rather longer than everyone expected to accomplish and it was not until February 1900 that Arthur was called home, and then only because of the extra pressure of work generated in the Office by the Boer War. In the meantime, Arthur spent his summer leave not on the boards, but apparently enjoying London society, garden parties, gallery exhibitions and a weekend at Osborne with Fritz and Ria. Arthur was sufficiently proficient at golf to play a game with Arthur Balfour, but not sufficiently bold to beard him on the faults of the diplomatic service. Arthur and Dolly had also to visit Lady Maud's family, the Pembrokes at Wilton, which they both dreaded, but if they had to endure the banalities of Lady Maud and her family, they also had the pleasure of Hubert Parry's company, which Arthur particularly enjoyed.

In the months before his removal from Copenhagen, Arthur had begun to write. He completed the manuscript of a novel. The story was about a morbid man haunted to death by the recollection of an awful incident which he considered a crime. Ponsonby doubted his ability to handle such a theme and it went unpublished, although he did persuade Edmund Gosse to read it and they subsequently had a talk about it. Arthur's contact with such a literary giant as Gosse was provided by his cousin Maurice Baring. Baring, whose own literary career lay in the future, was at this time Arthur's junior colleague in the diplomatic service and a great favourite of his aunt, Mary Ponsonby. Maurice had taken sides in the dispute over diplomacy as a profession with Mary Ponsonby, much to Arthur's disgust, but he saw and encouraged Arthur's literary ambitions and, even after the failed novel, suggested Arthur write a play. Literary success came at a much more mundane level; a piece abusing his profession was accepted by *The National Review*[13] and he published another article on Tycho Brahe.[14] As he had made no secret of his views, even going so far as to discuss them with a senior colleague, Francis Bertie, during his visit to London in the summer of 1899, everyone knew the identity of 'A Diplomatist'. Francis Bertie had encouraged him to apply for the exchange, pointing out that although he should expect to do a great deal of tiresome mechanical work in the Foreign Office, he would also be in a position to see how the various questions of interest in foreign politics were being treated. The major question of foreign politics in the winter of 1899–1900 was the Boer War.

The Boer War ended the complacency of late Victorian politics. It raised particular problems for the Liberals and their attitude towards Imperialism. The radical wing of the party, in particular, were outraged by the Boer War. The great debate that raged between Little and Big

Englanders swept aside all other issues. Families like the Ponsonbys were engaged at several levels. Mary Ponsonby was angered by the actions of the Imperialists who had engineered the war through the absurd criminal enterprise of the Jameson Raid of 1895 – 'The war is dreadful; my old hatred of the Raid crops up occasionally' – but concerned for the fate of her two soldier sons. Arthur's reaction to the war at first was also ambivalent – 'How thrilling all the news is – how terrible the enormous proportion of officers killed.' He was sufficiently nationalistic to be offended by the Danish newspapers' support of the Boer cause – papers which he had to translate for transmission to London, but also outraged by the sordid connection between the Rand capitalists and Imperialism.

During the early campaigns, Arthur was looking for a decisive military victory – 'It is very exciting now; it looks much better; our tactics seem good; I hope poor Buller will get a decisive victory: but they are terribly cunning and the last telegrams don't seem very hopeful.'[15] Mary Ponsonby was not so sanguine about Buller's chances of winning and went on to remark that 'when we win (if we do!) it will have been an inglorious war for us, quand tout est dit – people like Stead and Ouida and other hysterical shriekers make me sick'. Arthur was back in London working at the Foreign Office when the dramatic news of the relief of Mafeking produced unprecedented rejoicing in the streets of the capital. In stark contrast to his reaction to similar street scenes in 1914, Arthur was content to describe to his sister what he had seen.

> The excitement last night was tremendous. I was at the Opera with Hubert – There were cheers and God Save the Queen but the streets were astonishing. I saw one very respectable man walking by himself down Piccadilly waving a dinner bell. At the Savoy they all stood on the tables and then a man got the big drum, broke it in and made a collection for the Mafeking relief fund. He got £46! It is going on still today, quite digne people walking along with a union jack tied round their top hats.[16]

As for the Foreign Office providing an inside look at policy making, as Bertie had predicted, Ponsonby found himself hating it more than ever. The work amounted to nothing more than bustle and scurry about nothing. The focus of Arthur's discontent now centred on Sir Thomas Sanderson, the permanent under-secretary and head of the Foreign Office. Much to Arthur's chagrin, Sanderson had, in the six years since Arthur had served his apprenticeship in the Office, carried out there a number of reforms while ignoring the diplomatic service.

> Now do you know what is the state of the F.O. as regards the dip S. they take no interest. Lamps and Bertie vie with one another to see who can get the most of the Foreign Office work into their hands and as for pausing to consider whether the dip S. might not be improved it never occurs to them nor will it ever – they have no time for it . . . I go in the evening to Lamps and this is what I see.

How can you ask this despatch machine *anything* far less for me a junior to begin
'Don't you think the dip. Service might be reformed.'[17]

Nevertheless, Ponsonby decided to rewrite his article on the diplomatic
service in moderate and strictly official tones.[18] His reasoning was that, if
he had to remain in the profession, then the subject was of vital
importance to himself. The main recommendation was for the appointment of chanceliers to do the ordinary routine work of the missions, which
would not only free the secretaries from the boring drudgery of copying
and decyphering, but, by lowering the numbers recruited into the service,
make for earlier and swifter promotion to more rewarding and satisfying
work. The day after submitting his memorandum, Ponsonby, as usual,
played golf in the morning with Norton, hardly concentrating upon the
ball, wondering what 'Lamps' was thinking. After lunch, he 'tore off to the
F.O. feeling fearfully closeterial' but found that nobody looked any
different and everything went on the same until around 4 o'clock when
Tyrrell came in and, smiling at Ponsonby, said 'Come in to me in a
moment, will you?' What Tyrrell had to tell him was, on the whole,
encouraging. Sanderson's initial reaction had indeed been explosive, but

he had calmed down and in Tyrrell's opinion Lamps really agreed with much of the memorandum. The following day, Tyrrell reported that Sanderson had told him that the staff at smaller posts might well be cut down and chanceliers introduced. Arthur caught sight of Sanderson, but Lamps darted back into his room the moment he realised who it was closeted with Tyrrell, his private secretary. Ponsonby did not get to see Sanderson until after his return from holiday, and, when he was called in, he was spoken to at length and not allowed to say one word. A further memorandum of extracts from the various Commissions[19] was then asked for and produced by the joint efforts of Dolly and Arthur. Suspecting that his work might be shelved, Arthur persuaded his brother Fritz to show the memoranda to Arthur Bigge, but the Queen's secretary politely refused royal support for Ponsonby's reforms. 'I do not see how the Queen could be asked to burst the patent A.P. bombs!'[20]

Shortly thereafter, the newspapers began to carry disturbing reports about the health of Queen Victoria; her death was recorded in the Diary

> The Queen. The word, the name, the idea, the person, seem so extraordinarily familiar as I cannot remember any time when I was not very conscious of her existence. The excitement of her presents on Xmas Eve, the Xmas tree at Osborne and being taught to make a bow, searching for Easter eggs in the corridor at Windsor. The Queen's carriage with the well known outrider, watching it coming in and out from the nursery window at Norman Tower. Her visit to Kent House or Osborne Cottage when we all made our bow and she smiled and said something to us. Papa and Mama dining with her and coming home and telling us about it. In fact she was connected with every day of our lives . . . Before I went out to Constple she had me to dinner and spoke to me of my profession and her interest in the Armenian Question and again when I came home and again when I was married – she saw us both privately – never forgetting she knew what Papa was to her, what he had been to her, and she was not reminded but remembered herself to keep her eye on all of us in the middle of the hundreds who were dependent on her. She gave England distinction there is no other word for it. Not by brilliancy but by quiet strong excellence, nothing cheap, nothing common, nothing worldly and rotten, but supreme dignity and nobility inspiring a feeling of absolute security and strength with the entire and wholehearted confidence of her people. It was a very wonderful life.[21]

Back in the Foreign Office, Arthur was soon in hot water, telling Dolly that abroad was a very likely possibility – 'I am apparently useless to either service.' This further contretemps with officialdom took Arthur directly round to St James's to see his mother, and, not surprisingly, the row with the Office turned into a row between mother and son, for the prospect of going abroad again roused all the old antagonism Arthur felt against going around Europe making pleasant acquaintances. Mary Ponsonby was so upset, that the next day she wrote to Arthur to say that she had no wish to reopen the discussion.

Arthur immediately wrote back to say that he was sorry for having lost his temper and for being so unreasonable. He agreed that the best thing to do was never to broach the subject again. In the conclusion of his letter of apology, he expressed the view that it was not simply a question of a preference for one profession over another, but that he was literally bursting with energy and desire for work and had not the remotest prospect of getting anything from the Foreign Office. 'I know I am one sided in my views, but I am so terribly frightened of becoming quite resigned to it like *all* the rest of them.' With his reform project apparently shelved, Ponsonby seems to have lost all interest in the Office.

Most of the summer of 1901 was spent in an attempt to resolve the old interior problem that had afflicted him at Balliol, when he had lain in his bed unable to move convinced that he was a powerless individual alone in a predetermined world. He decided to write a pamphlet which was eventually published under the pseudonym Thomas Clune. 'Spiritual Perfection' contains a homespun political philosophy which rejected orthodox religious opinion on original sin and eternal life in favour of the concept of here and now, in which the true meaning of life was to be realised through an individual search for the common good of society. 'Everything' he wrote in his diary after a particularly acrimonious exchange with Fritz 'seems to drive me towards extreme radicalism. I am learning more of politics, hating more than ever luxury and the society point of view. Disagreeing fundamentally with the arrogant conservatism of the day keeps me constantly awake and buoyed with the hope that one day I shall be able to shake off convention and my damping profession.'[22] The Foreign Office had become the embodiment of his former psychological impasse and he, as a clerk, was simply wasting away his life, unable to contribute or even make an impression on 'Lamps' Sanderson, who had become himself, in Arthur's own words, a machine. Once this problem was satisfactorily resolved in Arthur's mind, it was simply a matter of time before he would find fulfilment in political life.

If the lack of a private income precluded a career in Parliament, it was not an obstacle to other kinds of political activity. The Liberal Central Association operated an office in Parliament Street where, if only Arthur could get a footing, paid political work could replace the Foreign Office and the unappetising prospect of being sent abroad again. So Arthur plucked up his courage and wrote to Herbert Gladstone who, as Chief Whip, was in charge of the Liberal Party organisation. He explained that he found the monstrous mechanical routine of the Foreign Office intolerable and had no intention of resuming the expensive farce of loafing about at foreign capitals. As he had not enough money for Parliament, but was a 'more faithful follower than ever of Gladstone-Morley liberalism', he wanted to give his services to the party if Gladstone knew of a suitable subordinate post or secretaryship. Herbert Gladstone agreed to see Arthur, who went round to Parliament Street to be interviewed on the day of the announcement of the postponement of King Edward's coronation. And so the matter was arranged.

Meanwhile, Ponsonby was put in charge of the 'flunkey business' associated with the coronation and was escorting a delegation of Korean princes around London. He took his party to Hurlingham to look at the polo, where the sight of masses of overdressed, painted women in trailing skirts distressed him. 'The band played Sousa, Stephen Adams and Mascagni, and it was all very characteristic of their elaborate struggles against boredom.' That day, they had tea with peaches on the lawn, which Arthur enjoyed, but by the end of the visit, retribution lay in wait, for perpetual strawberries and champagne cup kept him in the closet all night.

Before officially resigning from the Foreign Office, Arthur wrote privately to Sanderson informing him of his decision. In a rather tart letter, he pointed out that he had made up his mind to leave, not because he thought there was any chance of the Office being reformed, for he knew that was impossible, but because he had hopes of finding more congenial employment elsewhere.[23] To Mary Ponsonby, Arthur expressed feelings of immeasurable relief – 'you have agreed with me that the feeling of devoting one's whole life to work that is against the grain is impossible'. Sanderson was not quite the ogre that Arthur imagined him to be and, clearly upset by the abrupt letter of resignation, asked for and received a letter of explanation.[24]

Although Ponsonby's reform project did not achieve its intended object immediately, and Ponsonby, as has been noted, lost interest in his scheme, his resignation was part of a larger process which culminated in the Eyre Crowe reforms of 1906. These reforms transformed the Foreign Office and made the clerks policy advisers. In unravelling the complicated story of the events leading up to 1914, the role of the officials in the Foreign Office has attracted considerable scholarly attention.[25] For a long time, it was accepted that their Germanophobia had unduly influenced the foreign policy of Sir Edward Grey. It is now known that this was not the case, for Grey was his own master. Ponsonby's subsequent enthusiasm for democractic control of foreign policy, which included the reform of the Foreign Office and diplomatic service, probably reflects some embarrassment on his part at the unintended consequences of this first effort.

In a small outline of major events in his life written some time after 1920 the entry for 1902 has four items:

> lived in summer at cottage at Betchworth. Resigned dipl. service. Became in Nov. Sec. to H. Gladstone at Liberal Central Assocn. Oct. took Shulbrede on lease.

While the career change was undoubtedly a momentous event in Ponsonby's life, the last entry 'Oct. took Shulbrede on lease' was to be equally important.

Home for Arthur Ponsonby had been the Norman Tower of Windsor Castle. After the death of Sir Henry Ponsonby, his widow eventually settled at Ascot, and also retained a grace and favour residence in St James's Palace. On his various leaves from the diplomatic service, Arthur usually stayed in the St James's apartment and, after his marriage, Dolly and he also stayed with the Parrys at their country home, Highnam Court in Gloucestershire, and more especially at the Parrys' seaside home in Rustington, Sussex. On his return to London in 1900, the Ponsonbys rented a house, 9 Victoria Square, where their daughter Elizabeth was born and, as been noted above, in the summer of 1902 they lived in a cottage at Betchworth. Dolly was not strong and living permanently in London was impossible for her, so having made up his mind to leave the diplomatic service, Arthur began to look for a permanent residence for his family somewhere just outside London.

The story of the discovery of Shulbrede can now be taken up in Arthur's own words. It begins several years before the momentous bicycle ride from Midhurst, at a lunch hour meeting in a London pub.

When I returned to London in 1900 I came again across Strachey who had been transferred to the Colonial Office. Louis Mallet, a very amusing and charming man, was a friend of both his and mine. One day I was to join them at luncheon in a sort of cellar where a wonderfully unappetising meal was served. I was late and found them deep in conversation. Charles was in the middle of describing a house and I caught the words as I sat down. 'There is a vaulted hall and a large vaulted dairy and upstairs a timbered room with pictures painted on the wall' but on my arrival the conversation changed.

On leaving our little London house in Victoria Square we decided to go into the country which we both very much preferred to London. So in every spare moment I went off on a bicycle with a packet of sandwiches and scoured the Southern counties. One day in 1902 I found by pure chance at Midhurst an advertisement of Shulbrede Priory which was just drawn up for the press. I came, I saw and I was conquered. On returning to my wife at Rustington I described the house and as I did so, like a dream or more like an echo, the description sounded as if I had heard it before – the vaulted hall, the large timbered room, etc. etc.[26]

Shulbrede Priory was taken in October 1902 on a lease and purchased by the Ponsonbys in 1905. They never left. It became the perfect refuge for a sensitive man embroiled in public controversy. Deep in the fold of hills below Hindhead, Shulbrede Priory, situated on a road that goes nowhere, when discovered by the househunting bicyclist, had been bypassed for centuries.

An Augustinian Priory that came into the possession of the Earl of Southampton at the Dissolution, it passed into the hands of the Viscounts Montague of Cowdray for more than two centuries. By the nineteenth century, it had become little more than a picturesque ruin – the Gate House, which had been the chief remaining attraction of the building, had long since gone and the house was only considered suitable as a residence for a working farmer. The land was separated from the house at the end of the century and the Priory became a private residence.

The buildings that have survived the ravages of time consist of the south-west portion of the Priory, the refectory, a passage to the cloisters, an undercroft or crypt and, on the first floor, the Prior's Chamber. This last room contains an important fresco. High up in the corner by the fireplace, a wall painting from the early sixteenth century depicts the legend that all animals became articulate on Christmas Day. The animals are perched on roughly painted green hills with scrolls issuing from their mouths on which are inscribed Latin words resembling their natural cries. The cock cries 'Christus Natus Est', the duck asks 'Quando, quando?', 'In Hac Nocte' is the raven's reply; 'Ubi, Ubi' enquires the bull and the Lamb answers 'In Bethlem'.

In October 1908, the diary has this entry:

'What on earth do you do at Shulbrede during your holiday' so many people ask me and I don't know what to say. Anyhow the time flies and I never have time to finish or do all I want.

Shulbrede was home, and home was the most real part of Arthur's life: 'it continues to be the great tonic, the rock on which all else is built, the only thing that matters, attracts delight.'

Shulbrede brought Ponsonby and Charles Strachey very close together, and over the years their joint researches, which eventually produced a book on Shulbrede, kept them together. The epithet 'Shulbredian' was the ultimate accolade that Ponsonby gave to his special friends. Although Shulbrede was, and still is, isolated in its beautiful valley, the Ponsonbys were not without neighbours. Not far away was Woolbeding, where resided the Lascelleses, and, at Friday's Hill, lived the American Quaker expatriate family, the Pearsall Smiths, whose son, Logan, had a house even closer to Shulbrede, at High Buildings. Logan, who had been in Ponsonby's senior year at Balliol, was soon on friendly terms with the new arrivals and before long they made the acquaintance of Logan's relatives and friends including the art critics Bernard Berenson and Roger Fry.

The Frys, who were staying at High Buildings that summer, were soon on good terms with the Ponsonbys, particularly after Roger showed 'Shulbredian' inclinations, a subject on which Arthur was especially sensitive, as one of Dolly's friends had, on the very day of the Frys' first visit to Shulbrede, left the impression that she could not see why Dolly should choose to reside in a dirty dungeon. Ponsonby also made the acquaintance that summer of Goldsworthy Lowes Dickinson, whose book *Letters of John Chinaman* had intrigued all the Ponsonbys several years before.

The Pearsall Smith circle's most famous member, his brother-in-law, Bertrand Russell, had also lived in the vicinity, but he and Alys had moved away before the Ponsonbys arrived at Shulbrede. Although Ponsonby met him at a Smith Square dinner party in February 1904, he was not to get to know him well until the summer of 1911.

Ponsonby's delight in summer days at Shulbrede are faithfully recorded in his diary. Gardening, lawn-tennis parties on the new court, exploratory expeditions into the surrounding woods with Elizabeth in a wheelbarrow, and, further afield, towing Dolly in a chair behind his bicycle, filled his days. In September, however, it was back to London to the half-way house into politics in Parliament Street – the National Liberal Association.

With his wife now living permanently at Shulbrede while he worked in London, Ponsonby began to send her an almost continuous daily account of his activities. These letters, which are much more matter of fact than his introspective diary writing, are curious in that they are addressed, not as his earlier letters were simply to Dolly, but to Darling Greatley, Darling Ginger or Darlingford, and are closed sometimes by his initials, but more often by 'your own Taylor'. At home they called each other by many different nicknames. Arthur writes about his detestation of the perfunctory use of terms of endearment and goes on to say 'so strongly do I feel this that I call her by the surname of a reporter in the House of Commons years ago, by the name of an Eton master of the sixties and the occasional name of a town. She calls me by the name of a Spanish general of the nineties.' If Dolly under whatever guise received an almost daily letter, Elizabeth was not forgotten (see letter on page 30).

The Private Secretary

The decision of a man whose private views were becoming distinctly socialist to work for the Liberal Party reflects more on the political realities of politics in early Edwardian England than on the sincerity of Ponsonby's commitment to socialism. Socialism was a political ideal rather than a practical programme and many radicals set out to achieve its objectives through the established party of the left. Not that Ponsonby was in any position to influence the movement one way or another. He maintained an animated and interesting correspondence with Mary Ponsonby on politics and they discussed the ideas of Rosny in *Les Ames Perdues* and Paul Adam in *La Force du Mal* agreeing with them that the social system should

M 👁 🦌 🕸

👁 ✳ pe 🌲 R

quite 🕳. It is 🌧 here

and will 🪢 s🪀. I if/w

U and 🦋 er have 🥮

a 🔔 2 🌊.

🪣 🌲 🐱 ch 🦂 or

, 🐛 🏠 this weather.

👁 shall 🐝 very g🚶 2

🧍 2 ⛪. R we

2 go from Ru🐝👉 🥚

🏠 the 🚗.

Give a 🦋 from me.

👁 Xpect 🌲 stand/will all this

y 🧹 loving

🔪ibs

be reconstructed from within 'through the force of will of each man on his own spot and not by fanaticism or battering rams from without'. He confided in Dolly that he hated being an official liberal but was equally annoyed with the socialists' detestation of Liberals 'for years and years to come it is only through the Liberal Party that they can accomplish the gradual steps toward their objectives'. The Liberals needed the socialists as much as the socialists needed the Liberals in order to permeate the party with strong advanced views to check any weakening influence at the Rosebery end of the party.

The move from the Foreign Office to Parliament Street meant much more than simply a change of office address. Ponsonby now gave up golfing mornings and lengthy club lunches before a few casual hours of registering and docketing, and enthusiastically immersed himself in Liberal politics. Herbert Gladstone encouraged him to seek out new and promising liberals and, as a matter of course, he found himself attending meetings and discussion groups. One particular discussion group stuck in his mind. Canon Barnett, the dynamic force behind Toynbee Hall, was worried that in the coming election, rows between Liberals and Labour would allow some Conservatives to slip in. He was not himself concerned with the practicalities of a Lib-Lab agreement, but wanted to find out how far leading men could agree in principle and so collected together representatives of radical and labour opinion for a talk. In his memoir of Ramsay MacDonald, Ponsonby wrote that he now had no recollection whatever of who was there, with one exception – Ramsay MacDonald.

> It was the first time I had actually met him. He waited till several had spoken and then he put the case with great clearness, pointing out the difficulties, showing how impossible alliances must be for Labour which was just beginning to find its political feet and, while not dismissing questions of principle on which agreement might be found, he summed up against any absorption of the Labour party as a wing of the Liberal party. I was greatly impressed by his power of expression, his careful weighing of the pros and cons, and his loyal adherence to his own party's independence, which seemed to be based on a faith in its future.[27]

Thus began a political and personal relationship of extraordinary complexity that was to flourish under the banner of the Union for Democratic Control in the World War before foundering on frustrated ambition on Ponsonby's part and manie de grandeur on that of MacDonald in 1931.

Another new and more immediate friendship was made at this time with another promising politician, Charles Masterman. Masterman and Ponsonby first met when Arthur sent an article to the *Independent Review* of which Masterman was an assistant editor. They met and, in spite of Arthur's distrust of Masterman's ecclesiastical appearance and pseudo' cockney accent, they got on famously, Masterman in turn being prepared to forgive Ponsonby his court and diplomatic past. The bond that united them was their joint commitment to social justice. Dolly provided Charles with potting plants from Shulbrede for his South London home and, on one famous occasion, Charles walked over to Shulbrede, turning up on the doorstep shouting 'Bread, Bread', carrying no luggage, except a hot water bottle which he had in the pocket of his black overcoat.[28] Eventually, their friendship drifted apart over differences in attitude towards the World War, but in the years before 1914 they were extremely close. Masterman was a candidate for Parliament and Ponsonby helped his unsuccessful campaign in the Dulwich by-election of 1903.

Earlier in the year Ponsonby had himself become a candidate for the Tory-held constituency of Taunton. He had considered seeking adoption at Windsor, but was advised not to do so because of his court connections. His official time was now spent between work at the Liberal Central Association and nursing his constituency in Devon.

Work at 41 Parliament Street was mostly concerned with speaking engagements for the leading Liberals in the constituencies and arranging for prospective candidates to be interviewed by Herbert Gladstone. Ponsonby had to run the gauntlet of both the speakers ('several MPs think creation was arranged for them'), who wanted only certain geographically convenient engagements and of the constituencies ('another winter of writing to people to tell them that they can't have Lloyd George will probably make me take to drink').

From this position, Ponsonby was able to get a close look at the inner workings of the party and, in particular, the very intense debate that raged over the leadership of Sir Henry Campbell-Bannerman. Ponsonby's opinion of Campbell-Bannerman was equivocal, for, while he had admired the stand he had taken during the Boer War, he thought his subsequent leadership of the party lacking in dynamism. So keenly felt was this opinion that he decided to approach John Morley.

Ponsonby had found that wherever he went the leadership of the Liberal Party had become an open question. People had no confidence in Lord Rosebery and although they were loyal to Campbell-Bannerman, they had misgivings as to his powers of leadership. What they wanted was a man who would not only command respect but really inspire enthusiasm. He believed John Morley to be such a man, to whom the leadership should be put to not as a suggestion to be accepted or refused but as a duty to the party. The letter that eventually went to Morley was hardly couched in these terms and, needless to say, Morley was not to be drawn.[29]

Ponsonby's impetuous championing of Morley in 1903 should be seen as an intuitive reaction to the schisms in the party. Gladstonian liberalism was still attractive and Morley was, on most issues, Gladstone's heir; if he could be persuaded to enter the arena, then perhaps all would be well. That politics hardly worked in this way was soon to become apparent, for the Liberal League had embarked on an attempt to gain control of the party machine. The Liberal League's siege of Parliament Street was very powerful and gaining strength when Ponsonby first came to the Liberal Central Office. Herbert Gladstone told him that they aimed to capture the central organisation and the party chest through the ingenious method of pretended friendship with Parliament Street. As Ponsonby retold the story in his memoir on Campbell-Bannerman

> it was never open warfare but incessant intrigue . . . I cannot remember all the various fights with the Liberal League. They were incessant and at times very acute. We were on the defensive. But I remember we had from time to time to count heads among members of Parliament, watch their speeches on Home Rule and make lists of the sheep and the goats.[30]

As far as his Taunton constituency work was concerned, internecine rivalries inside the party paled into insignificance when Ponsonby confronted the problem of his opponent, Sir Edward Boyle, KC. Boyle was very rich and not too scrupulous about how his money was used in the constituency.

Political work had given Ponsonby everything that his life in the Foreign Office had previously lacked. This is reflected in the letters that he wrote to Dolly; whereas before they had been leisurely, concerned with social affairs, they were now much more direct and practical, the letters of an involved and committed person. Arthur was, at this time, living in London at Artillery Mansions for the working week, while on the whole Dolly stayed at Shulbrede. She was again pregnant and, in July 1904, their son Matthew was born. The confinement was difficult and Dolly's health suffered in consequence. After the purchase of the Priory, the pattern of their future life became stabilised. Dolly and the children lived at Shulbrede, Arthur worked in London. He would get away to Shulbrede at the weekends and occasionally commute to London from Haslemere. With golf relegated to his holidays, art – his former second activity – now became an all-consuming interest in watercolour painting. What with his work in Parliament Street, his hunting down of clues to the history of Shulbrede Priory with his friend Charles Strachey in the British Museum and the London Library, it was surprising that he found time to watercolour, but it was pursued to such good effect that Roger Fry thought he could get Arthur an invitation to submit to the New English Art Club (NEAC). One day in December 1903 Arthur was lunching alone when as he reported to Dolly

> I saw looming out of the dark two eyes well known tragic and frightening. I saw it was Mrs Fry and I was terrified. Roger was there too and a man and woman.

Roger who had got an odd black cover over one of his eyes came up and spoke to me and asked me to say a word to his wife which I did before they went. She asked after you and was in a state of great restraint she looked dreadful haggard and sad. He had brought her up to see the doctor but I gathered she was by no means well yet. It was most difficult talking to her, I became inarticulate and got dark red on mentioning Pearsall's name.[31]

Mrs Fry was never to get better, as she was suffering from a terrible illness which caused the brain to press against the inside of the skull.

Arthur's watercolours were considered to be sufficiently good to warrant an exhibition which was arranged by the Carfax Gallery in the autumn of 1905. Prices for the paintings were fixed from between £3 and £7 and, although the Gallery were very soothing and kind, Arthur found the experience 'very alarming'. Although he greatly enjoyed painting – 'in copying in water colour Fra Filippo Lippi's Madonna in the National Gallery, 7½ hours passed like two minutes' – the style of his paintings left critical opinion divided. Some critics remarked favourably on a charming tapestry-like quality of colour in his watercolours, while others thought his sensitivity insipid and bracketed him with Roger Fry, Rich and Tonks, as members of an 'archaiistic vortex'. In the event he sold 16 of 61 of his paintings and realised £53.11.0. Not that Arthur had much time to reflect for within a few days of his exhibition came the long awaited resignation of the government.

By the end of 1905 Ponsonby's appeal to John Morley to take up the leadership of the party was long forgotten, for he was now a firm supporter of Campbell-Bannerman, converted by his tactful handling of the Liberal Imperialists. Ponsonby had played a small part in maintaining the ascendancy of Parliament Street over the Liberal League and his successful work at the Liberal Central Association led Herbert Gladstone to propose to Campbell-Bannerman Arthur's appointment as principal private secretary to the Prime Minister. The original intention was that Ponsonby would serve as private secretary from the back benches. This depended on winning Taunton. Although Ponsonby cut heavily into the previous Tory majority, he just failed to add Taunton to the Liberal landslide. When the polls were counted, Ponsonby was beaten by 339 votes. In public he was gracious in defeat, congratulating Sir Edward Boyle for the manner in which he had personally conducted the election. In private he wrote that 'the triumph of the scoundrelly Tory agent and some of the chief bribers and of Lady Boyle with her unprincipled vulgar dishonest methods was an unpleasant thing to see'.[32] Limericks were, in those days, still a popular feature of election campaigns, and Taunton furnished the following:

> Said an eminent King's Counsel I
> Came a cropper in Hastings and Rye,
>   If I ride Protection,

I'll win this election.
Murmured Ponsonby, 'Think so? Just try!'

Campbell-Bannerman's condolences on hearing Ponsonby's defeat were naturally muted – 'I cannot profess to regret a result which leaves you with me'.

The Prime Minister's Office, if it can be described as such in 1906, totalled three, two private secretaries, of whom Ponsonby was the principal and Vaughan Nash the second, and Henry Higgs the Treasury secretary who looked after ecclesiastical patronage. There were two assistant parliamentary secretaries, but they never did anything. 'We never give them anything to do' wrote Ponsonby 'and Vaughan was impatient if they ever asked to do anything.'

Ponsonby was chosen for the job because his experience and qualifications perfectly complemented those of Vaughan Nash. Arthur was not a complete stranger to Campbell-Bannerman. They had first met at Osborne when Arthur had played the part of Tony Lumpkin in *She Stoops to Conquer*. Campbell-Bannerman well remembered the performance and the claque of footmen who were ready to burst into storms of applause if any of the princesses forgot their lines. He had worked with Sir Henry Ponsonby and, at their first interview, spoke warmly of the relationship when he had been at the War Office having to exercise a good deal of tact in getting rid of the Duke of Cambridge. The fact of Arthur's having cut himself off from society appealed to Campbell-Bannerman, as did his anti-imperialist views. Although Ponsonby was the principal private secretary, he looked after the less important part of the work, arranging interviews and engagements, and letter writing, while Nash, who had vastly greater experience, looked after matters of policy and guidance of the Prime Minister in dealing with public questions. Vaughan Nash and Ponsonby were very much a team. Nash was much older than Ponsonby, having been formerly a journalist with the *Daily Chronicle* and the *Manchester Guardian*. He was an expert on labour problems, and had played a significant role in the famous dock strike of 1886. He had been Campbell-Bannerman's secretary before 1906 and might have been expected to resent the intrusion, but being an extremely modest man, he appreciated the qualities that Ponsonby brought to the team. Nash was shy and retiring to the extent of walking on tiptoe when in Campbell-Bannerman's room and completely overawed by the social atmosphere that surrounded 10 Downing Street, whereas Ponsonby, although contemptuous of 'society', was completely at ease even in the most exalted circles.

The private secretary had in addition to his office in Downing Street a room at the House of Commons.

My room at the House is so tremendously impressive that I shall have to buy yet another pair of bags to be up to it. Gold and silver and a smell of russia leather thick carpets and sacramental messengers crowns and cushions and whispering cabinet ministers.[33]

Going to the House as an official rather than as an MP was naturally rather painful at first. 'I drove with CB to the House and I got a little corner seat where I saw everything. I had a talk with Masterman and many other MPs and could not help feeling just a qualm at being out of it.' But the pressure of work was so great, and the distractions of the House so time consuming, that he resolved to do his work mostly in Downing Street.

Neither Ponsonby nor Nash had the capacity or inclination to become political wire pullers of the magnitude of someone like Lord Esher. However, as both were radical Liberals they were concerned to protect their Prime Minister from the machinations of the Liberal Imperialists. They could only drive Campbell-Bannerman in a direction that he himself was prepared to travel along and this they did with great skill over the issues of South Africa and the House of Lords. But it is not these issues that must be first addressed, for the Liberal government was immediately caught up in the Moroccan crisis with unknown consequences both to the foreign relations of the United Kingdom and to Ponsonby's own future political life.

Although Ponsonby was appointed private secretary immediately after Campbell-Bannerman was asked to form a government, he was not privy to the process of Cabinet making. In view of the subsequent course of events in foreign policy in relation to the government's commitment to supporting a balance of power policy against Germany, Ponsonby's retrospective views, especially those written after 1914 in the memoir of Campbell-Bannerman, need to be treated with caution. To make matters even more complicated, Ponsonby admits that his memory of events in December 1905 was confused by the turmoil, but that, after the event, he had heard from Campbell-Bannerman himself the details of the construction of his Cabinet and of the 'plot' to send him to the House of Lords. Ponsonby, like many others, had made his own Cabinet list after Balfour's resignation and his choice for the Foreign Office had been none other than Sir Edward Grey, a choice not liked by Mary Ponsonby – 'I don't like your foreign affairs Edward Grey who can't speak a word of any language but his own' nor did she approve of her son's second choice, James Bryce, whom she thought more suitable for Education than the Foreign Office. She preferred either Lord Rosebery or Lord Cromer. In the memoir Ponsonby asserted that 'Haldane and Grey acted together and their feelings of animosity against C-B were pronounced and undisguised' but the evidence for this assertion is Ponsonby's recollection of Campbell-

Bannerman's reaction to a letter he received from Grey while at Biarritz at the end of 1907

> he received a letter from Grey with New Year's greetings. In it he expressed regret at the attitude he had adopted on the formation of the government saying that the two years of liberal administration abundantly justified C-B's leadership. I forget the exact phrase but it was a generous acknowledgement of his mistake. The letter will be among C-B's papers but I doubt if it will ever be mentioned. That Grey should have brought himself to write such a letter proves what an obstructive and obstinate position he must have taken up at the time of the formation of the government.[34]

As to the military conversations between England and France, Ponsonby honestly admitted that he knew nothing of it at the time, but then proposed the view that Campbell-Bannerman was the innocent victim of a Grey-Haldane conspiracy.

> It seems that Haldane went to Belgrave Square and told him of the French 'conversations' with a view to getting his sanction to them. Grey also must have made his statement to him then. To Haldane it appears he said 'that is purely a War Office matter go ahead.'[35]

Ponsonby continues the memoir by asking that two things should be borne in mind; first, the peculiar relationship between the two and the Prime Minister, and second that Campbell-Bannerman never talked the matter over with either Morley or Loreburn, his two closest colleagues. Such an important question required constant consultation and exchange of views. 'This he never had with either of them . . . So I am fully persuaded that C.B. never apprehended the significance of the conversations with France, nor did he see how we were being gradually committed. As a matter of fact I doubt if Grey did either.'

While none of this throws any light on what actually happened, what can be seen quite clearly is the emergence of secret diplomacy as a central feature of the radical critique of Grey's foreign policy. The irony of his being as close as it was possible to be to these events, yet at the same time completely unaware, was not lost on Ponsonby in 1914. It must be pointed out that the Anglo-French conversations, started so surreptitiously on horseback in Rotten Row in December in a casual conversation between Major Huguet and General Grierson, only came to the notice of the Foreign Office on 9 January. Ponsonby was at that time in Devon fighting for his political life and so entirely missed Grey's letter of 9 January to Campbell-Bannerman, who was at Belmont, informing Campbell-Bannerman that 'the War Office ought to be ready to answer the question what could they do if we had to intervene against Germany if the neutrality of Belgium was violated'.[36]

Just as controversy still surrounds the exact nature of the commitment given by England to France before the World War, so an equally acrimonious and more immediate controversy broke out over the new government's political settlement in South Africa. What was at stake here was not simply a question of either representative or responsible government being given to the Transvaal, but the bigger and more important question of reconciliation and co-operation between the victorious British and the defeated Boers. By giving South Africa back to the Boers, Campbell-Bannerman achieved a great act of statesmanship and in so doing clearly differentiated his new administration from his conservative predecessors. After a Cabinet meeting on 8 February, the Prime Minister remarked that he had struggled with beasts in Ephesus and had vanquished them.[37] In dealing with the question as one of principle and calling for a clean break with the past, Campbell-Bannerman taught his secretary a valuable lesson which was to serve him in good stead in later years.

Both the Moroccan crisis and the South African question were decided early in the life of Campbell-Bannerman's government when Ponsonby was still working his way into the private secretaryship. In his private correspondence the predominating theme is one of being rushed off his feet. To Dolly he confided:

> I simply hate being at the House there is a lot of waiting and loafing. Nash does all the important political work and I have only odds and ends of tiresome correspondence to see him about I get so sick of political talk I feel out of it ignorant and bored. I had dinner with Masterman but Sidney Buxton joined us and so did not have much of a talk. There was no room to get in the House and I came home at about 10.30 in absolute despair wondering if I could stand it.[38]

While this feeling may have been caused by his having to endure fulsome condolences from his Tory adversary at Taunton, it also reflects Ponsonby's disenchantment with practical politics as opposed to what he termed real politics.

On that particular evening, the arrival of Buxton at the supper table prevented Masterman and Ponsonby from discussing the really important issue confronting the Liberal Party, of how they were to use their great majority to redress the enormous social and economic inequities in Edwardian society. Masterman's commitment to this cause had been the original basis of the friendship as Ponsonby had put it in his diary. 'It was the politics of life of which we spoke not the politics of parties.'[39] There were to be many more days of boring politics before the Liberals finally began to address the real issue. The Campbell-Bannerman administration's chief weakness in Ponsonby's view was that it lacked a programme.

> The danger I think is that he [C-B] does not look forward enough nor do any of the Cabinet nor does the Cabinet as a whole. They deal with what is under their

nose; they have an uncomfortable feeling about what is coming on next week but they simply ignore what is to happen after that. The result is a dangerous lack of project and construction. The work of the session was heaped up higgledy piggledy like stones on a cart and some of them are now rolling off and some are being surreptitiously pushed off and it will not be much of a load that they will bring in at the end of the session.[40]

The experience of the first year and a half of their administration had taught the Liberals that their great majority in the Commons was going to be powerless in effecting real changes because of obstruction by the equally great number of Tory peers in the 'other place'. The House of Lords question now became the dominant issue in British politics. This was to be real politics with a vengeance, for any reform of the House of Lords was bound to challenge not simply the balance of power within the constitution between Lords and Commons, but raise the whole question of the class bias of English politics. The Ponsonbys were continually being reminded of this by the hostile attitude they encountered from any number of friends and acquaintances. Shortly after Ponsonby had become Campbell-Bannerman's private secretary, Dolly found that her friends regarded this not as an achievement worthy of congratulations, but a reprehensible if not treacherous desertion to the other side.

At the end of the year Arthur was persuaded to go to dinner at the house of an old Balliol acquaintance. He found there other Balliol men including his old friend Lord Kerry (later Marquess of Lansdowne), 'all bitter narrow Tories'.

The immediate issue that brought the House of Lords to the forefront was their killing of the Education Bill of 1906. This Bill was the centrepiece of the government's legislative programme. It sought to remedy the non-conformist objections to the Education Act of 1902, but, without plunging into the labyrinths of sectarian controversy that surrounded the gradual extension of state power into the jealously guarded privileges of the Churches in the education system, enough is said if it is understood that all sections of the religious community and the Conservative Party were opposed to the bill. Ponsonby followed the details of the debate with great interest and in the process formed distinctly unfavourable impressions, in particular of the Church of England hierarchy. He reported to Dolly

> As I went down to the House on Monday a brougham of the very smartest description with a pair of prancing horses dashed up and I saw 'that most unchristian sight a clergyman debonair lolling back on the cushions of this dashing carriage and pair'. It was Archdeacon Wilberforce eminently typical of that class.[41]

The strongest expression of disapproval came a few months after the bill had been killed when in his diary Ponsonby wrote

The Archbishop and his deputation stayed 3 hours were very heated and interrupted McKenna's speech 37 times. I've never seen such a high percentage of unpleasant countenances in a deputation except perhaps the licensed victualler deputation . . .[42]

The gauntlet thrown down by the Conservatives in the Lords was taken up in the Commons by the government's decision to oppose the Lords' amendments to the Education Bill *en bloc*. A motion to that effect was carried by an enormous majority in the Commons, but an equally large majority of the Lords, a week later, insisted on their amendments. The deadlock was now complete.

In the new year Ponsonby became much more actively involved in the government's plan to deal with the House of Lords. He took the view that the loss of the Bill was a great pity but that the Liberal Party itself was much stronger now than when it had come in. The controversy had resulted in general indignation against the House of Lords, without alienating the nonconformist supporters of the party, which further compromise would have inevitably brought about. The government accepted the challenge, but rather than taking it up directly by seeking a dissolution, they decided to set up a cabinet committee to examine the options open to it. Its deliberations produced the Lord Chancellor's scheme for a joint committee of MPs and Peers who would resolve issues that separated the two Houses. Ponsonby and Nash decided that this was hopelessly weak, and that they should clear it out of the road. Ponsonby's first opportunity to make his views known came at the dinner with the Archbishop of Canterbury, where he overate 'nay rather excessively banketted'. He told the Lord Chancellor that his scheme would never do.[43] Nash and Ponsonby had developed the habit of conferring together away from the routine and official atmosphere of Downing Street and on the Whitsun bank holiday weekend Nash went over to Shulbrede where their House of Lords counterproject was hatched.

Back in London, they began the task of converting the Prime Minister and then the Cabinet. The Diary records the progress.

Nash and I set to work at once. N. tackled CB and then we both had a conference with Ilbert [Sir Courtney Ilbert, the Clerk of the House] who entirely agreed that the present idea of tackling the Lords was ineffectual and he more or less fell in with our suggestions. I got hold of Herbert Gladstone too and made him see the futility and danger of the present scheme before the Cabinet. They none of them realize in the least degree the overwhelming importance of whatever action we take. I shall have to intrigue a good deal and get hold of the Lord Chancellor and other members of the Cabinet before they meet.[44]

His first Cabinet convert was Lewis Harcourt, whom he reported to Dolly on the 29th was thoroughly taken up with the scheme. And the next day after endlessly talking, running about and interviewing, he reported home that 'H of L scheme going very strong – most cabinet ministers won over – it will be up at the Cabinet tomorrow.'[45]

In that Cabinet meeting of 31 May, the Ponsonby/Nash scheme won enough support to dispose of the Lord Chancellor's scheme and the Diary records '1 June 07 Our House of Lords scheme progressing passed cabinet on Friday and is now circulated as a memorandum.' Following its progress beyond this stage was to prove more difficult for Ponsonby who was, as far as the Cabinet was concerned, 'without the door', and not privy to all the papers and information that was circulated within the Cabinet, but as far as he could judge he was confident that his scheme had taken hold. Campbell-Bannerman was due to speak in the House on 24 June. His health was not good and he caused anxiety by overdoing his social engagements. Ponsonby and Vaughan Nash had a good talk about the Lords over dinner on 23 June. Campbell-Bannerman had not done anything by 18 June and, in the end, the speech was only got out with the help of Vaughan Nash in a Sunday meeting, the day before it was to be delivered.

The central feature of the Ponsonby/Nash scheme, as elaborated to the House by Campbell-Bannerman on 24 June, was to separate the question of the powers of the House of Lords to interfere with Bills from the infinitely more complex question of the composition of the Second Chamber. The 1907 Resolution was therefore framed with this end in view. It said 'that in order to give effect to the will of the people as expressed by their elected representatives it is necessary that the power of the other House should be so restricted by law to secure that within the limits of a single parliament the final decision of the Commons must prevail'. As Ponsonby explained it to his mother, the Resolution was a first step and a Parliament Bill would follow later but that as it was of such vast importance it should be dealt with deliberately and slowly. No one has ever satisfactorily explained why Campbell-Bannerman did not follow up the Resolution with a Parliament Bill. Roy Jenkins' guess that he intended to give the Lords a further trial of perhaps a year certainly chimes with Ponsonby's view that a Parliament Bill should only come by slow deliberation.[46]

This ended Ponsonby's direct involvement. Eventually the scheme with various amendments went through and formed the basis of the Parliament Act of 1911. The private secretary's involvement arose, not so much from any desire on the part of Ponsonby to manipulate power, but from the particular relationship that had developed between the Prime Minister and his secretary.

CB is a splendid man to work through but he sometimes exasperates one by his want of initiative and energy. He gets through all he has got to do but it is a case of controlling a rolling ball, the pace and in fact the motion does not depend on him but on outside circumstances.[47]

The personal and domestic problems that surrounded Campbell-Bannerman's premiership were unknown to the general public, but not to his colleagues and, right at the beginning, Herbert Gladstone had warned Ponsonby that Campbell-Bannerman would have to have 'his attention focused on things of importance very often'.

As far as the official relationship is concerned, the point to note is that although Campbell-Bannerman was very punctual in his official work, he was also very easy going. He once told Ponsonby that he had never read a Bill nor a blue book through. This made life difficult for the secretaries, as they had constantly to guard against drifting. The work of the government was not helped by the excessive departmentalism of ministers who became preoccupied with their own problems and were all too often, in Ponsonby's opinion, in the pockets of their permanent officials. These tendencies were more than counter-balanced by Campbell-Bannerman's rocklike hold on principle. None of this would have amounted to very much if he had enjoyed good health, but this was not the case, for first came the death of Lady Campbell-Bannerman and then the slow, but inevitable, decline of Campbell-Bannerman himself. Ponsonby wrote in retrospect

CB's two years of Premiership were very far from being the unadulterated enjoyment of power and position. They were in reality to him a tragedy and I should not wonder if in his life of 70 years they were not the two years which brought him the most distress and suffering. This was not detected by the outside world who only saw his political success and popularity. But to understand more it must be realized that during the first year he was watching his wife dying with a solicitude and vigilance which completely overtaxed his strength and during the second year he himself gradually declined till he died within a few weeks of his resignation.[48]

Lady Campbell-Bannerman's illness was the extremely painful and incurable disease, diabetic neuritis. When Ponsonby came to Downing Street, she was already very sick and hardly ever left her bedroom. It was decided that Campbell-Bannerman would take his wife to Marienbad in the summer of 1906, and that Ponsonby would be with them. Ponsonby travelled out independently of the Campbell-Bannermans, arriving at Marienbad a week later on 15 August 1906. On his way out, he stopped at Ostend, where he inadvertently took a stroll to occupy an hour's wait at the railway station and found it to be

an astounding place, nothing but improper women with canary coloured boots and pink and white stockings, bands, jewellers shops gigantic hotels fat foreign children bearded foreign toffs and [an] air of unhealthy dissipation and sham amusement.

Marienbad, for all its chic status, was found to be

> nothing but new hotels and planted out gardens promenades and restaurants all modern and spic and span – deadly dullness could not go further. Crowds of people but not at all smart. The women that surround the King are a special sort of sham improper ladies.[49]

After spending the greater part of his first day in the 'Tet', 'the correct occupation' he was assured by Campbell-Bannerman, he accompanied the Prime Minister down to the station to meet the King. Ponsonby had not seen the King since he had left the diplomatic service. Edward VII had heard then that Arthur had become a socialist. He had said to Fritz 'There is drudgery in every profession and I don't think it at all clever of him to have left but very foolish not to have found out.' When Fritz attempted to play down the socialism by explaining that his brother was a keen follower of Campbell-Bannerman, the King had responded with a ginger beer noise. Knowing that the King thought a socialist was a person who put a bomb under your bed, he was not surprised to see his monarch looking rather nervous but Edward VII took the plunge and shook hands. In the face of this sterling display of fortitude, he determined not to allow himself to think of this sort of life getting on his nerves.

Walks in the pine forests, listening to an open air orchestra, and tennis with a diplomat friend all helped, but within a week he felt that he had been there two months and then his good resolutions were dashed by the discovery of the presence in Marienbad of the member for Taunton.

While Boyle could be avoided, the King could not. He was staying at the Hotel Weimar and Arthur nervously went to lunch. 'The K got up from his writing table and shook hands. "I hardly knew you" he said "all shaven and shorn. haholjohrelzockzek." (this is his ginger beer laugh.)' Among the topics of conversation was Dolly's father, his love of yachting and his prospects of becoming a member of the RYS 'wonderful man most energetic works too hard haholjohrelzochzek.' A further ordeal was in store at another luncheon party this time given by Campbell-Bannerman for the King and then a dinner in the Kursaal.

These trials were as nothing to braving morning walks on the parade. He had only one turn, but did not talk to anyone, although he saw Ivor Herbert, Boyd, Lionel Sartoris, Steed (of *The Times*), Mrs Harter, Lady Newry, Charlie Lawrence, Mark Lockwood, Beaucroft, Pinero, old Vaughan Williams, Goschen, Soveral, Sir Gilbert Parker and Gurney Boyle. It was all too much and the gloom was only lifted by Lady Romney's fury at having to leave a band concert to go and have lunch with the King.

It was by now apparent to everyone that Lady Campbell-Bannerman was not benefitting from the change of air at Marienbad and soon she became very ill, dying on 30 August. Ponsonby, rising to the challenge, handled all the difficulties of bringing her body back to Scotland.

These tragic circumstances had the inevitable consequence that the private secretaries now became more and more involved in the domestic side of the Prime Minister's life. After Ponsonby left Belmont Castle, the Campbell-Bannermans' Scottish home at Meigle, Vaughan Nash took his place and, while he was there, Campbell-Bannerman had his first heart attack. It was not serious and the news was kept from the press. Now there could be no question of his being left alone in London, so Arthur was persuaded to move over from his bachelor quarters in Artillery Mansions to Downing Street. Work now became more or less continuous. The most enjoyable part of Arthur's new daily routine was dining tête-à-tête with Campbell-Bannerman; he talked very freely with his secretary and the Diary records that one of his favourite subjects was 'the difficulty of ruling a democracy through a social aristocracy and the instinctive class feeling of English people'.[50]

A further entry in Ponsonby's diary reveals the Prime Minister in a lighter vein.

> This evening he was on a favourite theme of his which is his affection for inanimate things – walking sticks pencils even clothes. He treats them like old friends. At Marienbad he said to me one day pointing to a little old walking stick 'I never use this one but poor little chap he would have minded if I had left him behind so he always comes abroad with me'.[51]

Campbell-Bannerman liked talking over things and surveying the political field; they usually dined alone, but sometimes political colleagues would come and, if it should be Winston Churchill, they all had to act as audience.[52] When they were at Belmont, Arthur greatly amused Campbell-Bannerman by protecting his calves from the attention of his bulldog, Zuli, at tea-time by handing round the cakes carrying a fire guard over his legs as a defence. However, in spite of the easy going and friendly relations that prevailed at Downing Street, Ponsonby began to feel the strain of his position, although the arrival of Mrs Campbell, the Australian wife of Campbell-Bannerman's nephew, in Downing Street did something to help – 'Mrs Campbell does chatter dreadfully but I don't really mind her as she is very humble minded and tries to fit in.'[53]

In a retrospective look at 1906, Ponsonby concluded that his present profession was only a stepping stone and that he got impatient and bored with it unless he was overwhelmed with work which, fortunately, occurred pretty frequently. The problem was not simply that Downing Street kept him away from his family, only allowing him to get to Shulbrede from Saturday evening until Monday morning, but that being bound to Campbell-Bannerman blocked any possibility of entering Parliament. This heretofore remote prospect became quite suddenly attainable when, one day early in November, Jessie Herbert of the Central Office asked Ponsonby if he would like to stand in the Liberal interest for Huddersfield, which would be both cheap and safe. The offer was rejected. 'It only took me one minute to make up my mind.' The reasons being first that he could not leave Campbell-Bannerman, second that he would never fight a Labour man, and third that he doubted whether he could stand as a Liberal.[54] Ponsonby attempted to resolve this dilemma in several discussions with Vaughan Nash. After the first of them, he reported to Dolly:

> He is always very clear minded and not impetuous and merely idealistic like I am. He agrees absolutely in the main but his argument is – and it is a good one – that the English people will never join a party that conforms to a particular code or any 'ism' of any kind. In politics they like to be persuaded by practical legislation of the truth of any policy. He agreed with me that the Socialists lose many opportunities of stating their point of view however extreme it may appear. For instance on land tenure they might support the liberals but state their case for getting rid of landlords altogether and nationalizing the land. It is all very difficult.[55]

Ponsonby had known of the Lib-Lab electoral pact of 1905 and approved of it and so he came to the colusion that given the present state of the Labour Party, he would be in a stronger position to stand for Parliament as a Liberal, provided he had no Labour man to fight than if 'I created a sensation by calling myself a socialist and laying myself open, from my training and education influences which cannot be completely shaken off, to charges of inconsistency'.[56] While many upper class people continued to regard all socialists as potential incendiarists, this was never the Prime Minister's position. He and many other leaders of the Liberal Party were firmly convinced that the future of the two parties lay together. The previous summer, shortly after Lady Campbell-Bannerman's funeral, Ponsonby had been the delighted witness of an animated conversation between Lady Airlie, John Morley and Campbell-Bannerman during which she raised the question of the socialist menace. The Prime Minister had reassured her that even the most extreme Labour men were admirable members of the House and told her of the 'deeply touching' telegram he had received from the 35 Labour men at the Trades Union Congress 'we mourn with you at the grave side'. As Ponsonby had already decided that he could not leave Campbell-Bannerman, these discussions were for the moment of no practical import.

One inescapable part of any private secretary's lot was to sift the many applications for patronage and honours that at times piled up on the doorstep of 10 Downing Street. The patronage secretary, Higgs, dealt with the ecclesiastical world, much to Ponsonby's relief, but he had to cope with the demands of Campbell-Bannerman's colleagues for honours and appointments for their friends and protégés in the civil service, and even came into reluctant contact with the seamy and squalid purchase of honours by rich supporters of the party. The Prime Minister did not take much interest in the applications, so Ponsonby collected them together until the approaching publication day made a meeting imperative. Ponsonby had a list, Campbell-Bannerman had his own list and Whiteley, the Chief Whip, a third.

> 5 June 1907 The drawing up of the Honours List has taken up a good deal of attention and shows up incidentally a good deal of sordid and petty ambition.
>
> 16 June 1907 I was at work a good deal at the Honours List, a degrading occupation. Peers who pay for it, Baronets who badger for it and knights who are nonentities.
>
> 27 June 1907 I propped up that letter from Sinky [Elizabeth] on my table to encourage me and help me through this last honours day and it did. . .it's done now and as usual some of them have got their honour by a fluke or a mistake.
>
> 3 July 1907 The Honours List caused satisfaction. There were a good many rival claimants. Whiteley enjoyed the money squeezing part of it which I think is particularly disagreeable and it is rather a shock when one hears of bleeding also in very high quarters. But this is the inevitable result of the offensive custom.
>
> CB was really very amusing last night about Adam. He said he thought he behaved so abominably trying to put the blame on God 'the woman thou gavest me' instead of behaving like a gentleman and saying 'it was entirely my fault' and he made me laugh a great deal going through the Honours list this morning. 'Oh no, no, a horrid fellow. I won't make him a knight.'[57]

The Chief Whip was the party dispenser of patronage and his methods were so bare-faced that Campbell-Bannerman became alarmed. One day, in Ponsonby's office, the Chief Whip pulled out of his pocket £50,000 [in 1907 money] which had been paid for a baronetcy.[58] On another occasion, an old gentleman cried on Ponsonby's shoulder because the chances of his peerage seemed shaky. The King was not above getting his gambling debts cancelled by conferring a baronetcy and altogether Ponsonby found the subject to be very disagreeable. He thought it would be a splendid innovation if the published lists of the recipients of honours could be headed by a list of the names of people who had refused!

When the Prime Minister's office had to deal with artistic appointments, Ponsonby did not feel quite so detached and impartial. Soon after he arrived in Downing Street, the appointment of Director of the National Gallery had to be filled. Ponsonby, by now a member of the NEAC with one small exhibition to his credit, had very definite opinions on who should be appointed. His candidate was his friend and artistic mentor, Roger Fry. Fry was the leading candidate for the position and would have secured the appointment, but for the fact that Pierrepoint

Morgan had already made him an offer to build up the collection of the Metropolitan Museum of Art in New York that he could not refuse. The directorship went to Sir C. Holroyd. But Ponsonby and Fry had the satisfaction of seeing their candidate, Dugald MacColl, appointed to the Keepership of the Tate.[59]

A second appointment that personally interested Ponsonby was that of Lawrence Hammond to be Secretary of the Civil Service Commission. It had become apparent, late in July 1907, that the proposed appointment could not take place on account of illness and so Ponsonby took advantage of the opening to forward Lawrence Hammond's name. Hammond at this time was a prominent journalist supporter of the Liberals, having been editor of the weekly *The Speaker* before it became *The Nation* in 1907 and was desperately in need of a break from politics and journalism. The appointment could not have been more fortunately timed and gave Hammond the leisure to begin his classic study of social history during the Industrial Revolution. When their book was published the Hammonds were only too pleased to acknowledge their debt.[60]

The Honours business was not without its amusing side. During the conversation at Lady Airlie's shortly after Lady Campbell-Bannerman's funeral, previously referred to, Campbell-Bannerman was persuaded to tell the following anecdote. His first bishop was the famous medieval historian Stubbs. He recollected that Stubbs was a Christian socialist and that someone accused Stubbs of being politically a socialist. This Stubbs resented – 'What is the difference then?' asked the man. Stubbs replied 'The political socialist says "What *you* have belongs to me": the Christian socialist says "What *I* have belongs to you".'

Although Ponsonby had given up the idea of becoming a professional actor, his interest in the theatre never waned, and the list of plays that he attended in these years is truly remarkable. The theatrical sensation of 1907 was John Galsworthy's social realist play *The Silver Box*, which Arthur saw in April 1907. It was produced at the Royal Court Theatre, which, under Granville Barker and J.E. Vedrenne, was making theatrical history as the centre for a theatre of ideas. The first success of the new venture had been Bernard Shaw's *Candida* in 1904. In January 1907, the PM's office had received an application from Granville Barker for a knighthood for W.S. Gilbert, and, when the Barkers took a house close to Shulbrede in the summer of 1907, their common interest in the theatre blossomed into friendship and they discussed from a political point of view the plot of Barker's new play, *Waste*.[61] One Sunday, the Barkers brought George Bernard Shaw to tea, who won over Ponsonby by admiring Shulbrede.

Earlier in the year Ponsonby had made the acquaintance of Galsworthy at a dinner in the House of Commons.

brilliant company. I hardly uttered. Charles Masterman, Lehman, Winston Churchill, Robert Cecil, Shaw, 2 Trevelyans making or rather shouting fireworks across the table. Nevinson, Galsworthy (author of the Silver Box, one of the best plays I have ever seen) and Charles Buxton thinking and occasionally supplementing the conversation with profound scraps of wisdom. I doubt if I have the lungs I know I have not the intelligence to be a la hauteur of such company.[62]

The theme of *The Silver Box*, one law for the rich and another for the poor, was very close to Ponsonby's heart. After this success, Galsworthy began to work on a series of sketches for *The Nation* on a number of causes that he had become interested in. They were published in book form as *A Commentary* (1908). Included in them are two sketches recording his horrified reaction to prison life. His visit to Dartmoor had been facilitated by Ponsonby, who made all the necessary arrangements with the Home Office.

When *Waste* appeared, it attracted the attention of the censor, who had been active earlier in the year against Edward Garnett's play *The Breaking Point*. The literary community was outraged, and a protest committee was formed by Galsworthy, J.M. Barrie and Granville Barker. Barker rather rashly asked Ponsonby to use his influence with the Prime Minister to abolish the censor. The most that Ponsonby could do was to arrange for a deputation to see Campbell-Bannerman. A date was fixed for November, but the state of Campbell-Bannerman's health prevented the event from taking place. The deputation had, unknown to Ponsonby, planned a demonstration. This was organised by William Archer whose instructions have fortunately survived:

The Dramatic authors of England are to assemble in Trafalgar Square. Barrie will address them from the base of Nelson's Column and the Savoy orchestra will play 'Britons will never be slaves'. The procession will then form and will be headed by Pinero and Shaw walking arm in arm. Immediately behind them will come Garnett and Galsworthy each bearing the pole of a red banner with the inscription 'Down with the censor'. An effigy of Redford [the censor] which is being prepared by the Savoy property man will be carried by Frederick Harrison and W.B. Yeats and over its head will wave a banner carried by Gilbert Murray with the inscription 'Ecrasez l'infame!' Arriving in Downing St. Swinburne will declaim an 'Ode to C.B.'[63]

Bernard Shaw's subsequent tirade against the censor in *The Nation* was to be poor compensation, although Ponsonby's diary records that when he arrived at Downing Street on 16 November he found the Prime Minister recovered from his attack and delighted with Shaw's letter.

There can be little doubt that Ponsonby's close association with the literary community during the summer of 1907 had an unsettling effect.

The creative energies of Granville Barker and Galsworthy which had produced *Waste* and *The Silver Box* only served to highlight Ponsonby's dependent position in Downing Street. He wrote 'of course it is interesting to be near all the centre of political affairs and of Government *but* only as an onlooker – a sort of eavesdropper – not a participant'.[64] This comment was written under the stress of discouraging reports on Dolly's health. The doctors said there would be no question of her going to live in London. So there was no prospect of ever spending more than a short weekend at home while Campbell-Bannerman was in London. And there was the further daunting prospect of having to accompany him both to Scotland and abroad. However, it was not Dolly's health alone that unsettled Arthur. Clearly he needed to find an outlet for his creative energy. Just before the end of the session, Arthur invited Roger Fry, Charles Strachey and Goldsworthy Dickinson to spend the weekend of Matthew's birthday at Shulbrede. Dickinson made a particularly striking impression on Dolly, who recorded in her diary that they played 'Nuts in May' and she laughed very much to see Maggie hand in hand with Dickinson and Roger Fry, complete strangers to her, dancing backwards and forwards and singing.[65]

In the evening, the discussion turned on more serious themes and they talked over 'the preposterous money making ideal that is set up by most people'. Ponsonby decided that he would collect some essays from his friends on the subject. This was the germ of an idea that eventually became Ponsonby's first successful book *The Camel and the Needle's Eye*. In the meantime, he took another look at the manuscript of 'Spiritual Perfection' written five years before and talked over his idea of the perfect soul with Dolly.

Returning to London immediately after Matthew's birthday party, Ponsonby as usual attended the debates in the House. On 31 July, he reported to Dolly that when he arrived at the House to listen to the Cromer-Grant debate last evening he had missed both Campbell-Bannerman and A.J. Balfour but was unimpressed by the new Labour MP, Victor Grayson. On another occasion, shortly afterwards, J. Burns, the President of the Local Government Board and the first working-class man to sit in the Cabinet, came and sat next to Ponsonby under the gallery. As usual Burns got through a certain amount of self glorification, but then was very amusing and racy about members and their ways. He told Ponsonby how devoted he was to the place – he could not tear himself away hardly for an evening.[66]

All the time Ponsonby was waiting for the right moment to tell Campbell-Bannerman of his intended resignation. Finally, he seized the opportunity one evening after dinner when holiday plans came up for discussion. For a moment, Ponsonby noted Campbell-Bannerman seemed surprised, but soon settled down to the idea and was quite ready to discuss new plans. It was arranged that Ponsonby would go on holiday in September, go to Belmont in October, London in November and perhaps abroad with the Prime Minister in December.

After the close of the session, the Ponsonbys went to the Parrys' Gloucestershire home, Highnam Court. The party assembled there was of rather a different hue from the previous month's gathering at Shulbrede, Spencer Lyttelton, Jack and May Talbot, Lady Queensbury, Charles Graves, young Schuster, Lady Cynthia Crewe-Milnes and Muriel Herbert. Lady Maud was as maddening as ever, but Arthur always enjoyed meeting Hubert Parry and was particularly thrilled to hear played over on the piano his new tone poem 'The Vision of Life'. Early in October, he went up to Scotland, arriving on 7 October at Belmont, where he found Campbell-Bannerman very alert and playing the host admirably. Again an atmosphere, which he knew well, but hardly cared for:

> Such an infinite amount of talk specially here in Scotland about sport, deer, grouse, fishing, the Kings view, Lord so and so's view, anecdotes, books, etc. about it. To know nothing and care nothing about it is either to be regarded as a fool or be very superior.[67]

As Ponsonby was neither of these, he was left alone to be uncomfortable. A visit which was to take on significance only later was made on 22 October to Campbell-Bannerman's constituency. At Dunfermline, he was much struck by the high level of intelligence of the people and their very attentive and enthusiastic attitude. 'Curious picturesque little town weighed down by Carnegie's gold which they don't know what to do with.'

Back in London, Ponsonby was soon immersed in a continuous round of secretarial duties. At luncheon on 5 November with Herbert Gladstone, several other cabinet ministers joined them and a lively discussion on socialism ensued. Arthur reported to Dolly that 'John Burns was the most reasonable poo pooing the hysterical violence of Mckenna – I was in hearty disagreement with them all but being of an inferior order I held my peace.'[68]

The Prime Minister's illness had so far been a well-kept secret. His programme had been carefully managed to avoid undue stress, but early in November fate conspired in the close juxtaposition of the Lord Mayor's banquet on a Saturday night, a state visit by the Kaiser, and a speaking engagement in Bristol. The Lord Mayor's banquet was a heavy and tiring occasion when Campbell-Bannerman for the first and only time made the Prime Minister's traditional speech. On the following Monday he went to Windsor to join in the official welcome of the Kaiser by the King, 'C-B thought his smile and laugh unpleasant. The corners of his mouth were drawn up in such a way that you expected to see fangs.' Back to London for a Cabinet on Tuesday and then to Windsor again later that day for a state banquet. Back to London the following morning to the Guildhall in uniform for a formal luncheon and presentation to the Kaiser, where Campbell-Bannerman had to stand for over an hour, 'only the bloated aldermen reclining comfortably on easy chairs' – 'a lower type of humanity than city aldermen etc. is hardly conceivable – gross ignorant stupid and prejudiced'. Back to Downing Street 'where he gulped down a cup of tea' and finally off to Bristol, accompanied by Nash. It was all too much for him and he had his worst attack, which now became public knowledge. Ponsonby blamed himself for allowing such crowded days, but as the engagements were primarily royal, they were nearly impossible to avoid, especially as the public had been unaware of the Prime Minister's illness.

Campbell-Bannerman and Ponsonby set off from London on 27 November and spent a few days in Paris before going on to Biarritz, arriving there on 2 December. The atmosphere of rich overstuffed idleness that prevailed at the Hotel Continental in Biarritz was a severe trial for Ponsonby who could not bear to be idle. The fact that he was so close to his release made it even more difficult to bear. In an effort to distract Hugh Campbell, Campbell-Bannerman's nephew, who had absolutely no resources in himself, Ponsonby took to the golf course. He played badly and Hugh worse. 'I shall never take to it again as I am more than ever impressed with the futility of spending hours pursuing a little white ball.'

On his return to London, Campbell-Bannerman's predicament was again discussed with Nash. It was decided that Campbell-Bannerman would not resign but carry on, as the doctors thought a period of rest might work wonders on his cardiac asthma. The King and Asquith were informed and Ponsonby took his leave of Downing Street. Vaughan Nash took over as principal private secretary with the assistance of Montgomery from the Foreign Office.

Free at last, Arthur took Dolly away to Taormina. They returned on 1 April to learn that Campbell-Bannerman was seriously ill and that in the interval the by-election scene had gone from bad to worse – mid-Devon had been lost earlier and now the Tories had scored a smashing success at Peckham. Whiteley suggested that Ponsonby might stand for Montrose as John Morley was apparently going to take a peerage. Nothing more was heard of the proposal and, in any case, political life was now in limbo awaiting the Prime Minister's resignation and the formation of a new government with the inevitable round of by-elections for the new ministers (a practice that was not finally abolished until 1926).

Ponsonby saw Campbell-Bannerman for the last time on 4 April. They spoke of the consolations of religion. He lingered on for only a few more days, and Ponsonby was called back to Downing Street to help with the funeral arrangements. The service at Westminster Abbey was beautiful, simple and dignified. Arthur told Dolly that, although the Abbey looked wonderful, he was quite unmoved. What was more impressive to him was the intense reverence and sympathy on the faces of the endless crowd on the road across London to Euston Station and most especially the bands of railwaymen, standing by the line as the train went out, with their caps off.

There seemed to be some chance for a seat for Ponsonby being found at Dundee. This evaporated when, after his sensational defeat in Lancashire, Churchill received the nomination instead. The prospect of Parliament seemed more elusive than ever. Rumour had it that the Stirling Burghs were earmarked for Crawshay Williams, a parliamentary secretary to Winston Churchill. That Ponsonby might succeed Campbell-Bannerman was a possibility that had never been discussed. However, at luncheon after the funeral Ponsonby found himself sitting next to all the people that mattered and so it was arranged.

How curious it is the way things shape themselves. None of this would have happened if I had not *myself* seen the people in fact if I had not sat next the Provost at luncheon. Elibank (I could tell) would not have moved except in a very leisurely way and it required sharp and short action.[69]

Ponsonby was not to return to London until after his election as MP for the Stirling Burghs. His diary had been left at Shulbrede. When he finally got home on 25 May he wrote.

Here I am again having taken my seat in the House this afternoon as MP for the Stirling Burghs. It is almost incredible the rapid way in which events followed one another and here I find myself with my greatest ambition fulfilled.[70]

Notes

1. *Shulbrede* MSS., A. Ponsonby Diary, Introduction, 1871–1893. Material for Ponsonby's early life is mainly drawn from the volume of Ponsonby's diary in which he put down 'as it occurs to me the events and sensations of the first 22 years of my life before I actually began writing a diary in 1893'. There is also at Shulbrede a considerable amount of other material relating to his early life, including a fairly extensive correspondence with Lady Ponsonby.
2. Arthur Ponsonby: *Henry Ponsonby, Queen Victoria's Private Secretary. His Life from his Letters* (London, 1942).
3. *Shulbrede* MSS., 'Travellers on the Road'. In addition to Lady Ponsonby, this manuscript contains a number of pen portraits including J. Ramsay MacDonald and E.D. Morel; copies of which are to be found in the *Ponsonby* MSS in the Bodleian Library MSS., Eng.hist. C.684, but also Frances Warre Cornish, Benjamin Jowett, Charles Masterman, H.W. Massingham, Vaughan Nash, Dick Sheppard, Charles Roden Buxton and Charles Gore.
4. *Shulbrede* MSS., 'Travellers on the Road', Memoir of Jack Talbot.
5. *Shulbrede* MSS., A. Ponsonby Diary, I, 30 Apr 1894.
6. *Shulbrede* MSS., A. Ponsonby Diary, I, 20 Jan 1896.

7. *Shulbrede MSS.*, A. Ponsonby Diary 1897, an account of a trip to Jerusalem, Mar to May 1897.
8. *Shulbrede MSS.*, A. Ponsonby Diary, II, 7 Sept 1897.
9. *Shulbrede MSS.*, Fritz Ponsonby to Mary Ponsonby, 8 Jan 1898.
10. *Shulbrede MSS.*, A. Ponsonby Diary, II, 14 Feb 1899.
11. *Shulbrede MSS.*, Mary Ponsonby to Arthur Ponsonby, 26 Feb 1899.
12. *Shulbrede MSS.*, Mary Ponsonby's memorandum on Professions, Mar 1899.
13. 'Diplomacy as a Profession' by a Diplomatist, *National Review*, Mar 1900.
14. 'Tycho Brahe', *Nineteenth Century*, June 1900.
15. *Shulbrede MSS.*, Arthur Ponsonby to Mary Ponsonby, 24 Jan 1900.
16. *Shulbrede MSS.*, Arthur Ponsonby to Magdalen Ponsonby, 18 May 1900.
17. *Shulbrede MSS.*, Arthur Ponsonby to Mary Ponsonby, 26 Mar 1900.
18. Suggestions for Reform in the Diplomatic Service, *Ponsonby MSS.*, C.652, f.16–46, printed in Steiner (1969), Appendix 4, pp. 222–30.
19. *Foreign Office*, Librarians Department, Correspondence and Memoranda, 1848–1905, Vol. 3A, Memorandum, 17 Oct 1900.
20. *Shulbrede MSS.*, Bigge to Fritz Ponsonby, 30 Nov 1900.
21. *Shulbrede MSS.*, A. Ponsonby Diary, IV, 19 Jan 1901.
22. *Shulbrede MSS.*, A. Ponsonby Diary, IV, 16 May 1902.
23. *Ponsonby MSS.*, C.652, f.60, Arthur Ponsonby to Sir T. Sanderson, 5 Aug 1902.
24. Ibid., f.86–91, Sanderson to Arthur Ponsonby, 24 Aug 1902.
25. The Eyre Crowe reforms are discussed in Steiner (1969), pp. 79–82 and Jones (1971), pp. 111–35.
26. *Shulbrede MSS.*, 'Travellers on the Road', Memoir of Charles Strachey.
27. *Shulbrede MSS.*, 'Travellers on the Road', Memoir of Ramsay MacDonald.
28. Masterman (1939), p. 75.
29. *Ponsonby MSS.*, C.652, f.121, A. Ponsonby to J. Morley, c.15 Oct, 1903.
30. *Shulbrede MSS.*, Memoir of Campbell Bannerman, 1905–1908. This manuscript is recorded as being lost in Hazlehurst and Woodland (1974), Addenda, p. 167.
31. *Shulbrede MSS.*, A. Ponsonby to D. Ponsonby, 8 Dec 1903.
32. *Shulbrede MSS.*, A. Ponsonby Diary, V, 26 Jan 1906.
33. *Shulbrede MSS.*, A. Ponsonby to D. Ponsonby, 20 Feb 1906.
34. *Shulbrede MSS.*, Memoir of Campbell-Bannerman.
35. Ibid.
36. *Campbell-Bannerman MSS.*, B.M. Add MSS. 41218, f.49–53. See also Grey's most recent biographer, Robbins (1971), pp. 145–9.
37. *Ponsonby MSS.*, C.653. Leaves of a Diary begun in Downing Street, Jan 1906.
38. *Shulbrede MSS.*, A. Ponsonby to D. Ponsonby, 7 Mar 1906.
39. *Shulbrede MSS.*, A. Ponsonby Diary, IV, 2 Apr 1903.
40. *Shulbrede MSS.*, A. Ponsonby Diary, VI, 30 Apr 1907.
41. *Shulbrede MSS.*, A. Ponsonby to D. Ponsonby, 21 Nov 1906.
42. *Shulbrede MSS.*, A. Ponsonby Diary, VI, 23 July 1907.
43. *Shulbrede MSS.*, A. Ponsonby Diary, VI, 15 May 1907.
44. *Shulbrede MSS.*, A. Ponsonby Diary, VI, 26 May 1907.
45. *Shulbrede MSS.*, A. Ponsonby to D. Ponsonby, 30 May 1907.
46. Jenkins (1954), p. 57.
47. *Shulbrede MSS.*, A. Ponsonby Diary, VI, 27 June 1907.

48. *Shulbrede* MSS., Memoir of Campbell Bannerman.
49. *Shulbrede* MSS., A. Ponsonby to D. Ponsonby, 15 Aug 1906.
50. *Shulbrede* MSS., A. Ponsonby Diary, VI, 2 Nov 1906.
51. *Shulbrede* MSS., A. Ponsonby Diary, VI, 11 Dec 1906.
52. *Shulbrede* MSS., A. Ponsonby Diary, VI, 24 Feb 1907.
53. *Shulbrede* MSS., A. Ponsonby to D. Ponsonby, 14 Nov 1906.
54. *Shulbrede* MSS., A. Ponsonby Diary, VI, 6 Nov 1906.
55. *Shulbrede* MSS., A. Ponsonby to D. Ponsonby, 19 Sept 1906.
56. *Shulbrede* MSS., A. Ponsonby Diary, VI, 8 Jan 1907.
57. *Ponsonby* MSS., Political Diary, C.653, 5 June, 3 July; *Shulbrede* MSS, A. Ponsonby Diary, VI, 16 June; A. Ponsonby to D. Ponsonby; 3 July, 12 Oct 1907.
58. *Shulbrede* MSS., Memoir of Campbell-Bannerman.
59. *Shulbrede* MSS., A. Ponsonby to D. Ponsonby, 2 May 1906; A. Ponsonby Diary, V, 5 June 1906.
60. J.L. and B. Hammond (1911), Preface.
61. *Shulbrede* MSS., A. Ponsonby Diary, VI, 3 Aug 1907; Dorothea Ponsonby Diary, 4 Aug 1907.
62. *Shulbrede* MSS., A. Ponsonby Diary, VI, 14 May 1907.
63. Jefferson (1982), p. 120.
64. *Shulbrede* MSS., A. Ponsonby Diary, VI, 16 Feb 1907.
65. *Shulbrede* MSS., D. Ponsonby's Diary, 27 July 1907.
66. *Shulbrede* MSS., A. Ponsonby Diary, VI, 7 Aug 1907.
67. *Shulbrede* MSS., A. Ponsonby Diary, VI, 13 Oct 1907.
68. *Shulbrede* MSS., A. Ponsonby to D. Ponsonby, 5 Nov 1907.
69. *Shulbrede* MSS., A. Ponsonby to D. Ponsonby, 29 Apr 1908.
70. *Shulbrede* MSS., A. Ponsonby Diary, VI, 25 May 1908.

CHAPTER TWO

Radical MP, 1908–1914

The Garden Party Affair

The by-election campaign in the Stirling Burghs lasted three weeks before polling took place on 22 May. Ponsonby's Conservative opponent was William Whitelaw, the chairman of the Highland Railway, and grandfather of Viscount Whitelaw. It was a straight fight and Ponsonby took a strong liberal, but hardly radical, line on the main issues. In his election address, Ponsonby naturally dwelt at first on his connection with Campbell-Bannerman. As for policy, the priorities were, first to maintain free trade, second to defeat the House of Lords' opposition to the Small Landholders (Scotland) Bill, third the peaceful settlement of the education question in England, and fourth support for a vigilant and pacific foreign policy.

The constituency encompassed two large urban centres, Dunfermline and Stirling, and many much smaller towns along the north shore of the Firth. His meetings in Dunfermline and Stirling were large, tumultuous and enthusiastic affairs. Often, there were crowds of 2,000 or more, with overflow meetings to be addressed afterwards. Much more stolid and staid meetings were held in the smaller centres like Queensferry. Getting around was the chief problem, but that was solved by the arrival of Hubert Parry's Humber for the last few days of the campaign. When the polls were counted, Ponsonby had secured a record majority for the constituency, more than doubling his predecessor's majority of 1900.

A. Ponsonby (L)	3,873
W. Whitelaw (U)	2,512
L majority	1,361

Undoubtedly, Ponsonby derived some benefit from the general atmosphere of a miniature general election that surrounded the by-elections of Asquith's new ministers. Equally, the electors were obviously fascinated by an advanced radical with such an impeccable upper class, not to say royal, background. All the newspapers dwelt on the court connections of his father and brother, and of his having been a page to Queen Victoria.

These royal connections were an embarrassment before the election and were to become even more so shortly after. Within a few days of taking his seat at Westminster, a spur-of-the-moment decision on Ponsonby's part to go into the division lobby and vote against the King's visit to the Czar of Russia at Reval created a royal incident. To understand why Ponsonby took this step, it is necessary to appreciate the depth of feeling that prevailed in England against the Czar. This personal animosity, which was never very much below the surface, had been stirred by Campbell-Bannerman's denunciation of Czar Nicholas' suppression of the Russian Duma to the Inter-Parliamentary Conference in the Royal Gallery of the House of Lords in July 1906.

In May 1908, the newspapers were again carrying stories of the Czar's reactionary policies, so when the King's visit was announced there was a storm of protest, chiefly by Labour MPs, but also by some radicals. An opportunity to debate the visit arose when the Foreign Office Vote came on on 4 June, only days before the royal departure. The debate was both passionate and acrimonious, the Czar was referred to as the hangman of liberty in Russia, and Keir Hardie was only persuaded to withdraw use of the word 'atrocity' by the intervention of the Prime Minister. A tart reprimand from the Chief Whip advised Ponsonby that influence could be more effectively brought to bear by quiet pressure behind the scenes than by hostile votes. Ponsonby was unrepentant and there the matter should have ended, but when the King returned to London, it became apparent that he was very angry. Unavailing efforts were made to clear the air. The Whips' office wrote privately to Knollys, the King's private secretary, explaining that Ponsonby's vote was against the government and not against the King, and that if, as they had heard, the court was seriously considering excluding Ponsonby from the Garden Party, this would be a great mistake, for Fleet Street would create a martyr to principle and 'an incorrect impression might thus be given of His Majesty's character and disposition'. Ponsonby considered a letter to *The Times*, but, after talking it over with Nash, decided that a letter to Knollys would be more appropriate. Ponsonby took the same line as the Whips' office in emphasising that his vote had been against the government and that it was ludicrous to claim that he had been disloyal to the King.

Neither approach succeeded in deflecting the King's displeasure and Edward VII struck the names of the principal offenders from the Windsor Garden Party List. In subsequent interviews with the King's secretaries arranged to resolve the issue, Arthur found himself breathless with anger, but the humorous side of the situation kept breaking through. He reported to Dolly that 'I hear talk of us both as if we were outside the pale of civilisation. Many I hear say "it is that mysterious woman who lives in a cloister who is at the bottom of it"'.[1] Eventually a placatory letter for the royal eye was composed which repeated the earlier arguments, but now included an expression of personal regret. The King accepted the explanation and the closing of the incident was marked by an invitation to a State Ball at Buckingham Palace.

Ponsonby's domestic arrangements were more affected by these events than anything else. In mid-July he went into the division lobby to vote against the government once more, this time being impressed by Snowden and Keir Hardie's case against indirect taxation. However, he obviously could not stay any longer at St James's after this fracas and his friend Pearsall Smith was sent out flat hunting. A *pied-à-terre* was found overlooking Lincoln's Inn Fields which was for a time shared with Pearsall Smith and Roger Fry.

The editor of the new radical weekly the *Nation*, W.H. Massingham, extended an invitation to the new member to attend the *Nation*'s weekly luncheon. Ponsonby became a regular member of that famous gathering. He reported to Dolly that Massingham was wonderful; full of latent violence. Ponsonby had been, for a number of years, a firm supporter of the Lib-Lab pact. He now detected Winston Churchill, Wilson and his 'gang' trying to reconstitute the Liberal Party in the country as a preliminary to an attack on socialism.

> This simply from the point of view of tactics would be a most fatal mistake in addition to this it may break up the Liberal party as there are many of us who would not consent to attack Socialism. I for one am more convinced of the truth of it as an ideal than ever.[2]

To head it off he prepared a letter to the *Nation* which was published on 8 August 1908. The letter claimed to detect, since the general election, a move away from the Lib-Lab pact and cited the fatal effect in a recent by-election of a three cornered fight allowing a Tory victory. The Chief Whip responded privately to Ponsonby's letter by claiming that the lack of co-operation was not due to him, but was the responsibility of Henderson and the Independent Labour Party (ILP).[3]

There the matter rested; he had not overcome his suspicions of Winston, 'I have never believed and never shall believe in him', and recorded, one suspects with relish, J.M. Barrie's opinion 'he struck me as being a man who would like to have convictions if he knew how you got them'.[4] He had made his point.

> A party of Progress can only be made to agree in its attack on the party of reaction. You cannot expect them to be one on their Reconstruction theories. There must be and there ought to be different ideas as to what path to take in the future.[5]

Before the session ended, Ponsonby made his maiden speech. He chose to talk about Macedonia in the Foreign Office Vote debate. He had practised speaking to a sympathetic audience of seagulls on a deserted Sussex beach but now, after a few hectic days of preparation, he found himself listening to his own voice.

> My voice sounded to me like someone else's I was very nervous for the first few sentences losing words that I knew well but which ran away and hid in large white clouds in my memory.[6]

This was not apparent to his audience, for his speech was well received in a thin house. He spoke with a certain amount of authority derived partly from his Constantinople experience, but also from his more recent membership of the Balkan Committee. He made only an oblique reference to the Garden Party scandal at the end of his speech, when he reminded the House that as far as Russia was concerned, the sympathies of the British people lay with the oppressed rather than the oppressor.[7]

After the close of the session, Ponsonby came to the conclusion that he liked the life of an MP better than he thought he would. There was so much to do that the difficulty was to know in what to specialise. He thought the best course for the future would be to stick to foreign affairs, as very few took an intelligent interest in them. He would also try and tackle prison reform and possibly the reform of the diplomatic service.

Holidays that summer were spent partly at the seaside and partly at Shulbrede. House guests included Charles and Lucy Masterman, Arthur's Aunt Barby, who told Arthur of an interesting packet of letters in her possession (from her aunt Lady Caroline Lamb, when she was in Belgium nursing her brother Sir Frederick Ponsonby after the battle of Waterloo), J.M. Barrie and the Stracheys. Visits were made to Sir Harry Johnston, sick in his badly furnished but charming old house at Poling, and to the Zangwills, where Arthur assisted in the copyright performance of Zangwill's famous play *The Melting Pot*. In fact, theatricals proved to be the highlight of the summer, for Charles and Jack Strachey, who were staying at Vann Cottage, gave the first performance at Shulbrede of their puppet musical play *Madame Mushroom*. The heroine of the play was Elizabeth, who was allowed to stay up to dinner and to see the performance. Charles and Arthur toured West Sussex on bicycles and, one wet and windy day, were unceremoniously turned away from Petworth House by Lord Leconfield.

Finding a Niche in Politics

During the autumn session, Ponsonby hardly spoke and, when he did, was rather ineffective. However, right at the end of the session, he made a strong attack on the government's acceptance of the House of Lords' emasculation of the Miners' Eight Hour Bill. The government's weak-kneed action served to focus Ponsonby's attention on the House of Lords.

Making himself into a nuisance as far as government was concerned was something that Ponsonby was later to develop to a fine art. In 1909 he was still only a novice 'troublemaker'. As the new session was not due to begin until the end of February, Ponsonby had plenty of time to make preparations. He was convinced that the Liberal Party faced a general crisis in its fortunes which could only be overcome by taking on the Lords. This was a radical perspective and many moderates in the party preferred a more cautious policy of gradualism rather than confrontation. Progressive social reforms were being emasculated in the Lords so it would have to be reformed 'we must do more to help but first of all, in order to get a clear run, this rotten ignorant incubus obstacle the House of Lords must be moved out of the way'. He decided the best method to proceed was by moving an amendment to the Address. In deciding what form the amendment would take, he consulted with Lawrence Hammond, Sir Charles Dilke and Massingham. At lunch, Massingham and Ponsonby were joined by Masterman and then by Burns, who on approaching the table called out

'Waiter, bring me a chair this table needs leavening.' He was racy and amusing, as egotistical and self important as ever – Bitter against Lloyd George and Winston C 'Your budding Pitts and pocket Napoleons, Massingham don't pan out.'[8]

Shortly before the opening of the session, Ponsonby went to Oxford to a revival of *The Frogs*, in which he had acted 17 years before, and which Parry had set to music, and visited the Bertrand Russells at Radley. He found there Logan Pearsall Smith, Gilbert Murray, George Trevelyan and the Hammonds. They were all solidly behind him about the Lords.

The debate when it finally came on was something of an anti-climax. Only 14 Liberals went into the division lobby with Ponsonby; scared off, he thought by a rumour from the Whips that the Tories were going to vote with them and bring the government down, but also because of the 'hopelessly smug cautious undiscriminating attitude of the great majority of our men'.

He heard from Charles Masterman that the whole of the front bench was furious with him, and, from Elibank at the palace that, as his brother arrived at the levée, the King turned to him and said 'I suppose you have been reading your brother's speech!' He found the *Nation* lunch shy, but was buoyed by many letters of support from his radical friends. Barbara Hammond especially liked the part of his speech in which he had pointed out that the prosperity of the country did not depend upon the number of people who had incomes exceeding their needs.

The theme of the corrupting influence of excessive personal wealth had occupied Ponsonby for a number of years. He had originally contemplated a volume of essays, but when this did not work out, he had fitfully gone on by himself. Lloyd George's budget accomplished what Ponsonby's amendment to the Address had failed to do and, during the summer of 1909, in between the marathon sittings of the Commons, he completed the manuscript and it was published at the end of November by A.C. Fifield as *The Camel and the Needle's Eye*. The details of Lloyd George's Peoples' Budget hardly raise an eyebrow today, so accustomed are people to progressive taxation. In 1909, Lloyd George proposed to raise additional revenue to meet the cost of the new social services *and* battleships by introducing, among other measures, a super tax and three new land taxes. The uproar in the Commons was instantaneous and unrestrained; on the one side, 'vindictive, inequitable, unprincipled, reckless, improvident, tyrannical and Socialist' and on the other 'a war budget for raising money to wage implacable war-fare against poverty and squalidness!' A marathon of sittings then kept the House hard at work through the summer and then through the autumn. When finally the bill was sent up to the Lords early in November, there had been 70 days debate and 554 divisions. All-night sittings were a commonplace and Ponsonby took up his full share of the burden. He would have liked to speak but found that he never had any chance. He wrote a congratulatory letter to Lloyd George expressing the view that the budget had given the Liberals a splendid fighting ground. If he needed any stimulus to keep him up to the mark, he found it one night at 2.30 a.m., after a budget debate, on the Thames embankment.

> It was very quiet – each seat was loaded to the full with sleeping men and women the parapet round Cleopatra's needle was strewn with ragged human bundles one old woman finding no room on the seats was sitting crouching on the second bar of the railings trying to sleep. The moon shone across the river. No melodrama no sensational novel, no statistics can bring this misery home to us. We accept this state of affairs in 1909 as a matter of course.[9]

Equally disturbing was the hostile attitude he had come across in country houses in Scotland on a constituency visit in October. Shortly thereafter, he went to stay at Tangley, his brother's residence, 'without a suit case and with my things in a brown paper parcel which will shock Fritz's butler'. He had a great argument with Fritz about it all, but felt more keen on his book than ever after talking to them. Before the book was finished, it was seen by the Hammonds, then accepted with alacrity by Fifield, who had it in the bookstores within a month.

In the meantime, against Ponsonby's prediction, the Lords decided to throw out the Budget. 'It is incredible. I hate Toryism and its works more and more every minute of my life.' 'I saw the House of Lords at work. . .

The ill concealed selfish brutality and light hearted destructive spirit is simply amazing – incredible.'[10]

When the book came out, it immediately received very favourable reviews in the *Daily Chronicle* and the *Daily News* where headlines 'A Book of the Day', 'the Problem of the Rich: A Commentary on the Budget' reveal its topicality. All the reviewers, both public and private, were struck by the comparative budgets of the rich and the poor that Ponsonby had compiled. These dramatic contrasts were selected from real life – the record of a day spent by a shirtmaker and a day spent by a lady of society, the dress bill of one 'female' and the dress of another, the household books of one family at 9/5½d a week and another at £72 a week and so on. Hilaire Belloc thought that nothing could be better or more original than Ponsonby's comparison of Budgets. Belloc thought of another comparison, the phrases used by the rich about themselves and the phrases used by the poor about them – especially the country poor whom they fondly believed to be affectionate. Galsworthy's letter was typical:

I've been reading your book and liking it enormously as has my wife.

The money malady is one great (indeed the greatest – so great as to almost mop up all the rest) branch of the universal disease in this country the worship of facts or matter to the death of the worship of the essence or spirit of things. I'm right glad you've had the stamina to carry out your idea single handed. It's much more effective than it would have been cut up amongst a crew. It's a really valuable work coming from you. I believe it will go home and fructify.[11]

From the opposite side came a typical letter from Fritz:

I have read your book. Thank goodness you're not the Almighty, what a dreary world you would make it. In your laudable desire to help the Embankment and Railway Arch people you would reduce us all to a sheep faced torpid race bereft of all energy passion or ambition.[12]

This was further evidence of Fritz's ability to distort his brother's view, for while Arthur may have been a socialist, his message was essentially democratic. Earlier writers such as Booth and Rowntree had concentrated their attention on the problems of poverty. Ponsonby simply reversed the emphasis, arguing that the possession of great wealth was as great a menace to the existing social order and to progress as poverty.

While Ponsonby's parliamentary and literary achievements were concentrated upon the Peers versus the People, he was also active in other directions. Like many other radicals, he opposed the increased expenditure of money on Dreadnought battleships by the Royal Navy because the reasoning which Ponsonby saw being advanced to justify the increases was purely mathematical and bore no relation to the actual state of relations between England and Germany. However, he did not speak, failing to get called by the Speaker, although on one day, during the debate on the

Royal Navy, he got to his feet no fewer than six times. After voting against the government no less than three times in a week, he went into the Division Lobby on his government's side for a change – 'very reluctantly but it was the hideous jingo alarmist view of the opposition that made me do it'.

At the *Nation* luncheon following the debate, the feeling was summed up by Ponsonby as being gloomy and despondent

> We had a very full Nation luncheon everyone was there including old Rowntree himself who acted as a check on the usual violent language but we were all very gloomy and despondent and could see no escape from this terrible rush of all countries towards large armaments and no solution as to how it can be checked.[13]

Russian affairs were again prominent, although not quite so sensationally as in the previous year. Ponsonby was very active in the parliamentary Russian Committee and was instrumental in extending its membership beyond the confines of the House. New members included George Trevelyan, Herbert Fisher, Gilbert Murray, I. Zangwill, H.W. Nevinson, Bernard Pares, S. Rowntree, Canon Barnett and Charles Gore. They were all enthusiastic supporters of Prince Kropotkin and decided, as a riposte to the government's invitation to the Czar to visit England, to issue Kropotkin's memorandum on Russia. They received some visiting members of the Duma, led by Milinkoff, and Ponsonby narrowly avoided having to drink the Czar's health. Ponsonby spoke up against the Czar's visit in the House, the only Liberal to do so. He said in a 'manly' speech that it would be a calamity if not a single vote on the liberal side were raised in protest against the visit. 'You cannot help the Russian people' Ponsonby said 'by giving an official reception to their oppressor.'[14] In September, he organised a luncheon at the House at which he introduced Prince and Princess Bariatinsky to Kropotkin and his daughter Sasha. Also present were Massingham and Philip and Lady Ottoline Morrell.

> There were at first torrents of Russian but they were very good and broke into English. Sasha Kropotkin of course talks English like you or I she was deeply interested in all the things of the day specially politics and the theatre. Kropotkin held forth and was excellent in all the subjects he talked of, so simple and sympathetic full of deep human feeling and keenness. Princess Bariat: was almost off her head. 'I shall never no never forget this day. To meet Kropotkin whom I have worshipped all my life and to meet him here in the English Parliament House. no it is too much.' Lady O dressed in silver and grey but quite quietly for her kept Massingham going at the other end of the table. I wish you had been there as you would have enjoyed it as these sort of people are so natural and easy to get on with. We kept it up till 3.30.[15]

After the Lords' decision against the Budget on 30 November, the marathon session, which had begun in February, was brought to an end.

The government had only one recourse, an appeal to the electorate which was not without danger because of the Tories' money and influential press. The election dates were fixed for 10–15 January 1910. Ponsonby only went up to his constituency for one day before returning to Shulbrede for Christmas and the New Year.

The first election of 1910 in the Stirling Burghs was contested. Ponsonby's Conservative opponent this time was Mr Cochran Patrick. Before the polls, Ponsonby thought he would do well to get back to Westminster with a reduced majority. His majority in the 1908 by-election had been 1,361, now, in 1910, with an increased electorate he thought that he might drop to a majority of between 1,000 and 1,100. The campaign ran with exceptional smoothness, a parade in Dunfermline was led by no less than 'thirrrty pipers' and several meetings had audiences of around 3,000 eager supporters. He was told by one constituent, 'your appeal last night was gran', it's the talk of the toon'. Ponsonby's message was simple and to the point: whereas his by-election had been about free trade, this election was about the Lords. The question he asked was 'Are the Peers or the people to rule?' When the ballots were counted, he had increased his majority from 1,361 to 2,052.

On his return to London, Ponsonby consulted with his radical friends about the need to keep Asquith up to the mark. Charles Mallet was of the opinion that a memorial signed by a representative group of MPs led by Ponsonby would counteract the moderating influence of Haldane, Grey, Spencer and Crewe. Ponsonby decided to trust in Asquith. 'I want to trust Asquith. I cannot see how he can avoid taking a strong and straight course.' After seeing Charles Masterman shortly before Parliament assembled, he became less sanguine.

Ponsonby realised that it was not plain sailing for the government and that there were many dangerous rocks and shoals that had to be avoided. His radical friends were full of abuse 'Mar 2. dined at Morrells – Masterman, Wedgwoods, Epstein, many others. a good deal of violent abuse of the Cabinet and PM.' He was told by Logan Pearsall Smith that he had a duty to lead the radicals, a duty he declined confiding in his Diary 'I am like Matthew [his son] a slow developer.'

Ponsonby spoke in the debate on the Naval Estimates on 17 March. The debate, like Ponsonby's speech, went off like a damp squib. The House was only interested in the Lords. When that subject at last appeared on the order paper, Ponsonby found it impossible to catch the Speaker's eye in spite of having taken the precaution of approaching him beforehand. When at last he was able to get to his feet, he found himself not only being recognised by the House, but actually being cheered. The government had decided to pass through the commons three resolutions embodying the principles of its Parliament Bill; the first resolution dealt with money bills, the second with non-money bills, and the third with five rather than seven year parliaments. The debate over these resolutions was brought to a dramatic end when Asquith told the House on 15 April that he would ask the King for 'guarantees' before another dissolution in the event that the Parliament Bill was again obstructed by the Lords.

During the parliamentary recess the government's plans were unexpectedly upset by the sudden death of the King on 6 May. Ponsonby had earlier in the year been reading Queen Victoria's letters and it had occurred to him how extraordinarily alike the Royal Family were to servants in style, mind and taste.

> It comes from their being shut off from natural intercourse with ordinary human beings. They use funny old fashioned rather ungrammatical language and have the same love of funerals and diseases and are touching and fussy.[16]

While Ponsonby had reservations about Edward VII as a King, at least he felt he had been impartial and statesmanlike. He was not sure of these qualities in the new King. He described George V as 'a very undistinguished and uneducated little nonentity' although meaning well. He was equally disturbed by his crude Tory advisers, not excluding his brother Fritz. Needless to say, his public tribute, 'The Two Sovereigns' (By One who has known them),[17] was more circumspect in tone.

While at Shulbrede, the Ponsonbys received the Hammonds for a week-end visit. Laurence Hammond again broached the idea of Ponsonby 'leading' a radical group. Ponsonby refused to push himself forward and was only prepared to participate in a small radical luncheon group comprised of just seven radicals – Noel and Charles Buxton, Harvey, Whitehouse, Whyte and Rowntree. As always, Ponsonby revelled in the Shulbrede atmosphere.

> Yes the uneventful days at home are the best of all. They are crammed with events really. 'Another rose out' shouts Matthew. 'I've found the place where the wild narcissus grow' said Elizabeth to me on her way back from school yesterday morning. Have the ducks hatched their eggs yet? and will that packing case do to make into a hutch? This side of the greenhouse must be painted that part of the bed dug out. The post brings odds and ends. An hour or two is spent writing with the door open into the garden and a yellowhammer perching on the archway near the door and proudly showing me his green caterpillars before he disappears into a tiny hole in the wall. Perhaps a game of tennis or a drive in the trap with tea up on a hill and the marvellous beauty of the country in all weathers surrounding us on every side. Reading out at night. the companionship whether in silence or in speech in sympathy or in argument in giving or accepting advice – complete and perfect.[18]

The House reassembled early in June and Ponsonby was soon taken up with the proposed conference on the constitutional question. The radicals were not at all sure that the conference was a good idea, they feared compromise and did not entirely trust Asquith to run straight. At the *Nation* luncheon of 14 June, the conference was discussed a great deal, he told Dolly. 'Apparently there is nothing to be done or said and we must just lump it.' The same story was told the following day after a radical luncheon followed by a radical committee; all Ponsonby had to report was his embarrassment at being treated by Sir Charles Dilke as the only person whose opinion mattered. The most that could be achieved was a promise from Asquith to hold an autumn session of Parliament so that some parliamentary control could be exercised over the conference.

Equally frustrating for Ponsonby was the July debate on the question of women's suffrage. As might have been expected, Ponsonby had all along supported the cause of women's suffrage, but had drawn the line at the increasingly militant attitude of the suffragettes. One of the leading suffragettes was a long time friend of the Ponsonby family, Connie Lytton. At Lytton's request, Ponsonby supported Shackleton's conciliation bill and spoke in the House to that effect, only to see the bill sabotaged by the joint opposition of Lloyd George and Winston Churchill. At a *Nation* luncheon shortly before the debate, he had been warned by Masterman of the line they would take:

> I confess it irritates me when these two take up a definite line and encourage one another. It is never on very sound lines. Their speeches are unliberal and in condemning the bill, which admittedly was a compromise, they refused to see that it is the only possible way of getting women's suffrage through the House.[19]

The following week he saw the Pankhursts, who were extremely affable, but he only reported to Dolly that there were wheels within wheels on the future of women's suffrage, reserving full explanations for when they met.

After summer holidays in Sussex and Gloucestershire, he made a constituency visit to Scotland, unaware of the imminent breakdown of the Constitutional Conference. Parliament was dissolved on 28 November and the ensuing general election proved to be the most apathetic within living memory. Ponsonby's seat was uncontested so he stumped around the country helping other candidates. At the end of the campaign, he returned home to Shulbrede in an optimistic mood.

Elizabeth's birthday, 28 December, was made memorable for Arthur by the beautiful simplicity of a small bunch of flowers on Dolly's table in the Prior's chamber. 'A sprig of rosemary, some winter jasmine, an early purple anemone, a pink and a Christmas rose.'

It was the end of February before the Parliament Bill came up. Ponsonby spoke early in the debate and, drawing on his speaking experience in the election, spoke spontaneously without notes. By now everyone but the

unrepentant Tory Peers realised that the case was unanswerable. The Bill
was read a second time, early in March, and its progress through the
Commons was completed by the middle of May and then passed up to the
House of Lords. The role of backbenchers through many arduous sittings
late into the night was merely to vote; the mood of tiredness and *déjà vu*
stands out in Ponsonby's diary. The Lords then proceeded to massacre the
Parliament Bill, changing it beyond recognition, utterly declining to
accept the verdict of the two elections of 1910. Late in July, the Commons
met to consider their reaction. What followed was unprecedented in
parliamentary history. The Tory diehards howled down the Prime
Minister in a demonstration of disgusting brutality.

They were, however, beaten and all that remained was for the last act to
be played in the Lords. On 10 August, Ponsonby managed to squeeze
himself into the House of Lords where, half-suffocated by the heat and the
crowds of onlookers, he witnessed the passage of the Bill.

The Parliament Bill on the Statute Book, Ponsonby went off to the
Galsworthys' Dartmoor home, Manaton, where he reflected on the past
fortnight.

> The quarelling shouting vociferating turmoil of the conservative peers disputing
> amongst themselves as to how they could best head back the great democratic
> wave and in their discussions and with their scattered leaderless ranks stand up
> against the united front of the liberal Govt was a sight worth seeing. Now it is
> all over and the Tory newspapers are only filled with echoes of abuse and
> recrimination. The Parliament Bill is law and the doors of the H of Commons
> have been further opened to poor men by payment of members.[20]

Ponsonby was not at all impressed by the Liberal victory celebrations; he
found the triumphant face of liberalism unattractive. He could, however,
feel quiet satisfaction at his own small but not insignificant part in
proceedings which had preoccupied the world of politics ever since the
great election of 1906. The Parliament Act of 1911 contained provisions
in its preamble for the reform of the Lords, but none was attempted. The
Act dealt only with its powers. The separation of these two issues, as we
have seen, had been the central part of Ponsonby's scheme in 1907. Had
the Cabinet followed the Lord Chancellor's scheme at that time, the
reform of the Lords would have become a much more difficult, if not
impossible, proposition. Ponsonby, who absolutely refused to push himself
forward and would never have dreamt of taking credit where it was not
due, no doubt took pride in the little asterisk that he placed on his diary
entry of 21 May 1907. The sentence reads 'V. Nash over for the day. We
discussed House of Lords project and elaborated a counter-project* to take
its place.' At the foot of the page the entry reads 'This was eventually the
Parliament Bill.'

The Radicals and Foreign Policy

While Ponsonby's attention had been concentrated upon the passage of the Parliament Bill, he and the other radicals had played the role of interested but frustrated spectators. They now decided to seize the initiative in asserting parliamentary control over the executive in mounting an impressive three year campaign that was only to be interrupted by the outbreak of war in 1914. Their first object was to develop parliamentary machinery to scrutinise the vast and ever increasing military expenditure of the government on defence; second, to democratise the civil service; and, third, to set up a Foreign Affairs Committee of the House of Commons.

Trimming the power of the House of Lords altered the balance of the constitution not only between the elected and hereditary chambers, but also between the executive and the legislative. Parliamentarians had recognised the existence of this problem for some time and now the passage of the Parliament Act provided a suitable opportunity for discussion of remedies. Massingham took up the question in an editorial in *The Nation* in June 1911.[21] He argued that the Liberal Party should attempt to make the new Parliament a real force of criticism of the executive by extending the committee system to the great standing subjects of Parliament: finance, foreign policy, the war services, law, trade, education and local government. The idea of increasing parliamentary control over the executive by the use of the committee system had been most forcefully advocated by the ILP MP Fred Jowett.[22] Jowett's case was that the theory of the constitution gave the House of Commons control over the executive through their power of the purse, but that the working procedures of the Commons Votes of Supply made the idea of control a farce. Jowett further argued that the Ministers were the prisoners of their permanent officials. His remedy to what he termed 'single Ministerial control' was 'committee government' similar to the system operating in county and local government.

Jowett was quite right in thinking that his scheme was too radical to get the approval of old parliamentary hands but Massingham's editorials had not been written in a vacuum. In the great debate on the Naval Estimates of March 1911, the First Lord of the Admiralty admitted to an embarrassed House that if he had not actually misled members as to the size of the projected German building programme, he had at least been the dupe of his permanent officials at the Admiralty. This embarrassed admission had been extracted from the Minister by Ponsonby, who, in a great speech which he was told had reflected Gladstonian traditions, established himself as a leading radical critic.[23]

The radicals had consistently opposed the great increases in spending on the new battleships of the Royal Navy that followed the launching of HMS *Dreadnought* in 1906. The German response had been to take up the challenge of the Dreadnought by building their own big gun battleships leading to the infamous naval armaments race that continued almost without interruption until 1914. During his time at Downing Street, Ponsonby had been critical of the Cabinet for having failed to contain the rise in estimates for the Royal Navy. In July 1907, he had talked over the problem with Vaughan Nash well aware of the danger of the Admiralty overstepping the mark without telling anyone until it was too late. He had no very high opinion of Tweedmouth, the First Lord, whom he knew to be in Admiral Fisher's pocket and whom he described as being blundering and stupid. The motivation behind this criticism was undoubtedly economy and not pacifism. Ponsonby was always watching for signs of Imperialist tendencies in the government and naval expansion was just one more manifestation of Whig deviation. During his stay at Taormina in 1908, he met Felix Moschelles, an old artist, whose father had been a friend of Mendelssohn and, in their talks, he discovered that Moschelles was a keen pacifist. This set in train a line of thought that he pursued in his reading of Greene's *History of England* and he began to analyse the causes of wars. His attempt to write something on this theme at the time was a complete failure, but the connection with Moschelles was maintained after his by-election victory, and, in June 1909, he was persuaded to address the International Arbitration and Peace Association. A year later, the debate had widened to take in Anglo-German relations. Ponsonby was acutely concerned, not so much about the German building programme, but the alarmist and purely mathematical calculations of the Tory press bent as it appeared to him on nothing more than spreading panic. Although he did not speak in the debate and was eventually placated by a moderate and optimistic speech by Sir Edward Grey, he felt he ought to have said something about the national feeling on both sides, which was rather more pacific than the Tory press were indicating. The debate never caught the public's imagination as in the previous year, being overshadowed by the Lords Question and the death of the King. In the following year, as early as January 1911, the radicals recognising the danger, began to prepare their case.

> Golf in the morning with Vaughan and Massingham. Nash boys playing too and all to luncheon. CHHP[arry] had seen McKenna on his journey home from the Riviera and told us what he said. Both Massingham and I agree that in some ways the whole question of Naval estimates is becoming more serious even than the Lords question. But the difficulties to combat are great. No good attacking Govt without voting against it. impossible to get enough men to vote against it. The people in the country dont sufficiently realize the danger.[24]

The radical dilemma not to appear to be negative in just voting against the Naval Estimates was resolved by their proposal to establish an Estimates Committee. Ponsonby gave the House pause for thought when he pointed out that if members followed the government meekly into the lobby, they were in effect renouncing the control of the House of Commons of the Estimates. This point had been forcefully put a few days earlier in the editorial pages of the *Daily News*. 'Has the Admiralty misled the nation or wasted money? They are reduced to nothing and the Cabinet and Civil Service stand absolute and irresponsible masters of our fate.' A further editorial entitled 'The Armaments Debate' emphasised the futility of leaving the criticism of the Estimates to full meetings of the House of Commons.[25]

The government's response to this criticism was forthcoming almost immediately. When the House came to consider the Army Estimates on 14 March, J.M. Henderson moved: 'That the Estimates be referred to a Select Committee for the careful examination of the details of expenditure and that the report of the Committee be submitted to the House before further considerations of the Estimates.'[26] Acland, the Financial Secretary to the War Office, told the House that the government were actively considering the reforms. The *Manchester Guardian* in an editorial summary of the Debate on the Estimates welcomed the news:

> There is no one in the habit of reading debates on estimates who is not profoundly dissatisfied with the very lax control of the House both over the policy and of the details of Estimates. A preliminary examination by a Commons Committee with a report that would bring out the questions of policy and of administration raised by the votes would make these discussions in Committee as valuable as they are now haphazard and uninforming.[27]

In October 1911, the *Manchester Guardian* took up the issue by publishing two articles from the expert and distinguished pen of Lord Welby. Welby, a former Secretary of the Treasury, restricted himself to an historical review, but came to the conclusion that within the previous thirty years control within the Executive by the Treasury and the external control of the House of Commons over current and future expenditure was defective.[28] What the House of Commons needed to help it regain control over expenditure was a Standing Committee on Estimates which would perform the same function for Estimates that Gladstone's Public Accounts Committee of 1862 performed in relation to public accounts. Welby and Sir Francis Mowatt, another former Secretary of the Treasury, supported the radicals' parliamentary campaign, which was launched late in November 1911. MPs were invited to support a proposal to set up a Standing Committee on the Estimates whose function would be to review current expenditure.[29] The astonishing degree of all-party support that was forthcoming, when 244 MPs supported the memorial, decided the issue; and the Prime Minister announced that the government would create an Estimates Committee. Set up at the beginning of the 1912 session, the Standing Committee's structure paralleled that of the Public Accounts Committee. While its function deliberately excluded policy, it had the power to scrutinise some portion of the Estimates in detail with the assistance of departmental officials.

While the *Manchester Guardian*'s comments on the creation of the Estimates Committee were suitably circumspect, Massingham, in a *Nation* editorial entitled 'The Decline of Parliamentary Power', was much more forthright. 'The particular function of the Estimates Committee would be to select special branches of expenditure for review, in order to reassert the financial control of parliament over the vastly increased military spending programmes of the Admiralty and the War Office.'[30]

The Estimates Committee first cut its teeth on the relatively simple estimates of a small department, but in the summer of 1913 it examined the estimates for the Naval Services and in 1914 those for the Army.[31] One of the leading radicals, A.G.C. Harvey, served on the committee and Francis Hirst, in his memoir of Harvey, records that he was busy in the summer of 1913 'most laboriously and most carefully considering line by line the Estimates of the Admiralty'.[32] A.J.A. Morris's characterisation of the radicals' self-centred lack of objectivity in holding innumerable meetings, passing the same tired old resolutions which were always ignored, seems altogether to overlook the painstaking and detailed work of the Estimates Committee.[33]

The radicals never claimed the right to determine the policy of the government; however, they did want to know what was going on. In persuading the government to create the Estimates Committee, they had succeeded in a vitally important area in reasserting Parliament's financial control of spending.

Just five days after the Prime Minister agreed to set up a Standing Committee on the Estimates he announced the government's intention of appointing a Royal Commission on the Civil Service.[34] The radicals were long-time critics of the bureaucracy and, in the spring of 1911, radical opinion had been outraged by the revelations contained in the 'Holmes Circular' of the continued exercise of patronage in favour of the 'privileged classes'. The circular was a confidential memorandum that had been circulated by Holmes, the Chief Inspector of elementary schools, advocating the appointment of public school and Oxford and Cambridge men to the position of school inspector rather than elementary school teachers. It had come into the possession of Samuel Hoare, then a junior Conservative MP, and revealed to an astonished House of Commons on 21 March 1911.[35] The Education Minister failed to satisfy the radicals either then or in a subsequent debate on 13 July.[36] Shortly thereafter,

Philip Snowden succeeded in getting over 400 MPs to sign a memorial to the Prime Minister asking for a Royal Commission to be appointed to enquire into the appointments and promotion in the Civil Service. The memorial claimed to detect evidence of a movement to dispense with competitive examination in favour of an extension of the system of patronage.[37]

For the 'overseas' radicals, the Holmes circular was manna from heaven, for they had long been convinced that the bureaucracy in the Foreign Office represented an exclusive, aristocratic, uncontrolled and undemocratic caste. The appointment of a Royal Commission now gave the radicals, and Ponsonby in particular, a golden opportunity to express their opinions upon the necessity of democratising the Whitehall bureaucracy.

Ponsonby was the leading radical publicist of the outmoded traditions of aristocratic government. He was much more than simply an 'overseas' radical. In his parliamentary activities and in his articles and books, Ponsonby's central concerns were undoubtedly domestic rather than international. For Ponsonby, the international policy of Great Britain was very much the consequence of the failure of the Edwardian political system to rid itself of the reactionary influence of the 'governing class'. The radical attack on the Foreign Office was simply one aspect of a wider attack on the aristocratic system. In the years 1908 to 1911, Ponsonby's speeches and activities inside and outside Parliament had been more concerned with the House of Lords' issue than with democracy and foreign policy. In *The Camel* and in a new book *The Decline of Aristocracy*, as well as in a very telling contribution to the *Nation's* 'Life and Letters' column entitled 'Our New and Old Nobility',[38] Ponsonby laid out his case against aristocratic government. Showing a fine sense of the value of ridicule, Ponsonby drew attention to the following passage in *Little Arthur's History of England*:[39]

> The nobles of England are useful to the country. As they are rich enough to live without working for themselves and their families, they have time to be always ready when the King wants advice, or when there is a Parliament to make laws or when the King wishes to send messages to other Kings . . . As their forefathers were made nobles because of their goodness, wisdom or bravery, they have, in general, followed their example; and they have always next after the King, been the people we have loved best, and who have done us most good . . . So you see that noblemen have been of great use in England. When you are older you will understand this better and you will find out many reasons to be glad that we have noblemen in our dear country.

'Little Arthur', Ponsonby wrote, 'is now grown up and he is not quite sure that everyone believes what he was taught.'[40] In particular, Ponsonby questioned the quality of the aristocracy as a governing class. In his version of history, the alliance of the aristocracy with wealth in the nineteenth century had produced a venal plutocracy devoted to the ostentatious and vulgar display of wealth. In political terms, this added up to a struggle between aristocratic government and popular government. The chief landmarks in a century of parliamentary combat had been: the extension of the franchise, the establishment of local government, popular education, legal status for Trade Unions and the gradual admission first of the middle classes and then of the working classes into the House of Commons and, finally, the supremacy of the people's House over the aristocratic House.[41] While the victory of the Parliament Act had settled the House of Lords' question, there remained the problem of the governing class in general and the Foreign Office in particular. One of the most widely held of radical beliefs was that the aristocratic principle still reigned supreme in the Foreign Office and diplomatic service.[42] The solution to this problem was twofold; the authority of Parliament should be exerted through the use of the committee system and the procedures for recruiting the personnel of the Office should be completely overhauled.

Ponsonby was at this time working very closely with Noel Buxton in creating the Liberal Foreign Affairs Group. Radical opinion was well represented on the Royal Commission, and as the Foreign Affairs Group was the only significant outside group to give evidence before it, they had a clear field in pressing their case for the abolition of the aristocratic principle in the Foreign Office and diplomatic service. Buxton's attention had been drawn to the 'grave defects' in the diplomatic service by the seeming inability of the diplomats to effect any improvement in Anglo-German relations.[43] He attributed their failure to a conservative class bias which was absolutely out of sympathy with the aims of the Liberal government. In the notes that survive in the C.R. Buxton papers of an article Noel Buxton wrote for *Nineteenth Century and After*, the radical position is so clearly set out that it can be quoted in full:

Diplomacy
Test of social position through nomination abolished.
Also wealth test.
Extravagant entertaining no advantage.
Rich men enter diplomacy without intending a career.
Diplomatic and Consular services interchanged.
Consular service should have route for best men into diplomatic service.
English exclusiveness a disadvantage in diplomacy. Should be met by democratic system.[44]

The Royal Commission was appointed in March 1912 but only came to hear evidence about the Foreign Office and diplomatic service from April to June 1914. Ponsonby, now the chairman of the Foreign Affairs Group, gave evidence on behalf of his radical colleagues in Parliament. He prepared and submitted a memorandum[45] as soon as the Royal Commission on the Civil Service was announced, but he had to wait until 21 May 1914 to be called to give evidence.[46] The Liberal Foreign Affairs Group also submitted a memorandum.[47] Their attack concentrated upon the plutocratic aristocratic test for entry into the service. It was represented that open competition combined with adequate salary would effectively democratise the foreign service.

In reporting the government's publication of a White Paper in an editorial entitled 'Caste and Diplomacy'[48] the *Nation* declared that the triple barrier of nomination, selection and property test, which had produced a service by 'a certain class', should be abolished. Liberals who had pioneered the work of popularising diplomacy deserved a diplomatic service staffed by men of wide outlook and popular sympathies.

> Much we believe would be gained if in all branches of the service some study in such a centre as the London School of Economics were required.

When the report of the Commission was eventually published, it endorsed this opinion and recommended the abolition of the £400 a year property qualification, the removal of the necessity to be offered a nomination from the Secretary of State and the reconstruction of the Board of Selection on a broader basis.[49]

While it should be noted that recommendations of Royal Commissions have not always been immediately translated into practice, the radicals had the satisfaction of the endorsement of their point of view by a Royal Commission Report, with the promise of fundamental changes in the recruiting practices of the Foreign Office. Both the campaign to set up an Estimates Committee and the campaign to reform the Civil Service were significant radical achievements, achievements it should be noted in which Ponsonby played a leading role. There remains the third part of the pre-1914 radical campaign – the attempt to democratise foreign policy.

After their great victory over the House of Lords in the previous session of Parliament, the radicals who assembled in Westminster in October 1911 were confronted with the appalling information that the Agadir crisis had nearly led to war between Great Britain and Germany. Their periodic offensives against Grey and the Foreign Office were now resumed with a new intensity. It is generally agreed that the starting point was a meeting held at the New Reform Club on 14 November 1911, but it should be noted that the radicals had long since adopted a position on this issue. Fred Jowett argued the case in typically pungent terms in the columns of the Bradford *Daily Telegraph* in August 1908:

> Let the pigeon-holes at the Foreign Office be emptied and their contents exposed to the eyes of the representative men holding different political opinions. In a word let them have committees to satisfy . . . Let us have all the

cards on the table – the diplomatic cards as well – and then none will have reason to fear that the trumps are up the diplomatic sleeve.[50]

In December 1909 H.N. Brailsford proposed that seven to ten members of the House should constitute a Standing Committee for Foreign Affairs who would be consulted on all important issues and have access to relevant documentary material.[51] The *Daily News*, in reflecting on the issues raised by Lord Esher's lecture on Queen Victoria's influence on foreign affairs, had also discussed the ideas of a foreign policy committee earlier in the year. The *Daily News'* editorial[52] believed it necessary to create a small standing committee 'which would have the same right as the [US] Senate's Committee to question and control the Foreign Office on the tendency and even on the detail of its policy'. A few days later the *Daily News* printed a letter of support for a Parliamentary Foreign Affairs Committee from G.H. Perris, the noted radical journalist. The case was also supported by J. Swift MacNeill, the Irish radical, who possessed a keen scent for constitutional problems. MacNeill contributed an historical review of the 'pernicious constitutional anomaly' that excluded Parliament from questions of peace and war, without however suggesting any remedy.[53] In the debate that followed Ponsonby's talk at the New Reform Club, it was generally conceded that the problem was real and evident but there was no consensus about a remedy.

There were about 35 members of the New Reform Club present at the meeting, including Sir W. Byles, Sir Henry Lunn, H.C. Chancellor, Noel Buxton, Fred Jowett, W.T. Stead, A.H. Scott and L.T. Hobhouse; Lord Courtney was in the chair. Ponsonby suggested that the enforced ignorance of MPs on foreign affairs could be overcome by the appointment of an unofficial committee of MPs, drawn from the party in power, who would have access to accurate information from the Foreign Office which would also publish a weekly bulletin of Foreign Office News. The committee would be kept informed on the broad lines and objects of policy and would act as a channel of communication between the government and the Liberal Party. They would deliberate in private with the help of the Foreign Secretary, but they would in no way share responsibility for policy. Jowett disagreed with Ponsonby's proposal and suggested a non-party committee which would be more representative. W.T. Stead proposed that the group form themselves there and then into a committee to suggest some means of bringing the House into touch with foreign policy. And Lord Courtney in his summary of the debate expressed the opinion that if peace and economy were to be the guiding principles of British foreign policy, what was needed was not a parliamentary committee, but reasoning members always on guard against the fighting qualities of the nation.[54]

Given this lack of unanimity, it was not surprising that Ramsay MacDonald's parliamentary question to the Prime Minister asking for an enquiry into creating some means, by a committee or otherwise, for keeping Parliament in closer touch with foreign affairs, received a dusty answer.[55] However, there was nothing to prevent interested backbenchers from creating their own group along the lines of the Balkan Committee[56] and the same day that Asquith refused to consider the question, a backbench committee was set up by Noel Buxton and Ponsonby. Noel Buxton was elected chairman and Ponsonby vice-chairman of a Liberal Party backbench unofficial committee on foreign affairs. At this meeting, they passed two resolutions, the first deploring the bad relations between England and Germany and the second expressing the opinion that:

> in the opinion of this Committee it is not expedient for the Government of the day to contract engagements with foreign countries involving grave national responsibilities without the knowledge of parliament and while in no way suggesting any interference with delicate diplomatic negotiations which are best conducted in private, this Committee considers that more frequent opportunities should be afforded the House of Commons for discussing general lines of policy so that the country may be better informed with regard to our intentional relations and the actual course of foreign events. By this means the country would be in a better position to give genuine support, and the danger of alarms resulting from ignorance would be avoided.

The group set up sub-committees to hold watching briefs on particular countries as follows:

Germany	J.H. Whitehouse and J.C. Wedgwood
Persia and Russia	A. Ponsonby and P. Morrell
Arbitration	J.A. Baker and H.W.C. Carr-Gomm
Far East	A.G. Harvey and Sir Maurice Levy
Near East	D.M. Mason and A.M. Scott
Congo	Joseph King and Silvester Horne[57]

Other radical liberals associated with the group at this time were G.J. Bentham, A. Rowntree, W.H. Dickinson, T.C. Needham and T.E. Harvey. In order to familiarise other Liberal MPs with their programme, the group issued a statement entitled 'Liberals and Foreign Affairs'.[58] The result was a considerable increase in support. In addition to those mentioned above, thirteen other Liberal MPs[59] allowed themselves to be identified with the group.

The unofficial backbench group continued to be interested in the idea of an official committee and sometime in the spring of 1912 the whole question was thoroughly explored.[60] A meeting to discuss the Constitution of a Standing Committee of the House of Commons on Foreign Affairs was attended by Noel Buxton, Ramsay MacDonald, P. Morrell, G.H. Perris and

Ponsonby. The scheme suggested by Buxton, Morrell and Perris and opposed by MacDonald and Ponsonby was for a full-blown official committee.

Scheme
A standing committee of the House of Commons on Foreign Affairs to consist of from 60 to 80 members nominated by the Committee of Selection in proportion to the strength of the parties in the House.
  To meet at stated intervals and also in requisition. Proceedings to be usually open to press representatives, but no official report.
  Business to be conducted by means of resolutions proposed by members with notice (similar to the procedure of the House of Lords) and either accepted or refused by the Government. In case of a vote adverse to the Government it should at once be the Government's duty to bring the matter before the House.
  This procedure to be without prejudice to any existing means of discussing foreign affairs in the House, by debate in the Foreign Office vote or otherwise.[61]

Ponsonby's original proposal had been for a semi-official committee, the impracticality of which he soon discovered when the publisher Fifield asked him to prepare his talk for publication as a pamphlet. In his pamphlet[62] Ponsonby now urged caution because of the constitutional problem. A Foreign Affairs Committee could only be created 'after careful enquiry and deliberation by men of experience and full knowledge of constitutional law'. In the meantime, Ponsonby was only prepared to recommend small committees to watch carefully the foreign situation. What was needed was the full utilisation of existing machinery. There should be more frequent opportunities for discussion in the House of Commons, answers to parliamentary questions, laying of papers on foreign questions and pronouncements by the Foreign Secretary in the country. Not for the first time, nor the last, Ponsonby assured his audience that the group did not desire to pry into secret corners or interfere in delicate negotiations. Neither did they want to interfere with the Foreign Secretary's prerogatives. All they wanted was information and knowledge so that in matters of critical importance Parliament could exercise democratic control.[63]

MacDonald's opposition to a foreign policy committee was based on the general ground that control of foreign policy was a matter for the House of Commons as a whole.[64] However, Noel Buxton and Morrell felt sufficiently strongly about the need for an official committee to make their case in public.[65] Both writers argued the case for democratic control in general terms without suggesting how the constitutional difficulties standing in its way might be resolved. Morrell at least recognised that the difficulty existed, suggesting that 'the recent formation of an Estimates Committee as a means of controlling public expenditure, though with extremely limited powers, provides at least some precedent'.[66]

While these somewhat academic discussions were proceeding, another

Foreign Policy Group was set up by Hobhouse, Hobson and Courtney. This extra-parliamentary group was actively supported by the parliamentarians who believed it would provide a new forum for the discussion of foreign policy issues. But apart from one very successful meeting in November 1912[67] little more was heard of the Courtney group.

The radicals were, however, given an opportunity to press their case for changes in parliamentary procedure when the Prime Minister agreed to set up a Select Committee on Procedure in March 1913.[68] The government was responding to a widespread feeling that the position of the private member in the House had deteriorated in recent years and that it was now impossible for him to exert influence or take any important part in the proceedings of the House.[69] The government agreed that the membership of the Committee should represent the interest of private members rather than that of the government. The result was very satisfactory, for Ponsonby and Wedgwood of the Liberal Foreign Affairs Group were joined by the Irish member Swift MacNeill, a long-time advocate of parliamentary control of foreign policy and another ex-Foreign Office clerk, Robert Harcourt. The Committee held four meetings in the summer of 1913 and twelve more between March and July 1914, before being overtaken by the war. A draft report was presented to the Committee in 1914, but detailed discussion was deferred to the next Session.

The consensus of opinion that emerged after evidence had been taken from the three major party leaders, the Speaker and the backbench experts on procedure, Fred Jowett and Lord Hugh Cecil, was that the Committee could only suggest alterations in the practice and procedures of the Commons. Changes that involved the Constitution fell outside the Committee's terms of reference. This immediately put the question of creating an official foreign affairs committee out of court and so Ponsonby and the other foreign affairs experts were never able to do more than gather opinions which were almost entirely negative. Not one of the party leaders was prepared to consider the creation of a standing committee on foreign policy.[70] The Committee could not agree on a report for the 1914 session, adjourning on 22 July 1914.

The more immediate and personal impact of these events on Ponsonby's career are not without interest, for having made his mark in the House in the great Admiralty debate of 1911, he now had to live with its consequences. The question that had to be faced was what was to be the next move in his career? Was he simply to go on as before, or should he, like his friend Masterman, join the government and find fulfilment in office?

The radical group in Parliament had been unofficially led by Sir Charles Dilke. After his death, Ponsonby became the reluctant heir to this position. He was not at all sure that he wanted to lead, for, by his own rather exacting standards, his parliamentary friends were an uninspiring lot. Noel Buxton he described as single-minded, sincere, dependable, but somehow dull and uninspiring. Philip Morrell was unpopular, ill-mannered, second rate in spite of being conscientious and well meaning, Josh Wedgwood, an enthusiast, very original with charm and fire, but, Ponsonby wrote, 'if a man is fanatical I want him to be fanatical about my thing not his'. Murray MacDonald was worthy and disinterested, but heavy in hand and quite unable to carry any weight.

Outside of Parliament, Ponsonby had developed a close friendly relationship with Massingham and had become, by 1912, a long time member of the *Nation's* famous Tuesday luncheon party. Massingham obviously thought Ponsonby needed a push to the front and, carefully choosing the occasion of the sudden eruption of a naval scare in July occasioned by Winston Churchill's Supplementary Naval Estimates, began to champion Ponsonby as the leader of a new radical party. After speaking in the 25 July debate on the Committee of Imperial Defence, in which the House indulged in a 'welter of war talk', Ponsonby, in a characteristic speech of some force, took up Asquith's disclosure of the existence of a war book by wondering which department of government kept the peace book. He appealed for improved relations with Germany, describing the armaments race as insane.

While the House was unsympathetic, Massingham responded with a piece for the next day's *Daily News* pointing to Ponsonby as the prospective leader of a new independent party. The Tory press found this hard to resist, and a huge heading appeared in the *Pall Mall Gazette* 'Radical Revolt: Mr Arthur Ponsonby nominated as leader' and the article began 'Mr Ponsonby wakes to find himself famous'. His reaction was typically low key:

> I cannot tell you what a nuisance the Massingham article has been. Monday was a day of many divisions and the result was that everyone in the House came up to me and chaffed about it each in his own characteristic way and of course press men dogged me at every corner. The Tory press have taken it up and I shall have to suffer from it for some time. Massingham and de Forest were keen on a demonstration at Manchester in the autumn and I think something ought to be done in that direction. I was received at the Nation luncheon with loud cheers but Massingham sticks to his point and is very violent.[71]

In his Diary he wrote, 'I don't intend to lead anyone. I have not sufficient knowledge or experience – that may come some day. But I must agitate where I see real danger though I realise I am becoming increasingly unpopular in official circles.'[72]

He was quite right not to be taken in by the sensationalism of the press and stoically endured their continual references to him as 'Mr Ponsonby, who as page of honour to Queen Victoria . . .' as well as the Tory taunts in the House whenever the government's majority sank to a low figure of 'Where's Ponsonby, Send for Ponsonby.' Ponsonby was quite content to continue the informal co-operation that combined progressive members on specific issues in their various committees, such as the Balkans Committee and the newly formed Foreign Policy Committee. He talked over with George Bernard Shaw the idea of forming a new club as he put it 'on the debris of the New Reform Club'. The meeting, however, as with most of the projects of Bernard Shaw, ended inconclusively, Shaw being characteristically fantastic.

With the ribald sound of Tory taunts in his ears, Ponsonby could hardly wait to escape from London at the end of the session. The highlight of that summer holiday in 1912 was a river expedition. The family then went to the Parrys' Gloucestershire home at Highnam and, while there, he received a letter from the new Chief Whip, Illingworth, offering him the vacant whipship. This offer to join the ranks of the Government as a Junior Lord of the Treasury was the first rung leading to office and it carried with it a salary of £1,000, an important consideration to a relatively poor man who was living off capital to be in Parliament. It did not take him long to make up his mind to decline the offer. He wrote in his diary: 'When I imagined myself accepting I felt wretched at the very idea; now that I have refused I feel greatly relieved.' He was to remain an independent private member for the next six years. Had he known what lay in store for him, his relief might have been considerably muted.

Increasing opportunities of meeting the senior members of government encouraged Ponsonby to indulge his old habit from 10 Downing Street days of drawing up a report card on the government. Asquith and Grey were both given good reports.

Asquith is in a very much stronger position than he was a year or two ago. He has shown persistence and in addition to his wonderful talents he has shown a great deal more human feeling. He is less rigid, cold and machinelike. His speech on the 3rd reading of Home Rule was a masterpiece. The emotion was genuine and the eloquence was real. I don't think he has much control over his Cabinet. He is not really a strong man except in manner. On the other hand there is a certain strength in his dignity and perfect willingness to allow any of his colleagues to cut a dash if they want to. I am not sure that it is not better to have a man of judgment and calm but without great enthusiasm at the head of a cabinet which from time to time must be at sixes and sevens. His talents are so remarkable that on all sides he is accepted, an eminent and worthy figure for Prime Minister. His wife always has been and always will be a drawback to him. His house is unknown to the great majority of liberal members and it is as a public man and not as a private individual that he gains respect and support which can never quite amount to affection.

Grey is in some ways the most interesting figure in the Cabinet. To begin with he is a gentleman in the best sense of the word. Personal ambition and a desire to advertise himself I don't suppose he has ever felt for a single instant. This makes him a sharp contrast to many of his colleagues. His House of Commons manner has been a great service to him. It is very simple, very sincere, dignified and direct. He is rather aloof and unapproachable which makes a certain mystery that attracts. He is a liberal and is capable of passionate devotion to a cause but he is over-cautious and not really very able. He trusts the opinion of his permanent officials more than his own judgment and is therefore capable of making rather serious mistakes. He is out of touch with the party. I don't suppose he knows more than a score of them by name. He may be called upon one day to lead and it is very doubtful whether he would make a success of it. He has a great reputation in the country specially among Tories. His successes have been more due to chance, his failures to want of perception. He would be a good friend for Lloyd George and Lloyd George would be a good friend for him.

He was not so sanguine about either Winston Churchill or Lloyd George.

Winston Churchill is still a Tory democrat. He has really been perfectly consistent and never altered. He despises liberalism and has no remote conception of what it means though he can turn liberal phrases out better than any liberal. He is brilliant in his abilities. His speeches are carefully prepared and in some ways the best that are produced today. He is never spontaneous and has shown himself to be incapable of leadership in the House. He is far better at administration because he is most painstaking and thorough. Personal ambition is the keynote of all his actions and as his instincts are quite unsound he is a great source of danger. He has an unattractive personality – conceit and inconsiderateness mixed. He is in contest with Lloyd George for the limelight but he is unpopular in both parties. At the Admiralty he is intent on some great coup – that great coup may be war which he would enjoy immensely as he fancies himself as a strategist. He is really an Imperialist of the more crude and vulgar sort. But he is intensely alive, stimulating, active and will as long as he lives be a strong factor to reckon with.

To which portrait must be added a 1907 vignette from Ponsonby's days as private secretary.

Winston came in one evening and went up and had a talk with C-B who was sitting by the fire in his bedroom with a rug over his knees reading a French novel. Winston seemed considerably impressed when he returned to my room. C-B's solitude and imperturbable calm no doubt struck him but I think he imagined that a Prime Minister ought to be more ostentatiously Prime Ministerial.

Lloyd George is the popular figure, the great target for praise and abuse. It is personality and not talent that has made him. His instincts are true but he would not be above scheming to keep his position. One feels about his career that there is a breathless eagerness to keep up the crescendo of fame. He must be up and doing to maintain his reputation and to keep himself looming large in the public eye. His friendship with Churchill taught him this. The waning of his friendship with Churchill made him fear a rival and struggle all the more. He is a real democrat, full of humanity, with great charm and originality. He has imagination and force of character. He lacks judgment, reserve and discretion. The majority of the party are too frightened of him ever to trust him as a leader. He is not quite safe. He might let them down. He is over-ambitious and there is a strange blending of commonness and refinement in his character. He is a fighter and this is always appreciated in politics and he expresses sentiments which are a true reflexion of the popular mind. He is appreciated by both sides in the House of Commons. Circumstances may make him or mar him. He has strained his powers to the limit.[73]

The circumstance that seemed most likely to break Lloyd George in 1913 was the Marconi scandal, which was just another stumbling block to add to Irish Home Rule, Federal Home Rule and House of Lords reform that stood in the way of real advances in social reform. Ponsonby's solution to the dilemma of the government facing such intractable problems was to raise the whole constitutional question above party lines by getting the King to suggest a Conference. Fritz reported back on 4 July that he had broached the idea to both the King and Stamfordham. The King was interested as he dreaded the prospect of having to give royal assent to the Irish Home Rule Bill in face of Ulster opposition, but he had consulted Rosebery who was opposed to the whole idea. After talking things over with Rosebery, Fritz asked to talk to Murray MacDonald, whose pamphlet had set off this train of events. He was sufficiently persuasive to keep Fritz up to the mark, and the result was the King suggested a Conference to the Prime Minister as a way out of his being accused of betraying Ulster and causing a Civil War. Asquith deprecated the idea, but the King refused to give it up and arranged to talk it over with Lord Lansdowne.

The problem from the Prime Minister's point of view was that a Conference on the whole constitutional question, which Murray MacDonald and Ponsonby were advocating, raised more problems than it solved for the Liberal Party, particularly in relation to England, which would be swamped by the dominant Tory position in the South of England. These matters were talked over in October between Murray MacDonald and Ponsonby, and at a *Nation* lunch later in the month. Finding an unsympathetic audience, Ponsonby wrote an article on the whole question of devolution, which was published in the *Contemporary Review*. Entitled 'The Future Government of the United Kingdom' and published in November 1913, it attracted considerable attention for the courageous and spirited refusal to accept the impasse over Ireland. Devolution of the centralised authority of Westminster to a Dublin Parliament, it was suggested, should simply be part of a wider process of devolution in Wales and Scotland. After such a transition, the Irish question would not become one between Protestant and Catholic, or Nationalist and Orangeman, but between Progressives and Conservatives. Devolution would also solve the problem of the congestion of parliamentary business at Westminster. If such a programme were undertaken, Ponsonby was confident that the problem of the reform of the second chamber would fall into place and be more easily accomplished. These great constitutional questions should be settled, he argued, above party and a constitutional conference which would examine the whole question was infinitely preferable to a last ditch fight along party lines on the specific issue of Irish Home Rule.

Earlier in the summer, Ponsonby had heard, through his mother, that Fritz had heard that he was to be the next to be put into the government. He was inclined to believe that there was something in it, although as usual he also doubted his competence. The offer never materialised, and Ponsonby heard no more about it. That he was being considered, there can be no doubt, for at the end of November he received a summons by telegram to appear for the weekend at the Asquiths' country house at Sutton Courtney. Ponsonby only very occasionally went to large social functions and almost entirely avoided Asquith and his circle. If he was being looked over, he was not aware of it and no offer came from the Prime Minister.

Ponsonby's diary always contained a long year's end retrospective. In December 1913, he changed to writing on the prospects for the coming year.

> Politically the outlook is by no means calm. Home Rule and Ulster, Navy Estimates, House of Lords reform and the Tories perpetually trying to snap us out will make next session agitating. What depresses me is the attitude of Ministers. Asquith leaves things to chance and is rather interested if we get into a tight place so that he may display his skill in getting us out. Ll. George absorbed in his Land Campaign and not caring a button about anything else. Winston Churchill a Tory at heart making the Navy his hobby. Grey doing well by chance but by no means heart and soul engrossed in politics in the larger sense. The rest like McKenna and Lulu Harcourt men of second rank and no one with a broad grasp a long sight and a firm hand. And yet the other side are so much worse off and have not even a tradition of high principles that it may drift into calm waters simply on account of their ineptitude. I should not wonder if we did not have an election in the course of the year. I must realise that it is not enough to be busy I must take more trouble do more be less afraid of making a fool of myself and find opportunities for stepping more to the front. It is extremely difficult.[74]

Ponsonby had become chairman of the Liberal Foreign Affairs Group, succeeding Philip Morrell in 1913. For most of the parliamentary session the group was going about its normal business of promoting and sustaining interest in foreign affairs, such as hearing a talk from Norman Angell,[75] when the July crisis suddenly propelled Ponsonby, as chairman of the group, into the limelight.[76] Before the crisis, Ponsonby was working hard to secure the passage of his Bill to enable Peers to renounce their hereditary titles and, like many others, had hardly noticed the events following the assassination at Sarajevo. The first meeting of the group in response to the European crisis only took place on 29 July. Ponsonby forwarded to Grey a unanimous resolution signed by eleven members of the group which declared that, as no

British interests were at stake, there was no reason for Britain to depart from a position of strict neutrality.[77] Grey sent immediately for Ponsonby on receiving the resolution and pointed out that, for tactical reasons, he preferred not to be drawn in. His other remarks were all reassuring, including the assertion that 'we were absolutely free'. The group had arranged a further meeting for the 30th, which was attended by twenty-two members, which this time decided to direct a resolution to the Prime Minister rather than to the Foreign Secretary. The group again promised not to seek publicity but threatened to withdraw their support from the government if they made a decision to intervene. Although they were only speaking for thirty members, they told Asquith that nine-tenths of the party was behind them. Ponsonby then prepared to ask the Foreign Secretary an awkward private notice question on 31 July, but was advised by Tyrrell that Grey could not be in his place so that Ponsonby had better put it off until the following week.[78] In consequence the question was never put. A third meeting of the group was held on 31 July, when Ponsonby reported back on his letter to the Prime Minister and the question to Grey. They adjourned at 5.15 p.m.

Two further meetings were held on Monday, 3 August, one before and one after Grey's speech to the House. A resolution was passed by twenty-five votes to five in which it was still asserted that there was not yet sufficient reason for Britain to intervene and that the government should continue negotiating with Germany with a view to maintaining neutrality.[79] But by this time, the group's actions had been overtaken by events in the Cabinet which had, at its meeting on Sunday, 2 August, decided to make a *casus belli* of any German infringement of Belgian neutrality. After Grey's speech on 3 August, it was apparent that the majority of the Liberal Party and the country were firmly behind the government's decision. This applied as much to the Liberal Foreign Affairs Group as to the Liberals in general, for at the second meeting a further resolution 'that the violation of Belgium was a *casus belli*' was only defeated by a majority of sixteen votes to thirteen.[80]

In Ponsonby's papers, there is a typewritten paper[81] recording his opinion on this issue. Belgium, he wrote, is the only *casus belli*, but not sufficient to risk the Empire and the greatest catastrophe of history. Great Britain should accept the German guarantee of Belgian neutrality and if Britain remained neutral she would be strong enough at the end of the war to insist that Germany live up to her promise. If Britain entered a general European war she would be risking her existence to achieve a doubtful result. Britain was not bound either legally or morally to enter a European war to defend Belgian neutrality. Britain could not save Belgium from becoming a theatre of operations and her intervention would only add another army fighting on Belgian soil.

This rather formal account of the activities of the Liberal Foreign Affairs Group would be incomplete without reference to the searing white hot passions generated by the crisis. Ponsonby had gone away to Shulbrede on Friday, 31 July, confident that Britain would remain neutral. He was sufficiently disturbed by events to return to London on Sunday evening, where he walked alone amongst hysterical crowds gripped by war. The full impact of the war crisis on Ponsonby can be best appreciated by reading the three letters he wrote to Dolly at this time and his diary entry for the same period.

3.VIII.14

It is all very hideous and terrible but there is still hope. The streets were crowded when I arrived and evening papers were being sold at every corner. I found over a dozen members at the Club some already wavering because of Germany's entry into Luxemburg. I got some rapid dinner and we sat talking till 11. I then went to see Lulu Harcourt. He said the Cabinet had not split yet but it might and then there would be a coalition. The financial position is very desperate – no cheques or fivers can be changed. I have got two fivers which are apparently useless. I borrowed 5/– from Philip He is in a wild state very difficult and unreasonable and our meeting at 2 o'clock today is likely to be a job to manage. The streets last night at midnight as I walked from Berkley Square (I had no money for a taxi) made me sick. Bands of half drunken men shouting mafficking waving flags: bands of French waiters shouting vive la France the war fever beginning. Philip and Lawrence have both been in here this morning. The situation changes every hour. If Germany really mean to provoke us all is up. There is a danger that Winston will provoke an incident.

I really feel almost as if the world were coming to an end. Thank goodness I slept like a top.

You will find the trains are not to be depended on as all the railways are at this moment under the Government.

I wonder if your father has gone.

4.VII[I].14

I went down to the House early yesterday and talk and consultation and alarming rumours were kept up till 2 when my committee met. They were very difficult to handle as already marked differences of opinion were showing themselves. We adjourned and went into the House. There were chairs up the gangway and the place was packed. There was a horrible feeling of panic about the whole thing and the horrible raucous cheers which greeted the strongest anti-German passages in Grey's speech gave me a despairing feeling of utter hopelessness. We are accustomed to cool well balanced moderate speeches from him and to see him carried away by passion and presenting such an obviously biased view was most alarming. Philip very courageously got up and arranged that the debate should be continued on the adjournment. My committee met immediately again. I had great trouble in getting a resolution passed it took more than an hour. I was then torn to pieces by people who wanted to see me and finally had a few moments on the terrace with Massingham and a few others. A very hurried early dinner which I could not pay for as I have only 1/6 left. Then again the House crowded to the full and excited. Philip spoke not badly his case was good but his manner always irritates the House a little. Wedgw. was too wild. Keir Hardie dwelt on a bad point. I had almost decided not to speak but Philip urged me to. I had prepared nothing but I made up my mind to say a word. I had as I always do for some reason or other dead silence and wrapt attention. I shot out half a dozen sentences amid protests and a few feeble cheers. My reference to Grey's speech was much resented but I genuinely felt it at the time. I am sending you the Manch. Guard. which has a full report and you will have read PWW whom I saw later in the evening in a state of semi delirium.

The fact remains there *is still no need for our going in*. Belgium neutrality and independence can be preserved without our fighting Germany. The news is no worse this morning. But the uproar and excitement makes one feel we shall be forced further. Some of us are conferring with the labour party today.

5.VIII.14

It's all over. War is declared. Chaos reigns. Protest is futile. Maggie tells me this morning that Johnnie is ordered to Belgium. Those few of us still about 20–30 who believe the war is unnecessary and our action has been precipitate are combining with Labour. We met yesterday. Ramsay MacDonald presided and we meet again today. He dined with Philip and me last night at Bedford Square. Harley was there and as we talked the yells of the crowds kept on coming through the windows as an accompaniment to our conversation. I had a talk with Burns at the club. He has resigned and nothing will induce him to reconsider his decision. Morley goes too and Charles Trevelyan. It is splendid of them. Lulu of course has not gone and I hear Ch Masterman's attitude has been contemptible also Lloyd George's. I thought the Liberal League was dead. It has triumphed after all. Grey while declaring we were free had committed us to France all the while.

When our combination with Labour is announced today it will cause a certain sensation as we have never openly cooperated before. But those who think alike must stand together and watch. I must go and explain my position to my constituents next week. I dont know if they will support me. The House will probably be up on Saturday but we want to keep Parliament in being so as to have some control.

The horror and misery before us is immeasurable. If only in all countries it could result in the overthrow of monarchies and aristocratic governments there might be some hope for the world for it is they that make wars. If Germany had attacked us I should be in the street myself waving a flag but to plunge us into a war because of the technical interpretation of a treaty made in 1839 is criminal folly. I feel sick and have left off sleeping again.

Diary, 13 Aug 1914

Just a fortnight since I wrote and last night at 12.30 in the moonlight I saw Johnnie riding at the head of his battalion on his way to France to fight the Germans. Utterly incredible and yet true. England, France, Belgium and Russia and Servia are fighting against Germany and Austria. The long expected European war has come millions of men are gathering together all over Europe trains are stopped telegraph stopped commerce interrupted prices rising unemployment beginning ships blown up and we are all breathlessly waiting to hear who will slaughter the most. The face of the world has changed life has changed all the things I think worth while and was working for have broken down. I have no heart for anything and have to hear of hatred of passions of killing from morning till night and I have to think about it as one can think of nothing else. And what is it all for, why has civilization been hurled into the melting pot of barbarism why are we fighting why is anyone fighting? No two people would give the same answer and most people would say they didn't know. A dozen or so diplomats a score of Ministers and two or three monarchs have been offending one another so to make things straight they have ordered out millions of peaceful citizens to go and get massacred. The government have been telling us lies and we believed them. We were committed and we did not know it so without being attacked or our own interests in any way threatened we joined in. It is an end of Liberalism of social reform of progress itself for the moment. And no one can see what the future has in store.

As for me I played a poor wretched ineffective part. I was literally stunned it was so cataclysmic so utterly unlike anything that has happened in the history of the world before. One seemed to be standing on a quick sand with no foothold no one to look to no lead. I had a group of liberals for whom I acted as chairman and before we were actually drawn in we worked for neutrality but the rumours the pressure the doubts reduced our efforts to nothingness. When I twice blurted out a few disjointed sentences in the House not clearly knowing what to say but just blindly protesting amid an uproar of jeers and cries of impatience. I think the Govt have been wrong have acted both in recent events and in previous policy with a want of foresight, a narrowness of view and a want of straightforwardness that has been criminal. I cannot support them now and if my constituents disapprove of my attitude which I hear they do, they will have to get someone else. Ones efforts in public life now can be of little avail and yet if I leave it I am fit for nothing else. For the moment too one cannot argue about causes policy and motives all public interest is centred on one thing and one thing only which is national safety. It is all a hideous nightmare which never leaves one.

It has to be said that one of the unspoken assumptions of historians writing generally on Edwardian politics and society is that the political process had lost its capacity for compromise and progress. This assumption seems to underpin most of the previous specialist writing on the radicals and foreign policy, and has been most fully developed by the Arno Mayer thesis on the domestic origins of war. [82] What is suggested here is that the radicals were far from being utopian day-dreamers who were effectively isolated and silenced by their opponents. They had conducted a practical campaign to correct certain imbalances in the political process. It seems that not only had they identified certain problems, but their remedies had been accepted either in practice or in principle. The tragedy lay in the unexpected escalation of the Sarajevo crisis into a World War. The July crisis should not be cited as evidence of their failure, for the course of events would have been the same even if a standing committee on foreign affairs had been set up. For Ponsonby, the lesson of 1914 was not immediately clear. The country had, however, gone united into the war, the politicians seemingly powerless in the face of an almost universal war hysteria. The cause of peace would have to be carried directly to the people.

Notes

1. *Shulbrede MSS.*, A. Ponsonby to D. Ponsonby, 24 June 1908.
2. *Shulbrede MSS.*, A. Ponsonby Diary, VI, 6 Aug 1908.
3. *Ponsonby Papers*, C.657, f.152–5, J.A. Pease to A. Ponsonby, 25 Aug 1908. Ponsonby's reply is in C.655, f.144–7, wrongly dated 13 Dec 1907.
4. *Shulbrede MSS.*, A. Ponsonby Diary, VI, 14 Aug 1908.
5. *Shulbrede MSS.*, A. Ponsonby to Mary Ponsonby, 4 Apr 1908.
6. *Shulbrede MSS.*, A. Ponsonby to D. Ponsonby, 27 July 1908.
7. *Daily News*, 28 July 1908.
8. *Shulbrede MSS.*, A. Ponsonby Diary, VI, 27 Jan 1909.
9. *Shulbrede MSS.*, A. Ponsonby Diary, VI, 11 May 1909.
10. *Shulbrede MSS.*, A. Ponsonby Diary, VI, 26 Nov 1909.
11. *Shulbrede MSS.*, J. Galsworthy to A. Ponsonby, 1 Jan 1910.
12. *Shulbrede MSS.*, F. Ponsonby to A. Ponsonby, 11 Jan 1910.
13. *Shulbrede MSS.*, A. Ponsonby to D. Ponsonby, 31 Mar 1909.
14. *Hansard*, V, 8, 729.
15. *Shulbrede MSS.*, A. Ponsonby to D. Ponsonby, 22 Sept 1909.
16. *Shulbrede MSS.*, A. Ponsonby Diary, VII, 5 Feb 1910.
17. *The Nation*, 14 May 1910.
18. *Shulbrede MSS.*, A. Ponsonby Diary, VII, 19 May 1910.
19. *Shulbrede MSS.*, A. Ponsonby Diary, VII, 13 July 1910.
20. *Shulbrede MSS.*, A. Ponsonby Diary, VII, 17 Aug 1911.
21. 'The Parliament Bill and After', 3 June 1911.
22. Jowett (1909).
23. *Hansard*, V, 22, 1888.
24. *Shulbrede MSS.*, A. Ponsonby Diary, VII, 15 Jan 1911.
25. Editorial, 'Parliament and Policy', *Daily News*, 11 Mar 1911.
26. *Hansard*, V, 22, 2116.
27. *Manchester Guardian*, 16 Mar 1911.
28. *Manchester Guardian*, 24, 25 Oct 1911.
29. *Manchester Guardian*, 11 Dec 1911. The members of the committee were F. Banbury (U), G. Barnes (Lab), T. Burt (L), G. Cave (U), F. Cawley (L), A.G.C. Harvey (L), A. Henderson (Lab), J.M. Henderson (L), J.W. Hills (U), R.D. Holt (L), J.A. Murray MacDonald (L), A. Mond (L), C.T. Needham (L), C.N. Nicholson (L), H. Nuttall (L), A. Ponsonby (L), R. Rea (L) and E. Watson (L).
30. 16 Dec 1911.
31. Report from The Select Committee on Estimates; Naval Services. British Parliamentary Papers 1913 (231) VI, 299; Army, 1914 (429) VII, 181.
32. Hirst (1926), p. 91.
33. Morris (1972), p. 330, footnote 1.
34. *Daily News*, 21 Dec 1911.
35. *Hansard*, V, 23, 275–310.
36. *Hansard*, V, 28, 495–577.
37. *Manchester Guardian*, 21 Dec 1911.
38. *The Nation*, 24 Sept 1910.
39. Callcott (Dundas) (1835, etc.).

40. Arthur Ponsonby, *The Decline of Aristocracy* (London, 1912).
41. Arthur Ponsonby, *Democracy and Diplomacy* (London, 1915).
42. The most famous statement of this opinion is contained in the Fabian-inspired pamphlet of Robert Nightingale (1930), pp. 310–31, but see the dissenting opinion of this writer (May 1981), pp. 49–66.
43. Conwell-Evans (1932), pp. 77–8.
44. C.R. Buxton Papers, Rhodes House Library, MSS Brit. Emp. S405. C.R. Buxton, Box 1, f.9–10. Fully developed these notes become 'Diplomacy and Parliament' (Apr 1912), pp. 632–42.
45. BPP 1914–16 (cd 7749), Appendix LXXXVII, Memorandum of Mr Arthur Ponsonby, MP, July 1912.
46. BPP 1914–16 (cd 7749), Evidence of Mr Arthur Ponsonby, MP, Q.39249–39482.
47. Ibid., Appendix LXXXVIII.
48. *The Nation*, 11 July 1914.
49. BPP 1914–16 (cd 7748), Fifth Report of the Royal Commission on the Civil Service; Summary of Recommendations, 1, 2, 3 and 13.
50. Quoted in Fenner Brockway (1947), p. 122.
51. Brailsford (Dec 1909), pp. 122–31. Brailsford's ideas are discussed in Leventhal (1985).
52. 'The influence of the Crown', *The Daily News*, 8 Mar 1909.
53. Swift MacNeill (Jan 1911), pp. 209–20.
54. 'Democracy and Foreign Affairs', *Manchester Guardian*, 15 Nov 1911.
55. *Hansard*, V, 32, 1401.
56. Fieldhouse (1966), pp. 175–98. The Balkan Committee's most prominent members were the Buxtons, C.P. Trevelyan, Arthur Ponsonby and H.W. Nevinson. See Eyck (1982), p. 146.
57. *Daily News*, 7 Dec 1911.
58. Liberals and Foreign Affairs, *Ponsonby MSS.*, C.659, f. 133–34, printed in Conwell-Evans (1932), pp. 81–82.
59. Dr C. Addison, Percy Alden, Sir W.P. Byles, Baron de Forest, R.D. Denman, Leif Jones, Thomas Lough, P.A. Molteno, Sir C.N. Nicholson, H. Nuttall, Sir G. Scott-Robinson, Sir Albert Spicer, T.C. Taylor.
60. Morris (1972), 265–9.
61. *Ponsonby MSS.*, C.659, f.135. Constitution of a Standing Committee of the House of Commons on Foreign Affairs.
62. 'Democracy and the Control of Foreign Affairs', pp. 26–30.
63. In 1915 with the experience of the events of the summer of 1914 behind him, Ponsonby admitted that his confidence in the existing machinery had been misplaced and endorsed the idea of an inter-party standing committee. Ponsonby, *Democracy and Diplomacy*, p. 86.
64. *Manchester Guardian*, 20 Dec 1911, reporting Ramsay MacDonald's address to the Westminster branch of the ILP entitled 'Foreign Affairs and Democracy'.
65. Buxton (Apr 1912) and Morrell (Nov 1912).
66. Morrell, p. 664.
67. Morris (1972), pp. 269–70; Koss (1970), pp. 258–9; Gooch (1920), pp. 572–73.
68. *Hansard*, V, 50, 573.

69. Lord H. Cecil, Draft Report of Select Committee on House of Commons (Procedure), BPP 1914 (378), VII.
70. BPP 1914 (378), VII. Minutes of Evidence of A.J. Balfour, 1701–08, H.A. Asquith, 2279–87, Ramsay MacDonald, 2088–96.
71. *Shulbrede* MSS., A. Ponsonby to D. Ponsonby, 31 July 1912.
72. *Shulbrede* MSS., A. Ponsonby Diary, VII, 1 Aug 1912.
73. *Shulbrede* MSS., 'Some Members of the Liberal Government, Jan 1913'; Memoir of Campbell-Bannerman, 1905–1908.
74. *Shulbrede* MSS., A. Ponsonby Diary, VIII, 31 Dec 1913.
75. *Angell* MSS., A. Ponsonby to N. Angell, 25 Feb 1914 and N. Angell to A. Ponsonby, 8 May 1914.
76. Hazlehurst (1971), pp. 35–40; Morris (1972), pp. 408–11.
77. Hazlehurst (1971), pp. 36–7. Draft copy in *Ponsonby* MSS., C.660, f.49.
78. *Ponsonby* MSS., C.660, f.56.
79. *Ponsonby* MSS., C.660, f.65. Resolution of 3 Aug 1914, *Daily News*, 4 Aug 1914.
80. *Daily News*, 4 Aug 1914.
81. *Ponsonby* MSS., C.660, f.68–70.
82. Mayer (1967), pp. 286–300.

CHAPTER THREE

The Great War, 1914–1918

The Union of Democratic Control

Whatever doubts radicals may have had about Grey's speech in the House on 3 August, they were not felt by public opinion. Belgium was a *casus belli* that everyone could support. Germany had clearly run amok and must be stopped. The government held together with no major resignations and the radicals found themselves completely isolated. Politically, they were impotent in the face of the public's massive endorsement of Grey's foreign policy. It was neither the time nor the place for a debate on the origins of the war. The job in hand for everyone was to ensure a quick victory. Ponsonby's reaction to this predicament was not pacifist; he voted in favour of the £100 million Vote of Credit to finance the war on 6 August. 'I shall vote for the money. I want the war to be well conducted and no effort spared.' But at the same time he spoke out against 'the diplomatists' war' and, for his pains, was howled down by both sides of the House.[1]

Before Parliament was prorogued for the summer on 11 August, Ponsonby attended a number of radical meetings, both inside and outside the House. On 6 August, the Liberal Foreign Affairs Group decided to reconstitute itself to monitor the progress of the war.[2] Charles Trevelyan, who had resigned his junior position in the government on the outbreak of the war, as the senior Liberal of the group assumed the role of chairman with Ponsonby as vice-chairman. Altogether thirty-three MPs were reported to have joined the new group. On 6 August, when the group first met, Ponsonby entertained the idea of a Lib-Lab radical grouping. Ponsonby and Trevelyan had already met with Ramsay MacDonald and Arthur Henderson and discussed the creation of a small group of six to eight members on either side, who would co-ordinate policy and report back to their respective parties. Almost immediately, differences between MacDonald and Henderson over Labour's attitude to the war led to a break between the two and the resignation of the chairmanship of the parliamentary Labour Party by MacDonald. This smashed any prospect of a new radical grouping of the left forming immediately.

On the previous evening, 5 August, Ponsonby and Ramsay MacDonald had both been to supper with the Morrells at 44 Bedford Square. Also present were Bertrand Russell and E.D. Morel. They decided 'to start an organization to deal with matters later on when our national security has been assured'. E.D. Morel, the only outsider of this group, had been approached earlier in the day by Trevelyan to become secretary of the organisation, having displayed exceptional organising abilities in his campaign against the Congo Free State. It was also Trevelyan who made the initial contact with Norman Angell, who agreed to lend his support and that of the Neutrality League movement.[3] These five men, Ponsonby, MacDonald, Trevelyan, Angell and E.D. Morel, and their organisation, which shortly afterwards became the Union of Democratic Control (UDC), were to sustain the dissenting tradition in English politics through a crisis that had seen no parallel since the convulsions of the seventeenth century.

The wartime dissent of Ponsonby and his colleagues has received the critical attention of several scholars.[4] They have pointed out the limitations of the pacifist perspective on war and peace and have argued that their courage in speaking out against the war gave then an undeserved claim to wisdom. Their efforts to abolish war only succeeded in making it more terrible. Whatever value is placed on the quality of these insights into the problem, the fact remains that however much the dissenters were ignored by official opinion, the survival of liberal humanitarian values in English politics owed more to them than to any other group. What is often overlooked by historians of the right is that the threat to liberty in the Great War was as much an internal threat as an external one. If the dissenters did little to influence the course of the fighting, their dissent was a factor in combating the authoritarianism of a state embroiled in total war.

In this enterprise, the UDC was only one agency among others. Much of the movement's strength derived from the direct action of the No Conscription Fellowship and the Fellowship of Reconciliation. However, the key political organisation of dissent was the UDC. Its achievements were truly remarkable. In domestic politics, it played a vital part in the decline of Liberalism and the rise of Labour, and in foreign policy it had the immediate effect of challenging and eventually modifying the government's war aims policy. It succeeded in discrediting the old diplomacy with its reliance upon *raison d'état* and changed the way the nation thought about force and foreign policy. In the long run, it helped to modify society's attitude towards war. If there is any difference between attitudes in 1914 and those of today, it is that people have come to recognise that there are moral restraints on the exercise of power. In September 1914, all the UDC could do was to make preparations as the country was swept by war hysteria and no one would listen to anything except war news.

At first, it was to Ramsay MacDonald that Ponsonby looked for future leadership. He alone among the founders of the UDC possessed the charisma of a potential national leader, and so it was not surprising that Ponsonby reacted with alarm to the rumour that MacDonald was about to return to the chairmanship of the Labour Party to be bound thereby to the party's official support for the war. He wrote to MacDonald urging him to continue with the UDC.[5]

The Ponsonbys went to the Parrys at Highnam straight after Parliament had risen and while there he attempted to relieve his feelings by writing to the *Nation*. In this letter, which Massingham published on 22 August 1914, Ponsonby asked a number of questions about the course of international relations before 1914. These questions encapsulate the radical critique of the pre-war international system; the insane armaments race, the commitment to the balance of power, the secret commitment made to France behind the backs of the people, the hostility towards Germany and sympathy towards Russia, all culminating in a war in which no one clearly knew what they were fighting for, but which would kill millions and give victory to neither side. This letter was to cause untold trouble. It was taken up and answered in the *Spectator* in an article 'What We are Fighting For' on 29 August. The *Spectator* undertook to answer three of Ponsonby's questions. Ponsonby had asserted that nobody knew what Great Britain was fighting for. The *Spectator* said it was quite clear that they were fighting to prevent the German military caste achieving dominance, and to stop them making Germany the dominant world power. People were going to be killed, not because of a quarrel between ministers, but because the military caste in Germany had decided they would gain an advantage through war. And, as to who would gain anything, the *Spectator* said the whole world if the Allies won the war, for it would be a victory for individual freedom and a defeat for a despotic military caste. Ponsonby was tarred with the pro-German brush, and, within a matter of weeks, the first accusations of being supported by German money began to appear.[6] Ponsonby's *Nation* letter was reprinted not only in England, but on the continent in Sweden and in Germany, with the inevitable consequence that Ponsonby became labelled, as far as public opinion was concerned, as a pro-German.

While at Highnam, as Ponsonby told MacDonald, he had received Trevelyan's draft letter of the objects of the new organisation. The objects were three: (1) parliamentary control over foreign policy and prevention of secret diplomacy, (2) negotiations after the war with continental democracy to form an international understanding depending on popular parties rather than on governments, and (3) peace terms that neither humiliated the defeated nation nor artificially rearranged frontiers so as to provide cause for future wars. Ponsonby suggested that parliamentary control should not be put first because it was only the instrument not the object. The important object was (2) which he said

> should be wider and more explicit. We should work to inaugurate *A New European System* by which concerted action among all the powers for the settlement of international disputes must take the place of the attempts to create a Balance which has led to rivalry, suspicion and finally hostility – in fact a general European alliance which will prevent competition in armaments and secure the maintenance of peace.[7]

By the end of the month, Ponsonby was back in London attending both the meetings of the parliamentary Liberal Group and the UDC group. On 26 August, the UDC group met at 44 Bedford Square.

> We had a very good meeting at Philip's last night. Ch. Trevelyan, E.D. Morel, Rowntree and Ramsay MacDonald. We settled a good deal. There has been an extraordinary response to the letter and now we are engaged in getting men who have big bodies behind them. There seems a ray of hope when one talks with people who are entirely sympathetic. Of the many astonishing things I have heard, Noel told me yesterday of events which fairly took my breath away. As they are confidential I must wait till I see you.
>
> I feel more violent than ever. But I wish to goodness they would let us have the casualty list. I have had several more very sympathetic letters about my letter to the Nation and it is encouraging to think there is so much sane opinion about and that it will grow.
>
> Ottoline was very sound about the war and very violent. She was dressed in a sort of spotted curtain with beads and had a most evil looking American girl staying with her.[8]

However, doubts on the part of Arnold Rowntree and Philip Morrell, who wanted a much lower profile for the organisation, led them both to withdraw. To a certain extent, Ponsonby agreed with them and urged on Trevelyan a policy of caution.[9]

It had, however, become apparent that many other prominent liberals were only prepared to support the organisation privately. Adverse publicity from the Tory press, replete with references to a sinister secret organisation, finally convinced the committee to go ahead and publish the UDC's Cardinal Points.

> 1. No Province shall be transferred from one Government to another without the consent by plebiscite or otherwise of the population of such province.
> 2. No Treaty, Arrangement or Undertaking shall be entered upon in the name of Great Britain without the sanction of Parliament. Adequate machinery for ensuring democratic control of foreign policy shall be created.
> 3. The Foreign Policy of Great Britain shall not be aimed at creating Alliances for the purpose of maintaining the Balance of Power, but shall be directed to concerted action between the Powers, and the setting up of an International

Council, whose deliberations and decisions shall be public with such machinery for securing international agreements shall be the guarantee of an abiding peace.

4. Great Britain shall propose as part of the Peace settlement a plan for the drastic reduction, by consent, of the armaments of all the belligerent powers, and to facilitate that policy shall attempt to secure the general nationalisation of the manufacture of armaments, and the control of the export of armaments by one country to another.

Now that Ponsonby's name was attached to this second circular letter (it had been omitted from the first), he quite expected to have to face a howl of protest at his being pro-German. It came immediately from all quarters, his own family, his friends, his constituency and from perfect strangers.

Both Fritz and Johnnie were professional soldiers. Johnnie had taken his battalion of the Coldstream Guards over to France early in August. He was in the thick of the fighting at Mons and Cambrai, and was wounded in the leg on 14 September. Shortly before Fritz left to rejoin his regiment in France, he received a carefully edited version of Arthur's letter to the *Nation* of 22 August, which had been reprinted in a Swedish newspaper. Johnnie was asked to get an explanation from Arthur who pondered over his predicament in his diary

. . . how difficult it is for a wounded soldier full of the realities of battle and the spirit of action and sacrifice to understand a stay at home critic. It has made me feel useless impotent and almost criminal and yet in calmer moments I still feel most deeply that the future must be faced that my view of the war is right and that preparations for the future and the formation of a strong public opinion against these cruel brutalities and against the people being deceived kept ignorant and then driven to the slaughter by their governments is the most important thing of all. The war fills my mind day and night.[10]

For the time being, the differences in the family were patched up. Johnnie, who had always been more sympathetic, took it very well and Fritz, for the time being, held his peace.

The constituency problem was to fester for the rest of the war. MPs were expected to support the war effort, especially in appearing on recruiting platforms. The mounting criticisms of his anti-war stand from his constituency associations, and attacks in the Scottish newspapers, led him to affirm his full support for the government in conduct of the war as instanced by his support for the Vote of Credit. He also pointed out that before the war, he had actively criticised the balance of power, the armaments race and secret diplomacy, which had been the fundamental causes of the conflict. He added to this critique his belief in the futility of war. Neither the victor nor the vanquished would gain anything in the long run by force of arms. When the crisis broke, there had been no time for thought, reflection or advice. In this situation, Ponsonby explained, it would have been easy to forget everything he had said before and acquiesce, but he had not been able to do it, and made up his mind to join with others who were determined to work against the recurrence of the causes which had led to the disaster. Thus he was now fully committed to combat the spirit of militarism, to prevent any settlement which would leave grievances leading to future wars, and to ensure eventual democratic control over the conduct of foreign affairs.

Needless to say, these explanations were not kindly received. His constituency executive wanted Ponsonby to recant his heresies and, when they did not get it, it was only a matter of time before they were to ask him to resign.

Through the winter of 1914–1915, the members of the UDC executive committee began to get to know each other more fully. Ponsonby's initial comments on the group as it was then constituted were almost totally pessimistic. By the time spring came round, Rowntree and Morrell had both departed to join the ever increasing group of Liberal 'not-nowers', and Ponsonby's opinion of his colleagues had become, on closer acquaintance, more moderate.

Our U.D.C. Committee meetings take place in Trevelyan's House in Great College Street every Tuesday morning. We take ourselves rather seriously but we have been agreeably surprised at how seriously people take us and how our work extends.

Trevelyan has toned down in working with others. He is less aggressive. He is honesty itself, most ardent, most loyal, a good speaker and a kind friend. E.D. Morel is the backbone of the organization, indefatigable, quite disinterested, quixotically honest, very sensitive and fiery, rather dictatorial, very shrewd and a keen gardener. Ramsay MacDonald, who gets most of the public kicks and mud, gives a general impression to people that he is not to be trusted though no one yet has been able to tell me why or mention one occasion on which he has been false. He is very clever, a brilliant speaker, a good talker, a very pleasant companion, a snob but in quite a childish way. Norman Angell is a rather cold and reserved man with a subtle brain and a very good heart behind it. He has had an adventurous and curious career; he is essentially a man of inventive genius and initiative, but cautious to a fault and too frightened of making mistakes. J.A. Hobson has the best brain of the lot, a shrewd analytical mind, very sympathetic, an admirable adviser and a masterly exponent. Mrs Swanwick I know very little but she has never yet made a stupid remark and made very useful contributions to our deliberations. Judging by newspaper accounts one might suppose we were a dishonest set of unscrupulous plotters engaged in nefarious schemes just for the fun of hurting our country.[11]

The organisation had attracted some public support in both money and members, local branches were springing up and Ponsonby's speaking engagements were beginning to take him the length and breadth of the country. He found himself engaged in much more activity at the UDC than at the House of Commons. He spoke to an Oxford undergraduate group in December 1914, and in February went to Cambridge, where he stayed with Lowes Dickinson at Kings'. Early in March, he had gone to Gravesend and there addressed a meeting of 850. This was followed by the founding of the Bloomsbury branch of the UDC 'very odd and most embarrassing. Nearly all women and Ramsay MacDonald, Bertie Russell, Vernon Lee and several other of our lecturers in the audience. I did not feel at all at ease.'[12] Late in the month he went with Ramsay MacDonald to Bradford, where they spoke to a meeting of 1,500 people.

It was now time to face his constituents. His Stirling audience was entirely unsympathetic. They listened to Ponsonby's explanations, but did not accept them. They did not come to hear Ponsonby's reasons for his actions, they came only to hear him retract and apologise. When this did not happen, Sir William Robertson, the chairman of the constituency association, launched into a tirade, generally bullying Ponsonby for the benefit of his audience. Ponsonby was so angry that he could hardly speak and just managed to hold his temper. Shortly afterwards, he noted in his diary.

> There is a note of contempt in some people's attitude towards me. Robertson has it. And it is not entirely absent from CHHP who was over here on Sunday for luncheon.[13]

This was just the beginning of trouble, for bad news from the war in May, the sinking of the Lusitania, the publication of the Bryce Report on German atrocities in Belgium, added to the continuing horror of the trench warfare on the western front, led to a burst of anti-German hysteria throughout the country. Riots against suspected Germans and witch hunts for suspected pro-Germans led the UDC, for the moment, to curtail its activities. Fritz Ponsonby was not immune from these pressures, and the latent hostility, that the extremely conventional courtier felt towards his unconventional younger brother, broke out in a tirade directed at Maggie at Arthur's being a traitor and playing the German game.

None of the leaders was immune from similar attacks. E.D. Morel was savaged as a foreigner in the pay of Germany by the Daily Express, whose editor, Blumental, vied with Bottomley for the leadership of the gutter press. Ramsay MacDonald was subjected to a particularly venomous attack in Horatio Bottomley's 'John Bull' which revealed that 'James McDonald Ramsay' was illegitimate. Neither man was psychologically well equipped to deal with such attacks, and it fell to Ponsonby to shepherd his friends through these critical periods. The gift of friendship is a precious commodity, but Ponsonby gave freely. MacDonald called late one night and they talked. Ponsonby recorded in his diary 'He was utterly dejected.' Dolly's diary also contains a reference to this incident, 'Ramsay

MacDonald came in to A. last night when A. was sitting without clothes trying to get cool and had confided to him his despair at everything . . . he talked of suicide.'[14]

The antidote was work, and the creation of a national coalition government gave Ponsonby just the opportunity he was looking for to press upon his colleagues the adoption of a more positive and public stance on the war by the UDC. When the new government was sprung without consultation on the Liberal Party, Ponsonby was glad 'as the Liberal party in my opinion died in August last and this is only regularizing the situation . . . now we are to have men in the government whose views as to the war and its consequences are most pernicious'.[15] He conveyed to Johnnie the talk amongst the politicians that only more men and more munitions would drive Germany back. The answer he received confirmed his belief that the UDC should begin to press publicly for a peace by negotiation now, for Johnnie told him that, while all the soldiers were dammed sick of the whole business, the only way forward was ever-increasing bombardments to break through the barbed wire and machine guns that dominated the war in the trenches.[16]

Ponsonby had also been in touch with Charles Trevelyan and Ramsay MacDonald. He summed up the new situation in a letter to Trevelyan in which he reflected that the UDC should widen its scope to include not only the origin and settlement of the war in its campaign, but also the conduct of the war as the casualty rate on the western front of 2,500 a day was bound to lead to conscription.[17] He found Trevelyan substantially in agreement. The government's timetable, however, prevented any debate on the formation of the coalition and no other suitable opportunities came Ponsonby's way, so he sat through several depressing weeks feeling particularly helpless and inadequate.

A worse week. I have felt everything going wrong. The worst ideas prevailing, no sort of confidence in anyone, the wrong motives and the lowest reasons given on all sides for going on and on with the war. All the baser sort of people listened to. the best people snubbed and abused . . . One day I was racked and harrowed with a desire to speak in the House but took the wise, cowardly course of remaining silent.[18]

On 21 June, Ramsay MacDonald took Ponsonby to meet Jane Addams, the pioneer American social reformer and peace activist, who had just completed a round of European capitals. She was of the opinion that in spite of the strength of the military party in Germany, Bethmann Hollweg, the German Chancellor, seemed ready to open negotiations.[19] So Ponsonby decided to take a personal initiative. The Danish secretary in London, Torben de Bille, was a long-time friend, and finding him in agreement about the folly of trying to crush Germany, he suggested that the three Scandinavian Kings should take the initiative towards peace by holding a conference of neutral powers to draw up a peace plan. Needless to say, the Danes rejected the idea as imprudent.[20]

These failures were compounded in Ponsonby's mind by the harrowing experiences he was subjected to at Kingston-upon-Thames on 15 July. Pre-occupied with his new ideas, he seemed to have underestimated the savage strength of public animosity towards Germany and anyone who could even remotely be considered to be pro-German. The *Daily Express* decided to mount a campaign against the 'pro-German' UDC and a gang of patriots subsequently ambushed the small meeting that Ponsonby was about to address in the Surrey county town. At the Hall, Ponsonby was only hustled, but at the railway station the three UDC men were attacked again. Ponsonby received a violent blow in the face and was then forced into a small waiting room, where the windows were smashed and they had literally to fight for their lives. When the train came they had to fight their way on board.

> The actual fighting was the least bad part. I have never been in a scrap before and was surprised how little a blow on the face hurt. But the faces of these awful brutes standing round and insulting us I can never forget. It was like some hideous nightmare.[21]

The very next day, when Ponsonby rose to speak to a meeting at Leicester, he was again assaulted. This time, the toughs had been drinking in a public house beforehand and the soldier who got up on the platform only succeeded in knocking himself off his feet. To cap everything, he received news of a resolution from his constituency association keenly resenting his failure to support the government. 'All this' Ponsonby wrote in his diary, 'because we believe in justice truth and the triumph of the moral forces over the physical.'

Planning a New International Order

In the first period of the UDC's existence before the decision to take on the issue of the conduct of war and openly to advocate a negotiated peace, Ponsonby was active in another even more private group which began to explore the possibility of creating a completely new international order.

Belief in the triumph of moral force over physical was central to Ponsonby's thinking on international relations and in these troubled times occupied his thoughts a great deal. In the autumn of 1914, Ponsonby took part in the deliberations of what has become known as the Bryce group. The Bryce group was not actually the Bryce group at all, it was the Lowes Dickinson group, for the moving spirit behind the deliberations of the group that gave birth to the League of Nations was Ponsonby's academic friend from Cambridge. They used Bryce's name only because he was the most well-known member of the group. The other members, in addition to Bryce, Lowes Dickinson and Ponsonby, were Willoughby Dickinson, a Liberal MP, Richard Cross, a lawyer and the business manager of *The Nation*, John Hobson, the economist, and Graham Wallas, the LSE political philosopher.[22]

The first meeting of the group took place early in November at Lord Bryce's house. The diary records those present as being Norman Angell, Lowes Dickinson, Hobson, Graham Wallas and others. Subsequent meetings took place in Ponsonby's rooms in Lincoln's Inn Fields. By 18 December, they had progressed to discussing the constitution and powers of a proposed international council, using a memorandum of Lord Bryce's as a basis for their discussions. Ponsonby told Trevelyan that the whole question of the council was a thorny one, once you came to close quarters with it. He argued single-handed against the powers binding themselves to enforce obedience to an international council by force of arms. Ponsonby was not entirely convinced that an international council was the most effective way of mediating a dispute. He preferred the use of existing diplomatic machinery and, looking back at one of the obvious failures during the 1914 crisis, suggested that in order to avoid double, treble, or even quadruple negotiations, the powers should select a capital and use the diplomatic body there as a conference, as had been done in choosing London during the Balkan Wars. This argument for the concentration and simplification of negotiations was not a fundamental objection to the concept of a League of Nations; indeed, it continued to be a major part of the official British position almost up to the Versailles negotiations. So for the moment, he went along with the Bryce-Lowes Dickinson proposal to create an international council.

The sticking point soon emerged, for Richard Cross suggested that the council members 'should bind themselves by treaty to give moral and material support to any power attacked by another in breach of the agreement'. Ponsonby told the group that this would be a fatal mistake, for the great powers would object to policing the world, and would only agree to diplomatic pressure not backed by force. The council should work through diplomacy and conciliation by common action. In the event that coercive sanctions were eventually to become part of the powers of the councils, what, Ponsonby asked, would be the end result if a power refused to abide by a decision of the council? A break up followed by a majority and minority grouping, the formation of alliances, and the old evils perpetuated. The proposal was even more dangerous than an organised international police force. What Ponsonby wanted to see was the moral sense of nations made stronger; as peoples as distinct from governments became more articulate, it would never do to let nations subscribe to the false proposition that physical force was the only possible basis for the preservation of peace.[23]

Bryce was so impressed by Ponsonby's argument that he wrote to Ponsonby telling him that his notes were 'very weighty – the strongest argument I have seen against the force plan and personally I agree with most of it'. Bryce saw little chance of any government adopting coercive sanctions and little chance of their working if they were adopted.[24] Subsequently, he revised his opinions and insisted on retaining a coercive sanction in the draft 'else the whole thing will seem ineffective and pointless'. After the first intensive phase of the discussions ended in February 1915, the group continued to meet and produced further drafts in August and November 1915 and, finally, in June 1916. Ponsonby remained active in the group and intended to make one last strong appeal against armaments being the basis of the international council when he was struck down by lumbago and confined to his bed. He never departed from his belief that the use of force by an international council was taking the wrong road and rendered the whole scheme for a League of Nations worthless.

While the work of the Bryce group was a well-kept secret, the UDC, under Ponsonby's direction as their co-ordinator of publicity, had begun almost immediately after the outbreak of war to prepare and distribute a series of topical pamphlets and leaflets. The first pamphlet was E.D. Morel's 'The Morrow of the War'; this was soon followed by Norman Angell's 'Shall This War End German Militarism?', Bertrand Russell's 'War, the Offspring of Fear' and Brailsford's 'The Origins of the Great War'. Ponsonby was responsible for the fifth pamphlet, 'Parliament and Foreign Policy' published early in 1915. By the end of the war, the UDC had published 28 pamphlets, 47 leaflets and 18 books,[25] and a monthly journal which, during the war, was entitled *The U.D.C.*, but which soon afterwards became *Foreign Affairs: A Journal of International Understanding*. The success of the UDC in publicising its case against the war was phenomenal. Millions of copies of the pamphlets and leaflets were distributed for a nominal charge and the seal of success was delivered by the government in setting up a counter-organisation in 1917, the National War Aims Committee, funded from secret service money in a vain attempt to counter the UDC's campaign for a negotiated peace.

Ponsonby's pamphlet 'Parliament and Foreign Policy' was based on an earlier pre-war piece that had long since gone out of print. The new pamphlet covered much the same ground as before, but now it had the added impact of the 1914 crisis. Greater emphasis was given to the dangers of secrecy under the old diplomacy exercised by a narrow class of officials mostly living in permanent exile abroad. The whole foreign service should be reformed, so that the new foreign service would be representative of the whole people and less biased by the prejudices of one class. Emphasis was also placed on greater parliamentary control over foreign policy. Parliament was to give effect to democratic control by the following means: an annual two day discussion on the Foreign Office Vote; parliamentary sanction for all treaties and, specifically, no secret deals of any kind; war should only be declared with the consent of Parliament; and the people should be taken into the Foreign Secretary's confidence and instructed, instead of being mystified by his silence.

As has been described, Ponsonby gave evidence on behalf of the Liberal Foreign Affairs Group to the Royal Commission on the Civil Service. Although overtaken by the war, the Royal Commission continued to work and, in December 1914, Graham Wallas sent him, in confidence, the Report as it affected the diplomatic service. He was able to tell Ponsonby that virtually all his recommendations had been accepted by the Commissioners.[26] Given this news, and encouragement from Lords Bryce and Courtney and others, Ponsonby decided to develop his ideas into a book. After reading Ponsonby's pamphlet, Bryce agreed with Ponsonby that the danger of military and naval officers conferring with those of other nations had increased the danger of commitments being undertaken, which practically pledged the nation. He thought the way out posed difficulties and Ponsonby's third recommendation would be met with strong resistance from government. Courtney was also highly critical of the Committee of Imperial Defence; his solution to the problem was an enlightened Parliament and a liberalised Foreign Office. The Speaker, however, found no difficulty with the practicality of point 3. The only totally negative view came from Austen Chamberlain. He pointed out that, while he agreed that there need be a greater light thrown on foreign affairs, he was not at all sanguine about the peace proclivities of democracies or the prospects for any international organisation.[27]

It did not take very long to produce the book, as it had only 120 pages of text, and it was ready for publication in March 1915. *Democracy and Diplomacy: A Plea for Popular Control of Foreign Policy*, in spite of the non-contentious nature of the subject matter, was not immediately published, his publishers probably taking the view that the book would not get a fair hearing while the war was going on. However, after Ponsonby insisted, it was issued at the end of the year. Bryce, who had originally agreed to write a preface to the book, took the opportunity of the delay to renege on his undertaking, explaining to Ponsonby that it would be impossible for him to write a short preface as the subject was too complicated. Bryce's first difficulty was that people were ignorant of foreign affairs and did not care to be informed about them, so it was quite likely that they could be swept away by some national antagonism. The second was the constitutional problem of Parliament interfering with foreign policy, which was an executive responsibility of the government.

These practical objections reflect the pessimistic and conservative views of the ruling elite. The upper middle class has always known what is best for the rest of the general population and then, as now, was not really prepared to see democracy at work. Ponsonby had much more confidence in people. His view was that democracies were by nature pacific, more concerned with combating social evils and the forces of reaction than with racial, i.e. anti-German, animosity. Democracy was not mob rule; the jingo rabble-rousing of wartime had been encouraged and created by government. Whole peoples are not ignorant; they are either uninformed or misinformed. Ponsonby detected a growing spirit of internationalism within the working class which had not yet reached their rulers. These rulers, however, controlled foreign policy through secrecy and the maintenance of an elitist system. Secret diplomacy was a relic of autocratic and aristocratic rule. This extended into Parliament, where MPs were kept ignorant and their ignorance used as an excuse for not telling them anything. The remedy was open diplomacy and publicity. 'In foreign affairs frankness and publicity are the best securities for peace.'[28]

During the course of the year, Ponsonby had some interesting correspondence with Gilbert Murray, the Oxford academic, who was a firm supporter of the war, and John Galsworthy, whose views were very similar to those of Murray. Galsworthy raised the problem of force and, remembering the fracas at Kingston when Ponsonby had to fight for his life – 'It seems that this was wrong of you, my dear Ponsonby. I think it was extremely right.' Transposed to 1914, Galsworthy believed that Germany had been the aggressor with Great Britain forced to fight to defend herself. Murray's argument used another simile. He took exception to Ponsonby's assertion that in 1914 diplomacy had failed. 'In a sense of course diplomacy has failed just as one might say Law had failed whenever a burglar knocked down a policeman.' Ponsonby's answer to these criticisms was to assert that all the powers had contributed to the conflagration. If Germany's diplomacy was immoral, Great Britain's was stupid. The real analogy was a dispute in which the protagonists came to blows outside a court of law. The burglar concept, when applied to a whole nation, did not make sense, and diplomatic relations could be improved by changing its methods and machinery and altering the principles upon which it was founded.[29]

Ponsonby's ideas on moral force as the basis of international authority were developed first in an article which he published in an American journal for want of an English publisher, and subsequently in a 1915 pamphlet put out in England by the League of Peace and Freedom.[30] In these essays, he developed his critique of pre-war diplomacy based on the balance of power, which he argued was an impossibility; there never could be equipoise, only preponderance. In their search for primacy, the powers had built up their armaments until an inevitable conflagration had occurred. He predicted that no good would come of the war, it would simply create further problems and the triumph of might would produce a barren victory. Ponsonby was sure that humanity possessed a moral sense as yet latent, but nevertheless capable of exerting a moderating and pacific influence on international relations. The task before him was to keep that sense of idealism alive. It required a herculean effort on his part; that he was equal to it can be attributed to the particular quality of mind that his mother had noted years before when diplomacy versus law was being considered. It must also be said that he had that rare quality in a politician of being free from ambition.

While *Democracy and Diplomacy* was generally welcomed by virtually all shades of opinion as a positive contribution that would be useful in the future, the publication at almost the same time of Ponsonby's tract 'The Crank' immediately condemned him in the eyes of public opinion as an unrepentant pacifist. 'The Crank' is a short pamphlet about UDC policy done in dialogue form. The dialogue is between a professor and a secretary. The secretary is a pacifist, whose views had upset his employer who is considering sacking him. The employer invites the professor to judge whether or not his secretary was an unpatriotic pro-German who thought that his country alone was to blame for the war. The secretary proceeds to answer these charges and in the process advocates the four cardinal points of the UDC. His arguments, naturally, convince the professor and leave the employer in a quandary. 'The Crank' concludes:

> Well – em, well. He was worse than useless. Something of the crank in him too. It can't be helped, the fellow must go – yes, yes, he must go and there's no doubt about it. It's my duty not to keep him. Clearly. If he's not a crank, well, then he's a traitor.
> And yet . . . [lights a cigar].

The Campaign for a Negotiated Peace

In September 1915, Ponsonby was as strong as ever in his determination to find an opportunity in the House to express his views on starting negotiations to end the war. The utter blackness of the war situation and the probability of the introduction of conscription only made him more determined. He talked over the situation again with Trevelyan, Noel Buxton, Morrell, Ramsay MacDonald and Whitehouse, and found them in substantial agreement. Ponsonby, who had been upset by a personal attack by Hugh Cecil in the *Morning Post* earlier in the month, could ill afford another round of adverse publicity, and peace talk in the grim circumstances of the military situation of September 1915 would be considered almost traitorous. His diary comment on the 'great push' of 25, 26 and 27 September at Loos reveals his sense of frustration and impotence.

> I think these sacrifices are wanton, cruel and barbarous. I don't even believe in military victory. I believe by negotiation we could get just as much as we shall ever get by military action. Just as much that is to say as will make for a real lasting settlement. But the thirst for vengeance and triumph is so strong that speech is useless though I keep on preparing something to say in the House.[31]

In October, further discussions took place between Trevelyan, Ramsay MacDonald and Ponsonby. MacDonald, who had held a good many successful country meetings, believed that it would be possible to rouse public opinion from outside. Ponsonby disputed this. 'I am sure' he wrote to Dolly 'that House of Commons action is essential . . . There is black depression everywhere, people seem to realise that the losses were tremendous and now we hear Asquith talking about "at whatever cost". It is very depressing and one feels bound hand and foot.'[32] Equally disturbing to Ponsonby were the rumours he began to hear of dissension and trouble between ministers. Asquith was sick and upset by the conscriptionist plots of Lloyd George and Churchill. Grey was a broken reed and of no help.

> Everyone is discontented. Everyone wants to attack the government from one quarter or another. It is difficult to see how they can survive or who is to take their place if they fall.[33]

The opportunity to speak finally came on 11 November in the Vote of Credit debate. In spite of the 'fight to the finish' mentality prevailing in the House, Ponsonby found himself listened to attentively despite a few jeers from, of all people, Josiah Wedgwood. He was encouraged by John Burns, who came and sat near him and cheered him all the way through. Afterwards Trevelyan referred to an icy atmosphere and Ponsonby admitted that he felt wretchedly uncomfortable as he approached what he had to say about negotiations to end the war. The appeal to reason was made and it was received with deafening silence. The press almost entirely ignored what had been said, not only by Ponsonby and a week later by Trevelyan in the Commons, but also speeches by Courtney and Loreburn in the House of Lords.[34]

The press gave much more space to the events that occurred at the UDC meeting held at the Memorial Hall, Farringdon Street, London on 29 November. The break up of the summer meetings at Kingston and Leicester were as nothing to this occasion for not only did the riot take place in London, before a large crowd with the press in attendance, but was obviously and blatantly performed by soldiers in uniform. Incited by such headlines as 'Mass Meeting of Peace Cranks: Insult to London' which appeared in the *Daily Express* and the *Morning Post*, the Hall was stormed and the meeting broken up by the soldiers under the benevolent eye of the Metropolitan Police. The asinine conduct of the War Office in attempting to excuse the conduct of the soldiers by having Jack Tennant quote in the House a report on the incident by the Assistant Provost Marshall, which was a mass of lies, backfired and letters of sympathy and subscriptions poured into the offices of the UDC. It should not have had to be pointed out to Tennant that the suppression of free speech by military interference could hardly be reconciled with the preservation of democracy which other soldiers, so the government claimed, were defending on the western front.

At the end of the year, Ponsonby's review of 1915 made for sombre reading. The New Year in the House started with conscription and, although Sir John Simon, the Home Secretary, resigned from the Cabinet and made several brilliant speeches, the radical opposition only managed to muster 39 opposing votes. Ponsonby had a long talk with Simon one evening, who confided in him that he had misgivings that his, Simon's, resignation and speeches were responsible for the division in the country. Ponsonby told him that good as his speech was, it would not have that effect as the division of the country was there and very deep already. Ponsonby described the atmosphere of the House as being 'depressing beyond words' with Tories in uniform shouting and calling names with no thought of anything except the actual fighting. So depressed was he by the military frenzy, that he thought of retiring from politics altogether. 'I am useless. I am not sure I shall not stand aside when the election comes.'[35] After a successful Stirling meeting the following week, at which Ramsay MacDonald spoke, he had recovered his equilibrium. 'My desire to fight the forces of reaction and destruction is so great that I don't suppose I should ever have any peace unless I was at it.' He did not speak during the conscription debate but voted against it and as a result received the usual mailbag of abuse. One letter read 'I thought all Ponsonbys were gentlemen.' Ponsonby's riposte must at least have given personal satisfaction.

> I may not be a 'gentleman' although I do not think that is a question on which you, judging by the nature of your letter, would be a competent judge.
> I am a Ponsonby and am very proud to be one. My family have served their country in various capacities, chiefly as soldiers. I am also endeavouring to the best of my ability to serve my country in a way which may not be understood by those who are blinded with prejudice but which nevertheless I am glad to say is appreciated as disinterested, loyal and patriotic by a very large number of my fellow countrymen.[36]

Taking the bull by the horns, Ponsonby decided to move an

amendment to the address definitely asking for peace negotiations. Ramsay MacDonald was cautious, but as Snowden was as enthusiastic as Trevelyan, the move went ahead and a form of words agreed. Other amendments were also put down but the Speaker, afraid of controversy, would not take any of them. Instead he agreed to give the radicals an opportunity to speak on the Consolidated Fund Bill. The debate came on on 23 February. As Ramsay MacDonald prevaricated the speeches were made by Snowden, who led off, and Trevelyan, who were answered by the Prime Minister. Asquith had a typed sheet in front of him, which Ponsonby thought was a carefully worded sentence; it turned out to be his old tag from a speech at the Guildhall in 1914. He had nothing new to say. 'His was an ill-mannered, ill-tempered, barren speech repeating his old phrase and only adding some insulting remarks about Bethmann Hollweg.' Ponsonby followed the Prime Minister, told him off, but failed to move him.[37]

The UDC, having failed to get any new statement from the government on their war aims, now decided to go ahead and draw up their own statement. It contained four proposals:

(1) As a condition of negotiation Germany would restore the sovereignty and independence of Belgium.
(2) Germany should make reparation to Belgium, restore Serbia and evacuate N. France.
(3) The German colonial Empire would be restored.
(4) Alsace-Lorraine would only be transferred after a plebiscite.[38]

The UDC was not to know that these proposals were unacceptable to Germany, but from their perspective this was unimportant, for in their strategy their sights were firmly fixed on their own government. If it could be persuaded to adopt reasonable war aims, then there would be a way out from the ever-increasing prospect of being sucked into a war of attrition in the elusive search for a military victory.

It was small consolation to hear indirectly, through Fritz, that he had nettled Asquith, who condemned Arthur's speech to a sympathetic sovereign. Earlier in the month, Johnnie, who was now commanding the Second Guards Brigade at the front and had the Prince of Wales on his staff, had seen the King, who shouted, in his usual quarterdeck voice, that he knew before he opened his *Times* in the morning that he would see Arthur's name doing something wrong.[39]

In addition to elaborating their war aims, the UDC came out in 1916 in favour of the open door after the war ended. It appeared from the pronouncements of Runciman, the President of the Board of Trade, that the government was thinking of continuing an economic war against Germany after the shooting war was over. In March, a fifth point to the four Cardinal Points of the UDC was proposed and the Executive agreed to refer the matter to the branches. Ponsonby went up to Scotland to speak on the subject to the UDC branches there. Early in April, he addressed his biggest meeting yet, when an audience of over 2,000 people gathered in the Metropole Theatre, Glasgow, to hear him speak.

A more sobering experience awaited him the next day when he visited the Glasgow Tribunals. Conscientious objectors had been given certain assurances about compulsion, but the working of the Tribunals made few concessions. COs were scoffed at, persecuted and imprisoned.

> In the afternoon we went to the Tribunals. One special case of a conscientious objector – a U.D.C. man came on. It was held in a small room so as to prevent the public getting in. There was only room for about 12. My name was mentioned at the door with a request that I might be admitted. However in the crush I got a place and the request came to the chairman when I was actually in the room though he did not know it. It was most amusing, the mention of my name produced sneers and laughter from the members of the tribunal and the chairman very much irritated said 'tell him there is no room for any privileged people and if there is no place then he cant come in.' The conscientious objector was treated as if he were a criminal. He pleaded very well, they admitted his conscientious objection but peremptorily refused him exemption. It was an absolute farce.[40]

The government met the House in secret session late in April 1916 to report on the war. The UDC decided not to speak as they needed to be heard outside the House. Their opportunity came on 23 May in the debate on the Vote of Credit. Ramsay MacDonald was persuaded to support Ponsonby and Grey spoke for the government. The exchange was chiefly notable for Grey's hostility. He was not at all prepared to clarify the official position beyond what Asquith had said in 1914. Grey seemed rather to have resented Ponsonby's questions.

> He went for me tooth and nail. He was petty, ill-tempered, unprepared, unstatesmanlike and acrimonious. He did not, however, spoil the international situation entirely. I am very glad we did it because we were moderate and many approved of what we said even in the House and many more will approve in the country. One member came to me and said it was clear that Grey could never make peace. The truth is he is so utterly ignorant so swayed by his personal recriminations with Bethmann Hollweg so utterly incapable of taking a broad wise point of view.[41]

Through the summer, military catastrophe was only narrowly avoided at Jutland, at Verdun and on the Somme. Ponsonby was right in thinking that these events would make the war party more determined than ever to go on. Nor was he at all sanguine about the government's handling of Ireland, expecting them, rightly, to make a hash of it. When Roger Casement was sentenced and executed he wrote:

How idiotic his action. Of course morally speaking it is not really a crime. It is only the ridiculous sentimentalism of war that distorts the whole nation's vision and creates new so called crimes.[42]

During this year, the government stepped up its pressure against the UDC. In 1915, there had been two police raids on the UDC, actions initiated by Unionist politicians in the coalition, which were opposed by Liberal ministers. The publication of a collection of E.D. Morel's articles as 'Truth and the War', in July 1916, provoked a further outburst of official antagonism, but wiser councils prevailed and no prosecutions under DORA (Defence of the Realm Act) were initiated. But 'Truth and the War' was subjected to an export embargo as being liable to be used by the enemy for propaganda purposes. E.D. Morel, mindful of what had happened to Casement, began to fear that an attempt would be made to spirit him away to France. For the moment he was safe. More at risk were the UDC's leaflets. The following letter tells its own story:[43]

Darlingford,

Morel's book has been seized. Now about those parcels. Have they come? I said they were to be put on the shelf of Gibson's shed. Tell the children not to let the servants hear anything about what they are. The police may come at any moment.

Now if you could think out a scheme for having them removed to some house in the neighbourhood – I can think of one or two – *without telling me where* – I could then truthfully say that I had not got them and did not know where they were. I dont know that there is any immediate hurry and we can wait till I come down to talk it over. But if I telegraph tomorrow 'Yes, I think so' you had better try and think out something. It would be only a case of keeping them for a few months. Of course it must be someone who is sympathetic. If you can devise other means of hiding them without letting me know where, do it. If the police come just say they had better wait till I come down as you are not prepared to answer any questions on such matters.

I shall know more tomorrow.

> Yr own,
> Taylor

In the event, Matthew was asked to hide the parcels without saying where he had hidden them, and they were put in the loft above the garage. In spite of everything, Ponsonby kept plugging on. He tried to arrange a conference between members of the two Houses to see if simultaneous action might be taken to press for negotiations 'as they could not just sit with folded hands while the offensive went on for months hoping to massacre a sufficient number of Germans to make a difference'. The proposal fell through. Resignation and helplessness in face of the emerging casualty lists from the Somme precluded any action. After a brief respite from parliamentary duty early in August, spent haymaking in Gloucestershire, he returned to London to find his mother, who was now 84, suffering from recurring fits of weakness and visibly declining.

Even at Gilmuire the war intruded. Ethel Smythe, who came to see Mary Ponsonby, confided in Betty that she knew for a positive fact that the UDC was supported by German money. Mary Ponsonby died on 15 October 1916. Shortly thereafter, Ponsonby dropped a heavy box on his foot and broke a bone, so he was out of commission for the whole of November, but being a prisoner tucked up in the Prior's chamber at Shulbrede was anything but a hardship.

Now more than ever, Ponsonby came to appreciate his life at Shulbrede. 'Home is the only really repaying and solid part of life. It can either be a refuge or a sure foundation on which to base one's feet when one goes out to fight.' Arthur's sure foundation was Dolly. She has appeared so far in these pages as little more than the recipient of letters. Her seclusion at Shulbrede was the result of a combination of factors, of which the most important was her poor health. The exact nature of Dolly's maladies defied contemporary medical analysis. Eventually, it was decided that her physical weakness was caused by a combination of colitis and pyorrhea. As her temperament was finely sensitive and highly strung and her commitment to her family uncompromising, the result was often a nervous and physical breakdown. 'She was a lover of quiet days and turmoil and strife excited and exhausted her too much.' She struggled against constant suffering.

Dolly inherited from her father musical talents of a very high order. She never played the piano in public, but at Shulbrede Arthur was sometimes overwhelmed by the perfection of her playing. She was as much in love with Shulbrede as Arthur; the arrangements in the flower garden were her particular province and in the summer the gardens at Shulbrede were a blaze of colour.

Perhaps I have put all my eggs too much into one basket because I live almost entirely for her. She is reflected in the children, in Shulbrede – house and garden – in nature, in my work, in my books, in my pleasures and in my trials. To tell her, to get her sympathy, to ask her advice, to hear her opinion, to see her laugh and to get her praise, lie for me behind every thought word and deed. And in all fundamentals of religion, politics, art and social life we are in complete sympathy and agreement.[44]

During the war, Arthur and Dolly completed a book for young children of biographies of famous people. Entitled *Rebels and Reformers* and published in 1917, it is still in print.

Both Arthur and Dolly had definite views on the education of their children. Their somewhat unconventional views on religion and society were reflected in the plan they made for their children's education. For the first few years, everything was fairly conventional. The children were baptised, Charles Gore becoming Elizabeth's godfather, family prayers were established, and the ordinary routines of the nursery set in motion. In the course of time, the nurses gave way to governesses. One, a Miss Richardson, strongly Tory, was especially trying during the 1910 election gains.

> To find someone who thinks politics is merely 'a silly game' when one is devoting one's life to it is more than I can stand. Matthew, to relieve the silence at luncheon yesterday, turned to her suddenly and said, 'Have you got any warts?'[45]

In a more serious vein, Ponsonby thought out his approach to the religious upbringing of his children. More and more, he found himself out of sympathy with the practice of formal religion. This led to a breach with Charles Gore, who was upset by the Ponsonbys' refusal to allow Elizabeth to be confirmed, and by the publication of an article in the *Nation* on Public School Religion by 'an old Etonian',[46] which sparked off a furious correspondence, that had eventually to be curtailed by Massingham. Although he continued to go to Eton reunions and occasionally visited the school, Ponsonby was determined not to send his son there. His reservations were succinctly recorded in his diary after he and Fritz had attended the Pop Centenary dinner.

> Pop Centenary Dinner at Eton. Went down with Fritz. Saw many old friends. A very large number present. Speeches by Rosebery, Curzon and others. A great deal of self adulation, self complacency and overstrained praise of Eton and the public school system. I meanwhile am beginning to think that they have in them elements which may lead to the ruin of England. I can never cease to regret myself that I was never properly educated.[47]

More and more, he began to think in terms of sending Matthew to Bedales, the most popular, progressive school of those days. One evening in the House he had J.M. Barrie to dinner and heard from him of the Eton masters' 'ill-informed, Daily Mail, bigoted Toryism', which confirmed his opinion that Bedales would be more suitable for Matthew. The Eton versus Bedales argument was finally settled in Bedales' favour. Unlike his sister, who was an extravagant and extroverted butterfly, Matthew was solidly circumspect. After a day school in Haslemere, he went away to Bedales' preparatory school in September 1915. Among the papers preserved at Shulbrede are some envelopes which, illustrated wistfully with pictures of home, tell their own story.

Unfortunately, the school was not a success; the Headmaster was called away by war work and so Matthew was withdrawn and Arthur and Dolly put their educational theories to the real test of personally educating their

son. Through the auspices of the UDC, they secured the services of a
young one-legged pacifist to act as Matthew's tutor.

Inevitably, their circle of friends changed during the war. Almost
immediately, Charles Masterman enthusiastically embraced the war as the
only alternative to dishonour, and then both the Nashs and the
Hammonds took an opposite view of the war, with inevitable strains on
their relationship with the Ponsonbys. There was no open break in either
case, just a regretful and difficult drifting apart. The Nashs' eldest boy,
Christopher, joined the Grenadier Guards and after a meeting with the
proud parents, Ponsonby wrote in his diary, 'This might be fine enough in
people who believe in force and victory but in people who have held *their
views*, it is inexplicable. It makes a great barrier between us.' An even
greater shock was the news that Lawrence Hammond had enlisted and
joined the artillery. 'To think of a man of his fine nature and great
intelligence really believing in force and conquest . . . but he must feel it
very strongly or he would never have taken such a step for him with his
habits and general outlook is very heroic.'[48] Inevitably, he was drawn
closer to his colleagues on the executive of the UDC. The relationship
between the Ponsonbys and Trevelyans flourished, as it did on a different
level with the Morels. Arthur probably came as close as anyone to Ramsay
MacDonald, but he remained an enigma in spite of many Ponsonby
attempts to analyse that secret man's character. The Morels and
Trevelyans were new friends; the war provided very few others. Arthur
never went to the Morrells at Garsington Manor, although he occasionally
saw Ottoline in the distance and sketched her once for Dolly's benefit.

Shulbrede, because of Dolly and the children, never could become the
sort of refuge from the war that made Garsington famous. They
entertained guests occasionally, but usually it was for political conveni-
ence.

The house, which had been given a modern extension in 1914, was
undoubtedly difficult to staff properly. Servants preferred their picturesque
ruins to be on postcards. The war took away their one reliable
chauffeur/gardener, and the boy who replaced him had only to touch the
car to break it. Domestic help had been difficult before the war; now it was
almost impossible. The house needed four people to run it efficiently; with
two, life rarely ran smoothly. Not that Ponsonby ever complained. His
assessment after 15 years in the house was that it had stood the test.

Shulbrede after a fifteen years trial has stood the test. One's imaginings
generally overstep actual realization. But never could I have dreamed of a home
like this. Of course it has drawbacks, but they are stimulating and not irritating.
It is inconvenient and when radiators break and coal gives out it is cold and
necessitates a struggle. But aesthetically it is marvelously satisfying. The old
stone walls, the gable, the chimney stacks, the arches and vaulting, the beams

and tiled floors, the aroma of wood smoke, the blazing log fires, the lattice windows, the wonderful wooded hills, the peaceful meadow all and each are sources of unending satisfaction. The fact that there is always something to be done, new ideas, alterations repairs. It is such a mistake to finish finally even if one has the money something ought always be left to be done and to look forward to. And the garden every foot of which we have made ourselves with all its disappointments and its pests is a perpetual excitement. The place is a refuge of peace and a centre of interest entrancing and absorbing – making things feel really worth while, displaying the best side of life inviting in every nook and cranny occupation work and inspiration.[49]

Ponsonby's London *pied-à-terre* at Lincoln's Inn Fields did not survive the war. He had already decided to move when his mother's death opened up the possibility of sharing accomodation with Maggie. Maggie found a house in Chelsea. The arrangement lasted until the end of the war. Much the saddest part of the proceedings, from the historian's point of view, is contained in the diary entry for 10 August 1916:

Turning out drawers of old papers and letters I come upon interesting correspondence but it is no good keeping it all so I made a high pile in the middle of the room for the paper pulper.

War Aims Debate

Early in December, while Ponsonby was in Scotland making another fruitless attempt to placate his constituency officials, decisive events that were to change both the parameters of domestic politics and the eventual outcome of the war were set in motion by Lloyd George's ousting of Asquith on 4 December. While the Squiffites sat sulking in their tents, refusing either to support the coalition or to fight for a liberal peace, the initiative was passed indirectly to the UDC through the agency of President Woodrow Wilson, whose call to the combatants to state their peace terms on 18 December finally brought the whole question of war aims into the open. Wilson's peace without victory did not survive the German resort to unrestricted submarine warfare and the release of the intercepted Zimmerman telegram, which provided evidence of German hostility towards America, but America's entry into the war did not deflect Wilson in his efforts to secure a liberal peace. As Morel put it in February 1917, 'If she comes in she will come in on the programme of the UDC which President Wilson has made his own.'[50]

While America tottered on the verge of war in March 1917, the fall of the Romanoff dynasty in Russia provided, at least in the eyes of the UDC, further evidence of support for a negotiated peace. Arthur Henderson's infamous treatment at the hands of the Cabinet when he was made to wait outside the Cabinet door like a naughty schoolboy for wanting to attend a proposed meeting of the Second International, made it only a matter of time before he resigned and liberated the Labour movement from the coalition. Once out of the government, Henderson mobilised it behind the UDC's campaign for liberal war aims through a negotiated peace. The Labour Party's memorandum on War Aims was virtually indistinguishable from the UDC's platform.

Just how far the climate of opinion had changed from a year before, when a conspiracy of silence had enveloped the UDC, was revealed on 29 November 1917 when the *Daily Telegraph* published a call for a negotiated peace from the former Conservative Foreign Secretary, Lord Lansdowne.

Ponsonby, who shortly after his return from Scotland at the end of 1916 was notified that his Executive and Ward Committees had withdrawn their support, was much more than an interested spectator of these events, for his notice to quit raised the problem of his future political connections. In May 1916, Ponsonby had been approached by Herbert Bryan, the City of London branch secretary of the Independent Labour Party to join the ILP. If, Bryan asked, you believe that the Liberal Party has disappeared, that capitalism is the real enemy and that the policies of the ILP on war and peace are in accord with the UDC, why don't you join the ILP? Ponsonby politely refused; he did not want to give himself a new political label and preferred to go on working in collaboration with Labour without further alienating his Liberal friends.[51] He was to maintain this position until after the war, contesting the election of November 1918 as an Independent Democrat and only joining the ILP after the election in 1918. In 1917, the break up of the Liberal Party seemed to offer some more attractive alternative courses of action. If Lloyd George the great 'radical' of pre-war days had deserted the cause, there still might be hope that Churchill, the other great champion of radical causes, might be persuaded to come out and lead. To this end, Ponsonby arranged a meeting.

> I had a long talk with Winston Churchill and tried to persuade him to throw over Asquith and to come out more definitely, leading the Government on to a restatement of terms and moderation, foresight and attempt at settlement. He listened but was a curious mixture of shrewdness and stupidity. He does not believe in decisive victory but he still hopes the military situation may develop in such a way as to persuade Germany that she is to all intents and purpose beaten. On the causes of the war he actually admitted that diplomacy properly handled might have steered events into an avoidance of war. Anyhow he is not prepared to come out yet awhile.[52]

Lloyd George was not unaware that Churchill was running loose and, shortly thereafter, took the necessary precaution of appointing him Minister of Munitions.

This left Ponsonby with Ramsay MacDonald, as Simon was obviously not quite up to the mark as a leader of a new radical party. Several discussions were held in June. Ramsay was his usual baffling self; his qualities undeniable, his weakness the constant talk of his political associates. It seemed to Ponsonby that Ramsay's only objection to a new political alignment of the left was 'the old jealousy between him and Snowden'.[53] After the talk, Ponsonby listed in his diary the difficulties they were liable to encounter on forming a new party:

(i) Its urgency owing to the prospect before long of a general election with a large new electorate.
(ii) The split in the Liberal Party between Georgites and Asquithites both with party chests.
(iii) The likelihood of the failure and fall of Lloyd George.
(iv) The absence of policy initiative vigor and life in the Asquith following.
(v) The consequent collapse of liberalism.
(vi) The strength of the ILP its narrowness and ignorance.
(vii) The difficult question of leadership fundamental jealousy between Snowden who sees the necessity of action and Ramsay MacDonald who is the abler parliamentarian but is addicted to diplomatic tactics and drift.
(viii) The reluctance of Radicals to discard their liberalism or abandon the name of Liberal.
(ix) The suspicion of the ILP towards Liberals.
(x) The more individualist and moderate liberals who at present work for peace negotiations.
(xi) The absolute necessity of internationalism being the main plank of policy.
(xii) The international character of Socialism and the consequent probability of Liberals being left out of an international movement.
(xiii) The question of a name which would fuse the two sections and make for a 'union des gauches' in all countries.
(xiv) The radicals in the UDC better equipped and adapted for international work than the members of the ILP with very few exceptions.
(xv) The immediate preparations for a general election.
(xvi) The question of money.[54]

This did not prevent further discussions taking place, and Ponsonby met with Snowden at the offices of Hirst's paper *Common Sense* the following week. He reported to Dolly 'the outcome so far is a conviction with some of us that the moderate liberals should be shed. But the line of action is by no means clear.'[55] This was true.

At precisely this time, E.D. Morel was asked whether he would join the ILP and become once again a parliamentary candidate. He sought Ponsonby's advice, as the war had taught him that Liberalism was a fraud. Ponsonby quite appreciated that there was no real live parliamentary party for Morel to join and went on to remark

I agree with all you say about the old parties and so far as our little gang is concerned, while I think now and again we may have been of some use, I frankly confess we have been deplorably ineffective . . . But events are throwing us together and a certain force has been engendered which may strengthen us and make us effective. I have been impatient about this for some time past. I have hoped for developments which have not come off but I am rather more hopeful today. Things are moving . . .[56]

Arthur Henderson's resignation early in August was not immediately significant in Ponsonby's plans, although, ultimately, Henderson's reconstruction of the Labour Party made the idea of creating a new radical party redundant. Early in August, the two sides got together.

We had a very satisfactory and interesting luncheon of the members of a possible new party. The movement in that direction is gradually developing. If it were based on sympathy and identity of aim and policy, it could be formed tomorrow, but unfortunately, there are all sorts of mechanical difficulties owing to the ILP position in the Labour party. Radicals Ch. Trevelyan, Lees Smith, Arnold, Lambert, and self. ILP MacDonald, Snowden, Anderson, Jowett and Richardson.[57]

At the end of August, Ponsonby had made out a list of candidates and suggested to Trevelyan that when redistribution had been settled they should examine all constituencies with the ILP, noting incidentally that 'I had an elderly soldier here today who is bent on standing precisely on our lines but as usual does not know what to call himself'.[58]

After Parliament reassembled late in October, Ponsonby reiterated the need to get the progressive forces together, but recognised the difficulty of the divisions in the Labour ranks 'we recalcitrant Liberals are always conferring, but it is most difficult to know what step to take. We have got further conferences this week.'[59]

He was urged to come out as the radical champion, as 'the mantle of C-B [Campbell-Bannerman] fell on him', but this he refused to do, and the opportunity, if it could be called that was allowed to pass, for early in the New Year, Trevelyan used the correspondence columns of the *Nation* to challenge discussion. He told Massingham:

It is the first expression I think in public by a liberal member of the view that the Liberal leaders cannot lead democracy in the next stage and that the leadership has so far passed to Labour that we ought to either co-operate with it as comrades or associate with it as open allies.[60]

Trevelyan had hit the nail on the head, for there was no reason for Labour to make any move towards the radicals; the problem was strictly one for the radicals in the Liberal Party. Ponsonby's predicament was typical. He was receiving two whips in the House yet despised and despaired of both Asquith (who now appeared in his correspondence as 'Squith') and Lloyd George. His constituency organisation had disowned him and so his future inside the party was, to say the least, rather bleak. Ponsonby had been committed to socialist principles since the turn of the century, so he was not held back on that account. While he never could escape entirely from the class predicament, although he had separated himself from 'society', he lived a spartan life at Shulbrede, but in a style which cost something over £1,000 a year. Accusations of letting the side down and of deserting his class did not concern a man who had borne, with equanimity, the far more serious, but equally erroneous, charge of being a traitor to his country. He was held back by two considerations. The first was that the Labour movement was in as much disarray as the Liberal Party, divided over the war and rent with internal schisms. A new party of the left could become a national party, which the Labour movement before the war had never been. The second, and more immediately, important reason was that Ponsonby felt the need to submit his war-time parliamentary activities to the electorate of what had now become, by redistribution, the Dunfermline Burghs. For this reason he decided to allow himself to stand as an 'Independent Democrat'. Throughout the long acrimonious controversy with his constituency executive, Ponsonby had argued that his constituents, when given the chance, would approve his conduct in the House, so he felt obliged to stand on his war record and that meant standing as an independent. He stuck to this decision and it was as an independent that he went down to defeat in 1918.

As Ponsonby forecast, a party of sorts led by Francis Hirst began to exploit Lansdowne's initiative. It failed to materialise into anything permanent, for it was soon realised that the old gentleman's plea was simply for a return to the pre-1914 *status quo*. In the long run, more important newspaper reading than the Lansdowne letter could be found in the *Manchester Guardian* which began to serialise the disclosures of the Bolshevik press of the secret treaties engineered by the Triple Entente since 1914. Earlier in the year, the government had decided to step up its effort to silence the UDC. It was not above using a trumped up charge to get rid of E.D. Morel, who was imprisoned; giving secret service funds to the National War Aims Committee; and adding Regulation 27C to DORA to provide censorship of all war and peace literature. Ponsonby took up the slack with great effect. In its September 1917 issue, the UDC published 'First Class Lies'. This contains the germ of the idea that was to become Ponsonby's most famous book *Falsehood in War Time* (1928). The article is an exposé of official lies. Lies, Ponsonby wrote, were weapons just like poison gas. To show just how facts were manipulated in wartime, he quoted a series of newspaper extracts relating to the fall of Antwerp.

Kolnische Zeitung
'When the fall of Antwerp got known the church bells were rung.' [meaning in Germany]

The Matin

'According to the "Kolnische Zeitung", the clergy of Antwerp were compelled to ring the church bells when the fortress was taken.'

The Times

'According to what the "Matin" has heard from Cologne, the Belgian priests who refused to ring the church bells when Antwerp was taken have been driven away from their places.'

The Corriere della Sera, of Milan

'According to what "The Times" has heard from Cologne via Paris the unfortunate Belgian priests who refused to ring the church bells when Antwerp was taken have been sentenced to hard labour.'

The Matin

'According to information to "The Corriere della Sera" from Cologne via London, it is confirmed that the barbaric conquerors of Antwerp punished the unfortunate Belgian priests for their heroic refusal to ring the church bells by hanging them as living clappers to the bells with their heads down.'[61]

The 500,000 Russian troops in England with snow on their boots in August 1914, the British nurse mutilated and maltreated, the Belgian baby with its hands cut off, the German Kadaver story, corpses melted down for the manufacture of fats, etc. were all lies. 'So it goes on and the people are more and more hoodwinked and misled. The truth itself at last is not believed.'

In the House, on 19 December, Ponsonby used the Russian revelations as the basis of an impassioned attack on the government. As he told Dolly, he went at the government pretty hot and strong for over half an hour without a word of interruption or protest.

> You have prostituted the original disinterested motives for which this country entered the war and you have substituted for them a mean craving for vengeance and punishment, a sordid desire for gain and an arrogant demand for imperial aggrandisement and domination without the consent of the people secretly and surreptitiously making declarations all the while which were deceitful and false.[62]

Quite obviously, the government had to respond in more than a negative way. Lloyd George realised this and, having already disposed of Asquith, decided to respond by making a comprehensive statement on war aims to the Trades Union Congress on 5 January 1918. As Lloyd George made it clear in his war memoirs, the reasoning behind his decision was fear of a collapse in morale.[63] He fully intended to go on with the war in spite of the universal revulsion against the horrors of the Passchendaele offensive that had slogged through a sea of mud throughout the autumn of 1917. The significance of his speech lies not in what he said, but that he made it in response to the UDC. The UDC's penetration of the Labour movement, which had culminated in the Labour Party's Statement of War Aims, was now backed not only by the ILP, but by the Trade Unions, a constituency that Lloyd George could not ignore. It remained to be seen how effective the new alliance would be in translating their war aims into a successful peace.

Ponsonby correctly deduced that the terms offered to Germany were unacceptable. He thought that while German opinion might harden in interpreting Lloyd George's speech as a climb-down, the effect might be to strengthen Kühlman, the German Foreign Minister, and the moderates. The UDC's line, Ponsonby told Trevelyan, should insist on Britain joining the Brest Litovsk negotiations as 'the thing is going to develop openly into a struggle between democracy and the reactionaries'.[64] Ponsonby's initial surmise as to the Germans' intentions proved to be correct. While Ludendorff directed Germany's final despairing effort to achieve a military victory, the dissenters could only wait on events.

Curiously enough, this had also become the government's position, as Lloyd George revealed to Ponsonby in an interview on 27 June 1918. Lloyd George's position was that the government had to choose the right moment to open negotiations. The right moment was not now, because the government believed that Germany had won the war. They had to go on fighting until the Germans realised that the war had been a failure.[65] They had not long to wait, for in July the German offensive was clearly spent and Foch began the series of attacks that became by the end of August a German rout.

The prospect of a military victory brought no consolation to Ponsonby. His father-in-law was seriously ill and died in October 1918. As the jingo press called for a march on Berlin, he noted 'the end is coming . . . Revolution in Germany, Revolution all over Austria-Hungary. Bloody chaos that will spread further. This is the way war solves problems.' He summed up his views on the war in 'Ideas and Impressions':

The war has *increased*

Blatency, frivolity, vulgarity, materialism, lying, calumny, cruelty, vice, thieving, whoremongering, syphilis, disease, dirt, neglect, grief, money grubbing, cheating, charlatanism, arrogance, stupidity, ugliness and greed (actual instances of each could easily be produced)

The war has *diminished*

Love, sympathy, refinement, idealism, beauty, intelligence, gentleness, accomplishment, religion, honesty, truth, wisdom, tolerance and liberty.

Both in an extreme degree.[66]

Lloyd George then called an election to take advantage of the armistice and to maintain his wartime coalition. While the Tories agreed, the

Labour Party refused and Asquith also determined to run in opposition to the coalition. The Tories agreed not to run against 150 Liberals who agreed to support the coalition and who in consequence were given the famous 'coupon' – a facetious reference to wartime ration cards. This arrangement did not affect Ponsonby in Dunfermline who hoped only to face a Tory candidate, but the decision of the Labour Party to run a national campaign with as full a slate of candidates as possible was to have serious repercussions. Ponsonby was standing as an Independent Democrat and, in spite of Ramsay MacDonald's active support, the Fife miners remained unenthusiastic. At every meeting, Ponsonby had to face awkward questions about why he had not joined the Labour Party. When he went up to Scotland to begin his campaign, Ponsonby thought that there was a good chance that the miners would not run a candidate of their own. Nomination day was 4 December and on 28 November the miners still had not made up their minds. He told Trevelyan that there was furious opposition inside the Labour Party to the idea, but the danger remained and if it came off he would be dished. Much to Ponsonby's surprise, the Labour Party decided not to support the miners' candidate, Watson, at a meeting on 30 November; but, in defiance of the Party, he appeared on nomination day, and Ponsonby had to face the inevitability of defeat. The votes he needed to defeat Wallace would now be siphoned off to Watson.[67]

Ponsonby was also uncertain about the number of votes he would lose because of his opposition to the war. The local press was as virulent as ever and he was denounced by the Tory agent as an 'alien crank'. He sensed a good deal of silent obscure opinion which was against him on the war, but had no means of measuring it. He was heckled by some discharged soldiers and made no converts by refusing to go along with imposing a heavy war indemnity on Germany. The mood had clearly changed from the dark days earlier in the year when he had received the following letter from the front:

> I have just read with pleasure that you are going to address a meeting of your electors in Dunfermline. I don't need to hope, for I know you will have an overflow meeting, for by them listening to you they are hearing the truth. I have just been sent from France. I have been on the fronts of the Somme, Arras, Dixmude, and throughout Belgium, and received the 'Dunfermline Press' regular from home. The boys out there, who title you 'The Soldiers' Friend', liked very much to hear me read your letters in the above paper, and many a night, wearied in camp, would say, 'Come, Mac, give us Ponsonby', and I would repeat the following:-
>> 'Liberty and justice are not in the gift of any existing Government. Militarism and oppression are characteristic of them all. The war that has yet to come will be the war of united democracy against the stale traditions of discredited Governments.'

You told no lie; it came in Russia; it's to come in Germany and all the world over . . . I only ask you on behalf of the comrades to stick to your guns, and never mind those men who resign their agency from your committee, as Democracy is against their teaching. Stick it till the boys come home, and their vote will count to place you at the top of the poll higher than you imagine . . .[68]

It was the silent pro-war vote that continued to worry Ponsonby; he suspected that it was larger than most of his supporters thought and would be gathered in by Wallace. He returned to Shulbrede for Christmas and there awaited the verdict of the electors, which arrived by telegram on the evening of 28 December:

Wallace	6,886
Watson	5,076
Ponsonby	3,491

By Sunday the full result of the election was apparent. All the pacifists, Snowden, MacDonald, Trevelyan, the Buxtons, Anderson and Richardson, were beaten. All the leading moderate Liberals, Asquith, Simon, Samuel, McKenna, McKinnon, Wood, Runciman, were beaten. The jingo extremists, Bottomley, Billing, Butcher, Page Croft, were all returned with colossal majorities. The coalition totalled 473 seats against 59 Labour and 26 Liberals. 73 Sinn Feiners refused to come to Westminster. In his diary, Ponsonby wrote 'The whole thing is absolutely farcical. I am thankful I am not in. I should feel hopelessly isolated.' He put his defeat down to 'women and hanging the Kaiser and ingrained prejudice'.

Notes

1. *Hansard*, V, 65, 2089–90.
2. *Denman* MSS., Liberals 4(3) 1914, 1915 contains the minute book of the New Liberal Group.
3. Swartz (1971), p. 22.
4. Robbins (1976) and Howard (1978).
5. *MacDonald* MSS., PRO 30/69/1158, f.100–01, Ponsonby to MacDonald, 17 Aug 1914.
6. 'Sophistry and Self-Righteousness', *Spectator*, 26 Sept 1914.
7. *Trevelyan* MSS., C.P.T./73, Ponsonby to P. Morrell, 12 Aug 1914.
8. *Shulbrede* MSS., A. Ponsonby to D. Ponsonby, 27 Aug 1914.
9. *Trevelyan* MSS, C.P.T./73, Ponsonby to Trevelyan, 11 Sept 1914.
10. *Shulbrede* MSS., A. Ponsonby Diary, VIII, 9 Oct 1914.
11. *Shulbrede* MSS., A. Ponsonby Diary, VIII, 21 Apr 1915.
12. *Shulbrede* MSS., A. Ponsonby to D. Ponsonby, 10 Mar 1915.
13. *Shulbrede* MSS., A. Ponsonby Diary, VIII, 5 Apr 1915.

14. *Shulbrede MSS.*, D. Ponsonby Diary, May to June 1915.
15. *Shulbrede MSS.*, A. Ponsonby Diary, VIII, 18 June 1915.
16. *Shulbrede MSS.*, A. Ponsonby to J. Ponsonby, 14 June 1915.
17. *Trevelyan MSS.*, C.P.T./74, A. Ponsonby to C. Trevelyan, 22 May 1915.
18. *Shulbrede MSS.*, A. Ponsonby Diary, VIII, 17 June 1915.
19. *Shulbrede MSS.*, Wartime Diary, f.17.
20. *Ponsonby MSS.*, C.662, f.129–34, Bille to A. Ponsonby, 24 June 1915.
21. *Shulbrede MSS.*, A. Ponsonby Diary, VIII, 23 July 1915.
22. Dubin (1970) and Robbins (1967).
23. *Dickinson MSS.*, C.402, f.116–20, Mr Ponsonby's Notes, 10 Dec 1914. See Appendix, p. 239–41.
24. *Ponsonby MSS.*, C.661, f.190, Bryce to A. Ponsonby, 14 Dec 1914.
25. A list is in Swartz (1971), Appendix E, pp. 231–4.
26. *Ponsonby MSS.*, C.661, f.150, G. Wallas to A. Ponsonby, 6 Dec 1914.
27. *Ponsonby MSS.*, C.661, f.142–66. Correspondence about Ponsonby's book *Democracy and Diplomacy*, Dec 1914.
28. *Democracy and Diplomacy*, p. 113.
29. Gilbert Murray (1916), pp. 180–92 ; *Murray MSS.*, Vol. 30, f.3–6, A. Ponsonby to G. Murray, 2 Feb 1916; *Ponsonby MSS*, C.662, f.19, Galsworthy to A. Ponsonby, 12 Feb 1915, f.64, 6 Apr 1915 and in *Shulbrede MSS.*, 27 Nov 1915.
30. Arthur Ponsonby, 'International Morality', *The International Journal of Ethics*, Jan 1915; 'The Basis of International Authority', League of Peace and Freedom Pamphlet No. 10 (London, n.d.).
31. *Shulbrede MSS.*, A. Ponsonby Diary, VIII, 4 Oct 1915.
32. *Shulbrede MSS.*, A. Ponsonby to D. Ponsonby, 12 Oct 1915.
33. *Shulbrede MSS.*, A. Ponsonby Diary, VIII, 24 Oct 1915.
34. *Hansard*, V, 75, 140–60. In order to counter the semi-official silence, the UDC published the speeches as Leaflet No. 15b, 'Mr Ponsonby and Mr Trevelyan in the House of Commons'.
35. *Shulbrede MSS.*, A. Ponsonby Diary, VIII, 13 Jan 1916.
36. *Ponsonby MSS.*, C.664, f.5, draft letter, Jan 1916.
37. *Hansard*, V, 80, 737–42.
38. Swartz (1971), p. 76.
39. *Shulbrede MSS.*, A. Ponsonby Diary, VIII, 13 Feb 1916.
40. *Shulbrede MSS.*, A. Ponsonby to D. Ponsonby, 28 Mar 1916.
41. *Shulbrede MSS.*, A. Ponsonby Diary, VIII, 23 May 1916.
42. *Shulbrede MSS.*, A. Ponsonby Diary, VIII, 30 June 1916.
43. *Shulbrede MSS.*, A. Ponsonby to D. Ponsonby, 15 Aug 1916.
44. *Shulbrede MSS.*, A. Ponsonby Diary, IX, 30 Dec 1917.
45. *Shulbrede MSS.*, A. Ponsonby Diary, VII, 14 Dec 1910.
46. *The Nation*, 7 Jan 1911.
47. *Shulbrede MSS.*, A. Ponsonby Diary, VII, 14 July 1911.
48. *Shulbrede MSS.*, A. Ponsonby Diary, VIII, Sept 1915.
49. *Shulbrede MSS*, A. Ponsonby Diary, VIII, July 1917.
50. Swartz (1971), p. 137.
51. *Ponsonby MSS.*, C.664, f.80–2, draft to H. Bryant, 26 May 1916.
52. *Shulbrede MSS.*, A. Ponsonby Diary, VIII, 14 June 1917.
53. *Shulbrede MSS.*, A. Ponsonby to D. Ponsonby, 19 June 1917.

54. *Shulbrede* MSS., A. Ponsonby Diary, VIII, 22 June 1917.
55. *Shulbrede* MSS., A. Ponsonby to D. Ponsonby, 27 June 1917.
56. *Morel* MSS., file 116, f.2, A. Ponsonby to E.D. Morel, 19 July 1917.
57. *Shulbrede* MSS., A. Ponsonby Diary, IX, 10 Aug 1917.
58. *Trevelyan* MSS., C.P.T./78, A. Ponsonby to C. Trevelyan, 30 Aug 1917.
59. *Shulbrede* MSS., A. Ponsonby Diary, IX, 11 Nov 1917.
60. Morris (1982), p. 129.
61. *The UDC*, Sept 1917.
62. *Hansard*, V, 100, 2008.
63. Lloyd George (1933), vol. 2, pp. 1490–1.
64. *Trevelyan* MSS., C.P.T./79, A. Ponsonby to C. Trevelyan, 11 Jan 1918.
65. *Ponsonby* MSS., C.667, f.58–68, A. Ponsonby's Notes of an interview with Lloyd George
66. *Shulbrede* MSS., 'Ideas and Impressions'.
67. Marquand (1977), p. 232; McKibbon (1974), p. 108.
68. 'Changing Opinion', *The UDC*, Mar 1918.

Sir Henry Ponsonby, Queen Victoria's Private Secretary, Arthur's father, circa 1885

Lady Ponsonby, Arthur's mother, in her study at Gilmuire, circa 1910

Arthur Ponsonby as page of honour, with Queen Victoria, circa 1882.

Arthur Ponsonby as Leader of the Labour Peers in the Lords with his grandson Thomas (now Labour Chief Whip in the Lords) at Butley, 1933

Dolly and Arthur Ponsonby with Bess and Matthew and their two grandsons, Thomas and Nicholas, at Butley, 1933

Arthur Ponsonby with George Lansbury (left) Leader of the Labour Party and Clement Attlee (centre), Deputy Leader at the Labour Party Conference at Southport in 1934

Arthur Ponsonby reading at his desk in the crypt at Shulbrede Priory, circa 1940

Arthur Ponsonby, circa 1908

CHAPTER FOUR

The Labour Party and Foreign Policy, 1919–1924

A Socialist Aristocrat

To a certain extent, the result of the election had vindicated Ponsonby. Fritz Ponsonby's comment that it was 'only natural that, as a pacifist, your constituents should stone you as a false prophet' was, to say the least unbrotherly, and also wrong. The miners who had voted for Watson had done so out of misguided loyalty to one of their own; without his intervention, these voters would have gone to Ponsonby and he would have won by 1,681 votes. Both Ramsay MacDonald and Snowden were furious with Watson's intervention, but nothing could change the vote and the defeat left Ponsonby without a seat, without a constituency and out of work.

Ponsonby's main concern was, naturally enough, the Versailles Peace Settlement. In 1918, President Wilson had come forward as a champion of UDC principles. How far they would be translated into a durable peace settlement remained for Ponsonby and his colleagues an open question. The UDC, therefore, kept up its campaign for the principle of self-determination as against political and strategic reasons for Europe's new frontiers; for parliamentary control of foreign policy; for a League of Nations that would not be a League of Governments; and for disarmament, free commerce and the open door. From what little news that trickled out from Versailles, Ponsonby soon concluded that the peace settlement was going to be worse than he imagined could be possible because of the implacable hatred of Germany in France. He strongly attacked the secrecy surrounding the peace-making at Versailles. It had been announced that the plenary sessions would be open, but when the plenipotentiaries proceeded to do all their work in closed committees, Ponsonby characterised them as being 'like plumbers, who trade on the supposition that no one understands their job but themselves'[1] (the analogy coming easily to a man who grappled all too frequently with Shulbrede's ram tanks).

At the UDC executive meeting on 6 May 1919, Ponsonby heard from Charles Buxton that the Germans would sign under protest, trusting in public opinion in the Western democracies to alter the Treaty. He commented 'I fear their trust is very much displaced.' When the peace terms were published, Ponsonby could barely contain his indignation. 'Annexations, dismemberment, robbery and ruin. No faint pretence of justice or generosity. This after the war. This to finish it all. This the culmination of all the massacres and horrors.'[2] After Germany signed the peace treaty on 28 June, Ponsonby described it as 'a cold, meaningless formality . . . not the end of a tragedy but the definite beginning of further trouble'.

Ponsonby was particularly well qualified to comment on this aspect of the peace settlement for he had been, since 1908, a leading parliamentary advocate of the need for an Anglo-German understanding. Ponsonby saw in the punitive Versailles Treaty the culmination of a misguided policy that had antagonised Germany before the war, developed the myth of Prussian militarism in its war propaganda, and saddled the new republic with sole responsibility for starting the war in the Treaty's infamous clause 231. The way forward to the creation of a new international order lay in reconciling the new Germany rather than in punishing her for something that she had not done.

Ponsonby undertook a visit to Germany in the company of E.D. Morel in the summer of 1920 through the auspices of a group of scholarly moderate liberals calling themselves the Heidelberger Vereiningung. They first called on the leader of the group, Prince Max of Baden at Salem, and then further meetings followed in Berlin with Walter Schucking, Count Max Montgelas and Professor Lujo Brentano.[3] Naturally enough, the organisation, which was dedicated to proving that Germany had not been responsible for the outbreak of war in 1914, provided an opportunity for Ponsonby and Morel to interview Bethmann Hollweg.

> A most impressive picture of fallen Germany. He sat in a high Italian chair and said leaning forward with intense feeling, 'You made peace with us on Wilson's fourteen points and betrayed us in the Treaty of Versailles, you continued the blockade 6 months after the war was over and starved our women and children. These are facts I never can forgive or forget. Now our government is treated with such indignity that it cannot exercise any authority at all at home.' Tears welled in his eyes, he struck both the arms of his chair and got up and paced the room.[4]

The Independent Socialists were intent on discrediting the old regime and saw the UDC campaign against the peace treaties as unwittingly aiding these circles in Germany that advocated a war of revenge. For his part, Ponsonby pointed out to their German friends that the activities of the Independent Socialists, in emphasising Germany's sole responsibility for the war, were undermining their case for the revision of the peace settlement which rested on their belief in general rather than German responsibility for the war. Ponsonby was confident that the UDC was not strengthening German militarism; but others were not so sure that the threat to democracy in Germany was not the Treaty but still the old regime. He told Dolly

> It is the German psychology that is interesting. Not only are they in the dust but they are aware of it. They seem to have lost self respect they cringe and the stupid Independent Socialists go on emphasizing Germany's *sole* responsibility for the war not so much because they believe it as because they want for ever to discredit the old regime which they fear in the course of the May reactions might come back again. We are going to tell them on Saturday that this is a stupid line to take and it makes our own efforts for revision very difficult. There is fear of unemployment on a large scale of strikes and of more revolutions.[5]

On his return to England, Ponsonby took little time in publishing his experiences in Germany. Articles denouncing the continuing economic war against women and children in Germany appeared in the *Daily Herald* and the *Daily News*. While this appeal for justice to the downtrodden made a certain impact, a large body of opinion in England took the conventional view, as usual expressed to Arthur by his brother Fritz that 'it served them jolly well right!'. It served Germany right because Germany had started the war. This view embedded in the war guilt clause of the Versailles Treaty could not go unchallenged, because a fundamental tenet of the radical position on 1914 was general rather than particular responsibility for starting the war.

For Ponsonby, this raised again the problem of the course of British foreign policy before 1914. Ponsonby's position was that none of the Great Powers had had clean hands, least of all Great Britain which had pursued a balance of power policy behind the veil of secret diplomacy. Ponsonby had a ready explanation of how Great Britain came to make the secret commitment to France in 1906 that set off the train of events that led to intervention in 1914. He was convinced that it had been done by the Liberal Imperialists behind the back of the Prime Minister.

With the ending of the war, the debate over what had happened to British foreign policy before 1914 began in earnest, and was sustained by an ever-increasing flood of memoirs and biographies. One significant defence of Sir Edward Grey had appeared during the war,[6] and this was matched from the other side by the appearance, in 1919, of Lord Loreburn's *How the War Came*. This book raised the controversial question of the military conversations between France and Great Britain that had taken place during the Moroccan crisis of 1905–6, for Loreburn had been a member of that Cabinet and had known nothing of what was going on behind the scenes. Murray, writing in the *Nation* in September

1919,[7] fairly and squarely laid the blame for the Cabinet not being made aware of the military conversations with France on Sir Henry Campbell-Bannerman. Ponsonby could hardly contain his indignation, rejecting the accusation against Campbell-Bannerman as absurd. He wrote of Murray, who was a classical don, 'I wish he would stick to translating Greek which he does admirably.' A more plausible explanation in Ponsonby's view was that, as Campbell-Bannerman's closest associates did not know 'surely the most natural inference is not that Sir Henry Campbell-Bannerman, knowing fully the extent of our commitments, deliberately withheld the information from his Cabinet colleagues, but that Sir Henry himself had by no means been fully apprised of the exact nature of the understanding to which the Foreign Secretary had committed the nation'.[8]

Murray responded privately and pointed out to Ponsonby that the thrust of his argument was directed against the idea that the Anglo-French military conversations were part of a Liberal Imperialist plot. Murray had discussed the history of the incident fully with Grey, who explained to him definitely and in detail how he took the French Ambassador's proposals to Campbell-Bannerman. He added, 'I think Asquith went with him, but I am not sure. But as to the consultation with C-B, Grey's memory was perfectly clear. The strong differences of opinion within that Cabinet had made consultations disagreeable and had resulted in the growth of a departmental habit.'[9] As Murray seemed disinclined to return to Greek translations, Ponsonby undertook to educate him on political relations within Campbell-Bannerman's Cabinet. He pointed out that the relationship between Grey and Campbell-Bannerman was strained and difficult for practically the whole two years that Campbell-Bannerman was Prime Minister. A reconciliation had only taken place at the end of 1907. Haldane had actively intrigued on behalf of the Liberal League with Asquith acting as the bridge between the two factions. Ponsonby was ready to believe that Grey had reported his conversations with Cambon to Campbell-Bannerman 'but that by frequent consultation he made clear what exactly our commitments were it is impossible to believe'. Ponsonby had talked it over with Loreburn, who, with Morley, had been Campbell-Bannerman's closest friend. They knew his innermost thoughts on every question of policy and, as they were ignorant, Ponsonby concluded that Campbell-Bannerman had not grasped the significance of the conversations. Grey, in Ponsonby's opinion, did not do enough to keep Campbell-Bannerman *au courant*; Grey was not a Machiavelli and would never have deliberately concealed facts, but he was, in Ponsonby's opinion, completely in the hands of his Foreign Office officials and did not see the trend of the policy he was being forced to adopt. Grey had no knowledge of Europe and was at the mercy of his officials, as witnessed by his permanent under-secretary's remark: 'I am going to make Grey the greatest Foreign Secretary of modern times.' The negotiation of the Anglo-Russian convention of 1907 was not Grey's idea but Hardinge's and was a fatal step in alienating Germany and tying Great Britain to Tsardom. Grey was the victim and made himself the spokesman of a general drift towards alliances, balance of power, the alienation of Germany and preparation for war. Grey took the line of least resistance and was not strong enough to resist Benckendorff and Cambon, King Edward's prejudices and the vested financial interests of the city in Russia. Ponsonby concluded his letter, 'When I look at Europe sown thick with the seeds of future conflict, I think his policy was blind, stupid and disastrous.'[10] Murray, on receipt of this long explanation, quietly retreated behind a generalisation: the split in the Cabinet had indeed produced bad results and had led to one group not knowing the minds of the other.

The dust had hardly time to settle on this correspondence before Ponsonby received an appeal for further information on what had happened in 1906 from E.D. Morel, who suddenly realised that Ponsonby had been on the spot and might be in a position to know. Ponsonby did his best to answer Morel's queries and added some more details to his earlier explanation of the relationship between Grey and Campbell-Bannerman. He told Morel that it was clear to anyone who knew the relations between the two men that Grey did not, and could not, convey to Campbell-Bannerman the full import of the policy he was pursuing. The latter did not have the intelligence to understand what he was being involved in and Cambon pulled off a master stroke of secret diplomacy. Grey despised Campbell-Bannerman, mistaking his geniality for weakness. There was no doubt that if it had been made clear to him that the nation was being committed to an alliance with France, he would have realised the enormous significance of such a step and would at once have consulted Loreburn and Morley, as he always did on any vital point. Morel's second question concerned the role of Edward VII. Ponsonby pointed out that there was no case there, for, even in foreign affairs and the army, the King was deplorably ignorant. Hardinge was the man who mattered, working all he knew for a Russian *entente*, which meant a French and consequently anti-German policy.[11]

Early in the New Year, Ponsonby heard the disagreeable news that J.A. Spender, the former editor of the *Westminster Gazette* and himself a Liberal Imperialist, had been chosen to write the official biography of Campbell-Bannerman. He had long entertained hopes of doing the work himself. He wrote in his diary: 'it means the shelving and slurring over of an important political episode. I shall have to write something myself to put away in a drawer.' He was afraid that Spender would play down the differences that existed between Campbell-Bannerman and the Liberal Imperialists and so, when he sat down in the summer of 1920 to write his own memoir, he naturally gave full emphasis to that part of the inner history of Campbell-Bannerman's Cabinet. This mitigates to a certain extent the usefulness of the memoir as an historical document, but in writing the memoir Ponsonby drew on his diary and other contemporary material and, so far as the Grey/Campbell-Bannerman controversy is concerned, he was not at all guilty of rewriting the past to fit his current opinions and concerns.[12] It must be said that modern research into Grey's foreign policy has not resolved this issue and Ponsonby's version of events has stood the test of time.[13]

As for the general proposition that the war had been caused by the international anarchy of the nineteenth-century state system, the work of Lowes Dickinson swept all before it and it became standard in the 1920s to think that all the powers had been to some degree or other responsible for the war. As Germany could not therefore bear sole responsibility, then her treatment at Versailles had been unjustified.

Labour's Foreign Policy

With the emergence of the Labour Party as an alternative government, the time has come to assess the significance of the new approach that Labour claimed to offer in the foreign policy field. In projecting an international system that was based on the ultimate harmony of national interests as opposed to irreconcilable competition, Labour claimed not only to have found a new way forward but, taking as evidence the catastrophe of the Great War, the only way forward.

Ponsonby played a part in popularising this point of view through his journalistic activities and later in the twenties he was to make two highly original contributions, first to the pacifist debate with his claim to have discovered a value-free basis for pacifism, and second to the disarmament debate when he became the first advocate of unilateral disarmament. These developments are discussed in Chapter 5. In the immediate aftermath of the war, Ponsonby took up some of the practical implications of his earlier proposals on democratic control of foreign policy.

The Labour Party's first move in the foreign affairs field after the publication of their Statement of War Aims was to set up an Advisory Committee on International Questions. Its first meeting was held at the end of May 1918 with Sidney Webb in the chair and Leonard Woolf as Honorary Secretary. In its preliminary memorandum, it noted that the establishment of the committee was in itself a step in the direction of democratic control of foreign policy.[14] The setting up of the Advisory Committee should be placed in the context of a parliamentary debate initiated by Ponsonby on democratic control, in which was put forward a fully fledged scheme to establish an official Foreign Affairs Committee.[15] The Foreign Secretary was characteristically scornful.[16] Balfour was quite unable to appreciate the principle of parliamentary control, unlike Beatrice Webb, who saw the Labour leader's determination to get at the roots of foreign policy as a sign of 'a new type of politics – the initiation of social change from outside the recognised machinery of government'.[17]

The Advisory Committee decided to move forward by inviting Ponsonby as the expert on democratic control to make proposals on open diplomacy and another ex-diplomat, Sir George Young, to make proposals on the further reform of the Foreign Office and diplomatic service. Ponsonby's practical proposals were published as a Labour Party pamphlet in 1921.[18] In this pamphlet, Ponsonby set out a full programme of democratic control in order to abolish secrecy by changing diplomatic and parliamentary procedure to ensure full information and by establishing a new rule that all agreements should have parliamentary sanction. The need for a Foreign Affairs Committee was also reiterated. The second part of the reform programme dealt with the diplomatic and foreign services. George Young's original proposals[19] were so outrageous that they had to be toned down in the committee. Ponsonby's pamphlet noted that the Foreign Office had implemented some of the recommendations of the MacDonnell Commission of 1914[20] in that while it had abolished the nomination procedure and the £400 property qualification, it had not found any money to pay newly appointed attachés, so the net result had been to give 'official permission to any zealous young man (without £400 a year) to become a diplomat and go bankrupt in six months'. The only other proposal was the amalgamation of the Consular and Foreign Services. The more far-reaching Young proposals such as labour attachés and political appointees to all embassies were quietly shelved.

While it has been argued that the impact of Labour on foreign policy contributed to the decline of the Foreign Office in the inter-war period, the positive impact of the 'new' diplomacy has received short shrift.[21] The proposals emanating from the ACIQ reflect the emergence of public opinion as a factor in foreign policy formulation. As public opinion is a notoriously difficult concept to handle, the defenders of the old diplomacy have had a field day in attributing the failures of British diplomacy to the interference of public opinion. Some specific aspects are discussed in relation to the negotiation of the Russian Treaties of 1924 in the next chapter. In this context, the 'new' diplomacy represents much more than the rejection of aristocratic secret diplomacy that had contributed to the diplomatic débâcle of 1914. What lay behind the new diplomacy was the development of the idea that governments exist for the people and not vice versa. Ponsonby had, throughout his political life, a sure grasp of this essential principle of democracy.

It also needs to be said that Ponsonby's understanding of democracy and foreign policy was based on the confident assumptions of the Victorian era that there was nowhere any real conflict between the interests of nations. If the interests of the people were peace-loving, then it followed that governments caused wars. Their involvement in alliances and secret diplomacy, their colonial ambitions and the reckless accumulation of armaments were all capable of causing wars. The remedy lay in the restraining influence of an educated public opinion.

If there was a socialist element at all in this, it lay in the belief that the victims of international conflict were ordinary people who had paid for power politics with their lives in the World War. Some writers on Labour's foreign policy have attempted to correlate domestic with foreign policy in terms of the socialist objective of Clause IV of the 1918 constitution, arguing that as capitalism had been the root cause of war, there could be no peace in the world until international socialism prevailed.[22] This view ignores altogether the fact that the socialist objective was a figleaf cloaking the differences between the various sections of the party. The Labour Party was an electoral machine only differing from other political parties in that it was a machine devoted to gathering the votes of the working class.

Ponsonby's decision to join the Labour Party had little personal effect and his circle of friends and his relationship to them remained remarkably stable. It was a common enough view that Labour's recruits from the Liberal Party were all 'traitors to their class', but after surviving the maelstrom of animosity aroused by his dissent in the War, he was able to take up the peacetime threads of life with comparative ease.

The Ponsonbys' distinguished Sussex friends and neighbours had inevitably been disrupted by the war. The Bertrand Russells had migrated, along with Logan Pearsall Smith, to Oxford, although the Smiths kept Vann Cottage, which was still being used by Alys Russell. Alys Russell, with her forced and over-elaborated Quaker 'Thees' and 'Thous', was not an easy friend, and the Ponsonbys found more congenial company among the Russells, in spite of her vegetarianism, in Mrs Rollo Russell who ran a small hostelry at the Devil's Punch Bowl and Lady Victoria Russell, whose children, Anthony and Elizabeth, were friends of Elizabeth. The Granville Barkers' marriage did not survive the War; Ponsonby had been called upon as an impartial friend of both parties to play an intermediary role in the divorce. On the other hand, Roger Fry had built his famous house, Durbins, high above Guildford on the North Downs and remained a fairly frequent visitor, especially as his daughter, Pamela, was a friend of Elizabeth. New arrivals in the area included the Snowdens, who settled at Shere, the Joseph Kings, at Witley, the Webbs, at Passfield Corner,

Liphook, the Noel Buxtons at 'Houndless Water', and the Pethick Lawrences, who always appeared at Shulbrede in the summer for tennis. Curiously, Ponsonby's reaction to the wives of most of these political colleagues was uneasy. Beatrice Webb still left him, as she had done when they first met twenty years before, with the feeling that she had nothing but intellectual contempt for him, and, after a day with Mrs Buxton, he always felt inclined to give up public life altogether, so overawed was he by her tremendously impersonal public spiritedness. Ethel Snowden's head was turned and, like Ramsay MacDonald, liked nothing better than to talk to the Ponsonbys about court and society. Jos. Wedgwood escaped, perhaps only because Ponsonby never knew his second wife well enough to form an opinion.

The Ponsonbys, as usual, kept each other informed about Margot Asquith. After a weekend at The Wharf in April 1919, Maggie had found Margot playing bridge dressed in 'White silk fringes and a Hungarian night gown'. Much to her embarrassment, Count Bibesco insisted on talking about Margot two inches from Asquith's nose. 'Margot is almost a pathetic greenhouse she would try and dance like Carmen – which made one hot.' When Margot's autobiography appeared in November 1920, Ponsonby reviewed it under the heading 'Here's Me!'.[23] He read the book in the train with such absorbed amusement, that it attracted the attention of a fellow traveller, who asked Ponsonby with a chuckle whether they were married yet; the answer was in the negative, as he had only come to the sixth proposal. A few years later, Betty met Lady Ottoline Morrell at the Asquiths winning hands down over Margot 'with heavy black blob pouffes, spanish combs and a white crinoline covered with silver roses'.

Arthur's elder sister Betty, although still living in great style at Grey Abbey, remained entirely sympathetic, as did his other sister Maggie who had taken up social work with Dick Sheppard at St Martin-in-the-Fields and who introduced Arthur to Sheppard. Both Johnnie and Fritz regarded their younger brother's politics with bemused scepticism, but never allowed them to become a barrier. Johnnie remained a bachelor and took over Gilmuire, his mother's house at Ascot, before being posted away as DOC Madras. Fritz wrote a history of the Grenadiers' war-time exploits, returned to royal duty as Treasurer to George V and finally settled down not far from Shulbrede in the village of Wonersh at Great Tangley Manor.

Another marriage that had not managed to weather the war was that of Dolly's sister Gwen to Harry Plunket Greene. Gwen settled down in 1920 two miles outside Salisbury, not too far from the Pembrokes' country house at Wilton with all its childhood memories for Gwen and Dolly. Gwen's children, Richard, David and Olivia, were all growing up and Richard, the eldest, only a year younger than Elizabeth, was a particular favourite with Arthur. David, extremely tall like his brother, was the same age as Matthew. While Arthur and Dolly thought him to be a rather weak character, they were both of the opinion that Gwen's youngest, Olivia, still a teenager, had become too masterful and domineering.

At the end of the war, Elizabeth was learning the rudiments of acting in a London drama school. Arthur, who had himself thought of a stage career, watched her progress carefully, attending her performances in London and when she joined the Nottingham Repertory. The conclusion that he had reached early on in her acting career, after seeing her perform Barrie's Rosalind, that 'she cannot act well enough to make any mark on the stage' was confirmed in her apprenticeship in Nottingham. The trouble was that Elizabeth was completely stage-struck and refused to accept the verdict and continued to move around the fringes of the professional theatre. Her special friends were John Evelyn Strachey, still at Eton, but the possessor of a motor bicycle with a pillion seat, whose parents lived not far from Shulbrede at Newlands Corner, and her cousin Richard Plunket Greene, then still at Bedales. Richard Greene had all the mind, manners and conversation of a 14-year-old, and Strachey struck Ponsonby as being priggish and pontifical.

Richard Greene and John Strachey were both up at Oxford in March 1921 when Ponsonby came to address the university Labour Club. After discussing the various social and intellectual currents prevalent in the university, he came away with the impression of an odd, silly and perverse atmosphere. The cult of effeminacy was then running at full course and it was just as well that Ponsonby did not run into Jeffrey Prendergast who was in the habit, as Sir John Rothenstein recalls, of walking out in the street pulling behind him on a string his white woollen lamb on wheels. Ponsonby would not have been surprised at Strachey's antic in appearing at the wicket in a college match attired in a huge peasant straw hat ornamented with trailing pink ribbons.

Strachey was a Tory whilst at Oxford. Arthur was subsequently to bring him into the Labour Party. What was distressing to the Ponsonbys in these essentially harmless activities was the unrelenting frivolity of the young, whether in the ceaseless banging out of ragtime on the Shulbrede piano or in their general approach, which Ponsonby characterised as being '"gather ye rosebuds" or rather wrench every bud from the tree regardless of the future – gulp it all down greedily, squeeze all the juice out of the fruit at once – follow inclination, scoff at tradition, rush and tear through life without thought, without regard, without reflection, but anyhow keep smiling'.[24] While he could analyse the situation and correctly attribute the problem to the great wave of unrestrained feminine advertisement brought about by the sex dislocation of the war, he could find no solution to the immediate problem and, although he had many a family talk with

Elizabeth, the result was complete failure. He barely consoled himself with the thought that something he said may have been remembered.

In complete contrast to his sister, who could not stand Shulbrede, Matthew Ponsonby retained his youthful affection for the house and, as he grew older, became an enthusiastic part of the archaeological explorations that Ponsonby and Charles Strachey undertook in order to complete their researches into the Priory. 'M hard at work on the back of the cupboard kept filling the dining room with gigantic stones and clouds of dust.' Matthew who had eventually gone to school at Leighton Park still needed a tutor to prepare him for his Oxford Responsions. After a great deal of difficulty, he finally passed and in October 1923 went up to Balliol.

MP for Sheffield Brightside

Ponsonby's political activity in 1919 was restricted to UDC affairs. Although he had joined the Independent Labour Party, he saw very little of his Labour friends Snowden and MacDonald, other than occasional visits to the 1917 Club in Gerrard Street amidst the 'parked cars and the equally stationary, though more aged, whores' of Soho.[25] At these meetings, the usual topic of conversation was the hopeless character of the leadership and management of the Labour Party in the Commons. Ramsay MacDonald talked airily of the necessity of revitalising the centre of the ILP, but nothing practical seems to have been done. Once Ponsonby went to the House 'it was a curious feeling, so many strange faces amidst such intensely familiar surroundings'. He only talked to the police and the doorkeeper. In October, the same pessimistic tone prevailed in spite of Arthur Henderson's smashing by-election victory at Widnes. He found Ramsay despondent about prospects, and complaining that all the best Labour men were being ousted by Trade Unionists attracted by an MP's salary of £400 a year. By this time, Ponsonby had received no fewer than six invitations to stand from local ILP branches. He rejected them all in favour of a nomination contest with Watson at Dunfermline, which he lost. 'My utter rejection by Dunfermline was curious. The Tories opposed me, the Liberals ousted me and Labour turned me down. And when all connections were then cut after a membership of eleven years not one single soul wrote a line to me.'[26]

All the ex-members of Parliament of the ILP assembled at the 1917 Club at the end of October to arrange meetings and talk over candidates. Although Ponsonby found MacDonald and Snowden solicitous of his orphan status, he was left, for the moment, high and dry. The meeting was concerned to counter the animosity towards them coming from the Trade Unionist leaders and other officials of the Labour Party. In support of this campaign, Ponsonby undertook a speaking tour in the North East in November and noted that the feeling of the north was very good and it looked as though Labour would sweep the board there. On his return to London, Ramsay MacDonald spoke to him about the possibility of his standing for the Brightside division of Sheffield. Things moved rapidly. The selection conference was held in mid-January and rather to Ponsonby's surprise he found himself once again a candidate for Parliament. The reason for his surprise was that the Brightside constituency was as complete a working class constituency as it was possible to find in the industrial heartland of England, and his opponents were working men candidates presenting their case to an entirely Trade Unionist selection conference. The conference was an ordeal and he heard afterwards that it was his answers to questions that won him the necessary votes. 'One of the defeated men was very angry and did not conceal his disappointment.'

Although there is no way of knowing how Ponsonby answered his questions, it can be safely assumed that he made a moral appeal, using arguments from his new book on religion and politics for the Socialist Library. *Religion and Politics*[27] appeared in print in 1921. In this small book, along with a further short piece of dialogue writing entitled *A Conflict of Opinion*, which had been published in 1919, Ponsonby set out his views on Socialism as an ideal.

Ponsonby had long since severed all practical connections with conventional religious observance and, even before the war, he had come to regard 'The Church' as an obstacle to the spiritual development of mankind. Ponsonby now completely rejected the supernatural aspects of religion. He particularly objected to what he saw as the Christians' dogmatic concept of a God, and conventional church-going with hymns and prayers and sacraments compartmentalised into a mechanical routine practised exclusively on Sundays. Ritual, ceremonial and formalism excluded the inner meaning and the spiritual significance of religion, which was to him the most comprehensive and universal instinct possessed by man. Religion, for Ponsonby, to be real had to be interwoven into the whole texture of life. Life, he believed, consisted of simply a series of opportunities for the exercise of physical, mental and moral faculties. It was not possible for anyone to isolate himself from the community in which he lived; every act, besides being individual, was also social. Socialism as a political ideal was concerned at root not with palliatives such as higher wages and better living conditions, but with the constitution of the whole social system. Socialism aimed to get at cause and origin to prevent the birth of evil and was the embodiment of an idea of complete social unity. Ponsonby's ability to articulate such ideas lifted him head and shoulders above the other candidates, even if grappling with such important fundamentals left him feeling like 'a leaky fishing smack coming up alongside of a big liner'.

Another factor in his selection was undoubtedly the fact that, while there existed a degree of antagonism in the movement between Trade Unionists and the ILPers, it did not really extend to Ponsonby and the other recent converts from the Liberal Party. It is quite true that the Labour Party's great strength after the war was that it remained, in spite of its new constitution, a party with strictly a working-class membership, but when it came to MPs, the party's experience of working men at Westminster had been disappointing. As Ponsonby put it in his diary, 'the underlying truth is that working men rather mistrust their own kind'. Ponsonby's name and reputation established by his pre-war radicalism and war-time dissent were part of the bargain. If he was a fish out of water in Sheffield Brightside, he was, in the eyes of his selection conference, a business proposition who could be relied upon to win the seat for Labour. Not that an election was even remotely in the offing in the immediate future. The next election was nearly three years away and it was not until November 1922 that the Brightside Labour Party realised what a good bargain they had made.

Shortly after his return to Westminster, Ponsonby referred to his four years away from the House as wonderful and divine. A large part of his time was spent in reading, writing, gardening and golf; quiet days at Shulbrede largely out of the public eye. He took up the Shulbrede book, which the war had interrupted, and brought it to a successful conclusion, although as usual he did not make any money on the venture. The idea of writing a book about diaries and diarists was conceived after reading Barbellian's *The Journal of a Disappointed Man* and *A Last Diary* which had been the publishing sensations of 1919 and 1920. Their impact was not simply because the author used the artifice of a pseudonym and faked his own death at the end of the first volume, but because the diaries possessed intrinsic literary merit and great psychological insight into character. Ponsonby described *The Journal of a Disappointed Man* as one of the most tragic books he had ever read. After he finished the second volume, he went up to the London Library to reconnoitre the field and came away determined to pursue the project. He was soon deeply involved and spent the greater part of his reading time in 1921 immersed in this work. Pepys, Evelyn, Windham and D'Ewes were all absorbed in a matter of weeks. In March, he was undeterred by Fanny Burney's and Wesley's eight volumes. The London Library exhausted, he had resort to the Reading Room of the British Museum, reading there in intervals between political meetings the diary of Edward VI and Ashmole. Quite naturally, this preoccupation with other people's diaries made Ponsonby self-conscious about his own volumes. He had never before analysed his own motives in writing and now began to be conscious of a 'prying eye examining, criticising, laughing and ten to one getting me all wrong even worse than I get myself'.

Further diaries kept Ponsonby hard at work for the whole of the summer of 1921. In September, he completed Greville and Lady Holland. By November, the last diaries on his list were proving difficult to locate, but the manuscript was finally completed with 120 diaries reviewed, and many more read. It was accepted by Methuen and published early in 1923.[28] A delighted author finally found himself reading splendid reviews and soon enjoying rather more than the usual 5/11½d. in royalties that his previous books had brought in.

Ponsonby was particularly pleased with the review in the *Times Literary Supplement*, whose reviewer immediately spotted that the essential point about his book was its exploration of the relationship between the diarist and his diary. Often considered a humble literary form, diaries as distinct from autobiographies and letters possess unique qualities. 'The diary was one plain song of life, proceeding with all that reality which stirred them hour by hour, in style no doubt without beauty, but still a labour of love, picture of circumstance, confession of faith.' After reading another extremely satisfying review in the *Observer*, he wrote to Stella Morel that Methuen, who had agreed to publish *English Diaries* after rejections by Chatto & Windus and the Clarendon Press and who kept a magnificent garden, would now be able to engage an eleventh gardener on the profits.

By the time *English Diaries* had appeared, Ponsonby was once more a Member of Parliament. The long awaited election took place on 15 November 1922 following the break up of the Lloyd George coalition in October. Ponsonby had stepped up his speaking engagements in Sheffield in 1922 in expectation of an election. His meetings in 1921 had, on the whole, been very poor affairs. In January 1922, he held two meetings, both small, and came away feeling depressed, but, by March, with the spur of press speculation of an early election, the tone of his comments began to be more optimistic.

Letters addressed to 'Comrade Ponsonby' he took in stride, as they were generally sympathetic, and, from the fact that he took the effort to record it, so also did he the following exchange of pleasantries:

> To Farnham for shopping. Scene: The Spinning Wheel, old furniture and antiques kept by Harry Philipson Stowe. Enter Lady Stowe and daughter while I was talking to him.
>
> AP. This is a wonderful place only one wants a pocket book full of bank notes.
>
> Lady S. But you don't approve of that.
>
> AP. Oh, I have my off moments.
>
> Lady S. You mean your *sane* moments. I thought you said in a book that nobody could earn more than 500 a year.

AP. No I never specified any sum and I said people could not *spend* more than a certain amount without doing harm.

(Conversation drifted on to Shoolbreds, a local store)

AP. I wish they would send their van again into the district.

Lady S. It is that abominable 8 hours day that prevents them. Will you promise me if ever you get into Parlt again to try and abolish the 8 hrs day.

AP. Certainly not. I shall try to make it a 7 or 6 hours day so as to make these rich firms employ more people.

Lady S. Look here, Mr Ponsonby, I am going to speak quite plainly to you. That a man of your birth and position and upbringing – who attended on Queen Victoria – should go with Labour is perfectly disgraceful – disgraceful there is no other word for it.

AP. You see I am in a better position to know the faults of my own class than many of the Labour people themselves. They often throw stones at the wrong windows. I can show them the right windows.

Lady S. I call it disgraceful.

AP. Well I shall expect a telegram of congratulations from you when I get in at the General Election.

Lady S. Well you won't get it.

Harry and Alice meanwhile were shyly laughing. Lady S. in her funny dictatorial bossing way was quite serious. I like her.[29]

At the end of March, Ponsonby had with him at Sheffield Ramsay MacDonald. He had promised to speak for Ponsonby and, in turn, suggested that Ponsonby accompany him to Egypt, a journey that Ponsonby could not afford, but which MacDonald undertook. The meeting was a great success, and Ponsonby began to predict that, if an election came soon, he would do fairly well. In July, Sheffield held a large 'No More War' demonstration in which Ponsonby took part. He had only recently met Fenner Brockway, the founder of the No Conscription Fellowship, the war-time predecessor of the No More War Movement – 'I liked him very much, though such goodness is beyond my reach.'[30] After this meeting, Ponsonby began to reflect on the possibility of another war. He thought it was at least ten years away and would only be prevented by the Labour Party if it acted with great boldness and determination.

Ponsonby's election campaign in Sheffield was, thankfully, shortened by the proximity of the Municipal Elections. Labour registered impressive gains in these elections and the enthusiasm carried over into the general election. 'From start to finish, it was one long triumph: 37 packed meetings – scores of eager and active workers . . .' The place went mad, people appeared who had never appeared before. It was a huge 75 per cent poll and the majority was beyond the expectation of the most sanguine.

A. Ponsonby (Lab)	16,692
Tudor Walters (C)	10,949
Majority	5,743

As Walters' majority in 1918 had been 5,383, this represented a complete reversal of voting preferences. The results nationally were just as good for the Labour Party. Ponsonby had predicted they would win something under 200 seats. They won 142 seats and became, for the first time, the official opposition. The Conservatives, who won 345 seats under Bonar Law, formed the new government. The Liberals divided between Asquith and Lloyd George were in third place with 117 seats.

After three weeks in Westminster, Ponsonby came to the conclusion that he liked the Labour men. He characterised them as both alive and alert. His position in the House was in stark contrast to that of the war, when he was virtually alone and faced with the daunting prospect of saying what others would not say. Now there were plenty of men ready to speak, so Ponsonby sat quietly and did not get to his feet until just before the Christmas recess. He felt the need to make his mark in the House, but, at the same time, he was deterred from pushing his way to the front for fear that the party would resent it. He even suggested to Ramsay MacDonald more in jest than anything else, that if Ramsay would make him a Peer, it would be rather fun to preach socialism in the House of Lords. In his year end review, he wrote that, as far as politics was concerned, he was buoyed up with hope for the future of socialism and resolved to try and assert himself more than in the past.

Ponsonby's journalism was now taking up a good deal of his time, for in addition to numerous occasional pieces, he was contracted to the *New Leader* for a weekly article on parliamentary affairs and to *Reynolds News*, a Sunday paper, for a weekly report on foreign affairs. For this last, he received £4 a week, which, in his always precarious financial situation, was not to be despised. With the return of parliamentary duty, a London house again became a necessity and the Ponsonbys took the plunge in buying an attractive but dilapidated eighteenth century house. The house, 40 Smith Street, Chelsea, was only ready for occupation after Easter. It was to be the Ponsonbys' London home until 1931. It was from this house that he organised and ran the Peace Letter campaign of 1925 and 1926 with the solitary assistance of his former UDC secretary, Mina Wallis. Even with a London home, the quickening pace of political life along with the two weekly articles severely curtailed Ponsonby's diary-writing. He found no time to write during the greater part of February and throughout the whole of March.

When Parliament reassembled in June, Ponsonby found his position little altered. 'Parliamentary work and my position in the Labour party seems to become more and more difficult.' He once again attempted a private member's bill to abolish hereditary titles, his previous effort in this direction having been overtaken by the outbreak of war in 1914. The time seemed propitious for such a move, as Ponsonby's interest had been attracted by a news item from Ottawa, where Mackenzie King presented an address to the King asking that no more titles be conferred on Canadians, and, closer to home, Lloyd George's blatant exploitation of the Honours system for replenishing the party chest had become something of a scandal. These factors notwithstanding, and, in spite of a fine rhetorical flourish from Ponsonby in introducing the Bill, it was treated as a joke by the members opposite and did not proceed beyond a first reading.[31]

Before the end of the session, he spoke on a more important theme. It looked for a time as if he would be sidelined by illness. But after two weeks' enforced rest, ordered to bed by his doctor to get some relief from piles, surrounded by enthusiastic letters and reviews of his book on English diaries, Ponsonby returned to the House. Much to his surprise, he managed a successful intervention into a disarmament debate, speaking just after Asquith, in front of a full house, and scored a debating success over the former Prime Minister.[32] He not only warned the House against the dangers of a new armaments race, but graphically described the horror of a war from the air.

The political news early in November 1923, that a general election would be fought on the old Tariff Reform controversy, filled Ponsonby with dismay.[33] He regarded the issue as irrelevant to both Europe, where the French occupation of the Ruhr had set the former Allies at odds with each other, and to the continuing problem of high levels of unemployment in Great Britain. He went up to Sheffield to fight the election in bad humour. As usual, he did not know where the money was to come from and then his opponent turned out to be a local working man with a brilliant war record. He did not spare himself and spoke at over 30 meetings, this being considered the best way of exposing the candidate to the electorate, which now numbered 38,000. Light relief was provided by a limerick competition with Charles Strachey. Ponsonby's limerick was so awful that it shall remain decently buried, but Strachey's was quite deft:

> A Liberal lady of Brightside
> Was often a bit on the tight side,
>   But since hearing AP,
>   She drinks nothing but tea,
> And has promised to vote on the right side.

The fight, like so many in the 1923 election, was three cornered. However, the Liberal candidate was anaemic and the working class Tory was seen by the electorate as a stooge of the bosses and won no votes from his connection with Vickers. When the votes were counted, Ponsonby, in spite of being labelled a dirty pacifist and a bloody aristocrat, had a 5,000 majority.

A. Ponsonby (Lab)	14,741
Capt. M. Sheppard (U)	9,408
Clough (Lib)	3,684
Majority	5,333

Limericks apart, the majority garnered in the two general elections of 1922 and 1923, which made Sheffield Brightside a Labour stronghold that has survived intact to the present day, was the product of sustained hard work and organisation on the part of the constituency association and Ponsonby's electoral agent, William Asbury. Fortunately, while no trace remains of the dreary rows of slum housing streets divided by 'ginnels' where Ponsonby spoke, as Matthew told a friend, to 'swarms of little dirty children and women looking at my father as if he was a sort of curio', there has survived in the UDC papers a memorandum of Ponsonby giving details of his Brightside organisation.[34] Starting from the premise that it would never be possible to reach 38,000 electors, Ponsonby's whole object was to get together a sufficiently large band of workers who could, between them, reach every elector. The most important sections of the Ward Committees were its women's sections. The women were especially important on polling day for they took care of the children while the mothers went to the polls, and even went to the length of organising the loan of boots and skirts to enable the women electors to appear respectably at the polling station. Ponsonby's effort was directed at these voluntary workers and very careful arrangements were made to use every one of the volunteers to create an atmosphere attractive to the mass of very poor people of being on the winning side.

Democratic Control of Foreign Policy

Nation-wide, the Conservatives lost over 90 seats, with Labour gaining 50 and the Liberals 40. So the standing of the parties in the new House was now Conservatives 258 seats, Labour 191 and Liberals 159. Ponsonby was as much in the dark as everyone else at this tangle, for no single party had a majority and the Liberals, who held the balance of power, were unable to coalesce with either party. Ponsonby thought the best course would be to force the Tories and the Liberals into a coalition so that Labour could hit hard at them both. This failed to take into account the fact that the Conservatives had lost the election and would be defeated when Parliament met. In such circumstances, the King was bound by constitutional precedent to ask the leader of the next largest party to form a government. Ponsonby was at home nursing a bad cold while the politicians of all shades scrambled around speculating on the outcome. The madcaps on the right, who were predicting the end of time if Labour assumed office, were put firmly in their place by the King, who decided that Labour must be given a fair chance. On 10 December, when Ponsonby finally dragged himself up to London, he heard that 'the majority opinion seemed to be in favour of Labour accepting if MacDonald is sent for, which seems probable after the Tories are defeated. I was converted to this idea, provided it was not accompanied by any agreement with other parties of which there seemed to be no question.'

After the *New Leader* luncheon, at which these views were aired, Ponsonby walked away with MacDonald, who told him that Jimmy Thomas was to be Foreign Secretary. This astonishing news took his breath away, but he said nothing for fear of upsetting MacDonald by complaints which would sound like sour grapes. In Ponsonby's view, Thomas was entirely unsuitable, in spite of being a politician of the front rank and a confidante of MacDonald's. In his view, Morel, Charles Trevelyan, Noel Buxton or even Tom Shaw would all be better choices. So when he got home, Ponsonby leaked the news. His papers contain two references and an omission to this episode.[35] The omission first. In his rough notes on JRM [Ramsay MacDonald], written after 1937, he wrote 'MacD wanted Thomas as foreign secretary. By means of Brailsford [the editor of the *New Leader*] and others I engineered a press agitation against it as soon as I heard of it.' Significantly, this passage was left out of subsequent drafts of his memoir on MacDonald. In his diary he wrote, 'I wrote a few letters hoping as there is still time that such a false step might be avoided.' One of his correspondents was Charles Trevelyan, who said that there certainly ought to be a pacifist at the Foreign Office and that the only tolerable solution would be JRM himself.[36] Ponsonby had arrived at that conclusion and had already written directly to Ramsay MacDonald. As Labour would be unlikely to hold office for more than a few months, Ponsonby thought the combination of Prime Minister and Foreign Secretary quite feasible.

> The incredible seems about to happen. We are actually to be allowed by an extraordinary combination of circumstances to have control of the F.O. and to begin to carry out some of the things we have been urging and preaching for years. To give this job to J.T. is simply to chuck the opportunity away.[37]

On 18 December, he heard from Massingham that Thomas would not get the Foreign Office and that Ramsay would take it himself. He noted 'But with the daily difficulties in the H of Commons, the question is, can he?'

When Commander Grenfell called on Ponsonby to discuss the recognition of the Soviet Union, Ponsonby told him it was improbable that he would be connected in any way with the Foreign Office. Then added, 'I only wish to goodness I could be.' He asked himself, 'Where am I going to come in?' and then more characteristically, 'Am I going to come in at all?' On New Year's Eve, he went over to Passfield Corner to talk the situation over with the Webbs. They knew nothing and had not been consulted by MacDonald. On 15 January, he still had not the remotest idea what was to be his fate. He had been to a small dinner party on the 6th given by Birch Crisp and found MacDonald there, but he had no chance of any private discussion and only 'gathered that he had been making out his plans carefully with regard to policy and no doubt too with regard to persons'. He wrote in his diary

> I hardly expect to get anything I shall really like and I do not think there is the smallest chance of my being in the Cabinet. But if I can get something where I can contribute, do something, help effectually, and be of some use, I shall be quite satisfied.[38]

He was called in to see MacDonald on 21 January to be told that MacDonald wanted Ponsonby's help and that they would work together. His satisfaction was only spoiled by the exclusion from the government of E.D. Morel. Apparently, there was only one post available for him, under-secretary at the Colonial Office, and Thomas flatly refused to have him.

So Ponsonby was back in the Foreign Office after twenty-two years. 'It was a curious sensation at first – a few of my contemporaries, Crowe, Tyrrell, Wellesley, Gregory and a few office keepers. There I am in a huge room, private secretary and all with the great difference that I have got a real say in policy.'[39] He was soon to find that this was an over-optimistic assessment of a parliamentary under-secretary's position at the Foreign Office.

Although Labour were in office, they were hardly in power. They were a minority government who could be turned out by the Liberals at any time. So the opportunity to create a new international order was more apparent than real. The government's task was not made any easier by the stridently partisan and vocal activities of the left-wing backbenchers in the party, whose expectations were hopelessly unrealistic. Notwithstanding these difficulties, Ponsonby almost immediately took up the legislative aspect of parliamentary control of foreign policy.

If Ponsonby was the acknowledged expert on this subject, E.D. Morel had been, during the war, its leading propagandist. That complex and oversensitive man was the only one of the active political leaders of the UDC left out of the government. To say that he was bitterly disappointed would be an understatement; he was desolate and his anguish did nothing for Ponsonby's composure:

> These personal matters upset me too much. E.D.M. first and foremost . . . I ought to have said to J.R.M. both of us or neither – But when he offered me my place I had no conception E.D.M. was not to be in – I went to him at once afterwards and even then I was not quite sure. But I reproach myself now.[40]

Morel now embarked on what his biographer has described as frenzied efforts in pressing the government to introduce a resolution on parliamentary control of foreign policy. Morel asked to be allowed to introduce the resolution from the backbenches as a token recognition of his contributions to the cause. The parliamentary timetable was too full to allow this, but it did not prevent Morel from making a nuisance of himself to the degree that Ponsonby at last began to lose patience, feeling that he had become 'just a sort of peg for him to hang his performances on'. The government had inherited from the outgoing government the new peace treaty with the Turks, the Treaty of Lausanne, and it occurred to Ponsonby that this could provide an opportunity to introduce parliamentary control. Although sensing that MacDonald was only lukewarm, he secured his approval and read out his memorandum on parliamentary control at the conclusion of the Lausanne Treaty debate.[41]

If MacDonald was far from pleased, so also was E.D. Morel, who wrote complaining that the government should have introduced a Bill guaranteeing the nation against secret diplomacy. Ponsonby, ever sensitive to his friend's feelings, painfully went over the ground for his benefit, pointing out that Morel should bear in mind that Ponsonby had made the statement which he knew was out of order and raced through it so as to get it down in print, and, in spite of its ineffectiveness, if he had not done it, it would not have been done at all during the session. This was all that Ponsonby could do, given the difficult circumstances of the parliamentary timetable. A Bill was out of the question and a resolution extremely difficult, for, although it would not require as much parliamentary time as a Bill, the two days it would require were simply not available. The 'Ponsonby Rule', as Ponsonby's measure soon became known, established the constitutional convention that the ratification of a treaty should be delayed for twenty-one days, giving the opportunity for debate, while the text was laid before Parliament. As he pointed out to Dolly, the credit for the measure was his alone for

> unless I had said what I did about parliamentary control of treaties it would never have been said at all this session. J.R.M. is much too correct and frightened of offending official susceptibilities. I attach more importance than he does to being faithful to our promises, he attaches more importance than I do to being 'statesmanlike'.[42]

A vital aspect of democratic control was the need to know what had happened in the past and, as the great debate on the origins of the War had been recently fueled by both German and Russian documentary revelations, the Labour government had to give serious consideration to lifting the veil on British diplomacy before the war. The Foreign Office, who regarded their Labour under-secretary as a rough, indecent disturber of their smooth official routine, were more amenable to this than they had been to the Ponsonby Rule. The ball was set in motion by Morel when he put down a question on 20 February 1924 on the publication of pre-war British documents. Ponsonby was able to assure Morel that the Foreign Office would look into the question and that the Prime Minister supported the move to throw more light on the origins of the war. G.P. Gooch and H.W.V. Temperley were chosen as editors of the series by Ramsay MacDonald, although the first public announcement of the project was not made until after the Labour government had been defeated at the general election of November 1924.[43] If no progress was made on creating a Foreign Affairs Committee, the Ponsonby Rule and the *Origins of the War*[44] were both major accomplishments. Neither would have come to pass but for the Labour government.

The Russian Treaties

Of much more immediate relevance to the political situation of 1924 than the more long-term issue of democratic control in the field of foreign policy was Anglo-Soviet relations. From the time of the recognition of the Soviet Union in the very first days after taking office, until the bombshell of the Zinoviev letter in the last days before the general election in November, Ponsonby was almost totally absorbed in the negotiation for a Russian treaty. The first steps towards recognition of the Soviet Union by Great Britain had been taken by Lloyd George, who had concluded a Trade Treaty with the Soviet Union in March 1921 which also gave *de facto* recognition and the exchange of diplomatic representatives. Any further improvement in Anglo-Russian relations had been wrecked at the Genoa Conference when the Soviets concluded the Rapallo Treaty with the other outcast nation, the Weimar Republic. The Bonar Law Conservative government then took a hard line, so that nothing further was done before Labour came to power in 1924.

The question of *de jure* recognition of the Soviet Union had become an article of faith with the rank and file of the Labour Party, although it should be noted that there was no love lost between the British Labour leaders and those of the Soviet Union. MacDonald had always believed in achieving socialist objectives through a policy of gradualism and rejected totally the communist belief in the necessity of revolution to overthrow the bourgeois order. Recognition of the Soviet Union by a Labour government would be, for its left wing, a dramatic and symbolic rejection of what Labour had perceived to be a malignant and hostile attitude towards the Soviet Union on the part of the National Coalition. For the right wing of the party, recognition would break the Cordon Sanitaire and bring Russia back into the community of nations opening up the possibility of important economic benefits. Given the precepts upon which Labour's approach to international questions was based, recognition of the Soviet Union was bound to be one of the first acts of the new government. In fact, it could not come quickly enough for the left wing of the party and Ponsonby found himself deluged with complaints. The government came into power on 22 January and on the 30th Ponsonby wrote in a footnote to Dolly that he had 'been losing his temper a good deal with people who, because Russia was not recognized the first day J.R.M. came in are saying that he and I are betraying the cause. I have stopped a demonstration and let fly at 2 or 3 people. Hamilton Fyfe is very helpful, Brailsford is a snake in the grass.' The hold-up was due to the natural reluctance of the King to receive an ambassador representing the assassins of his cousin, but they had only to wait two more days, for *de jure* recognition was given on 1 February. Ponsonby was sent to the palace to reassure the King, through Lord Stamfordham, that, for the time being, there would only be an exchange of chargés d'affaires.

Recognition did not simply involve the King in the disagreeable task of having to receive Bolsheviks at Buckingham Palace, for the Russians had agreed to settle all questions arising out of recognition. These included the validity and status of treaties concluded before 1917 and the claims and obligations arising from Czarist war debts and Soviet counterclaims arising from the intervention, and debts to individual bondholders and dispossessed property owners. Once these problems had been satisfactorily settled, the government expected to reap economic benefits. The restoration of Russian credit in the London money market would open up trade between the two countries. British exports of manufactured products to the Soviet Union were expected to make a significant contribution to lowering unemployment.

The preliminary meetings started at the end of February. The Russians were prepared to make a number of concessions, as long as they did not compromise their principles. Above all else, their economic programme needed machinery which could only be imported; for this they needed a sterling loan. The preliminary position adopted by the British team was that the Russians would not be given direct credits. The Russians were expected to raise the money they wanted in the City, this in spite of the fact that the bankers had issued an uncompromising set of preconditions for a loan, which clearly compromised the principles the Russians were so determined to protect. MacDonald, fully occupied in other directions, then handed control of the negotiations over to Ponsonby. However, the Prime Minister, who had never learnt to delegate, did not give his under-secretary authority, and so Ponsonby soon found himself in a difficult position. In the face of at best lukewarm support from the Foreign Office, universal press hostility, and the indifference of a large number of his colleagues, it fell to Ponsonby to sustain the whole negotiation. In the Foreign Office, the parliamentary under-secretary had long ago ceased to count. As Ponsonby could make no decisions without MacDonald's approval and access to the Prime Minister was limited, he soon found himself in control, but without authority. It was not a very satisfactory position in which to be placed. However, he made the most of it although noting in his diary 'the position entails the disadvantages without the advantages of a permanent official and the disadvantages without the advantages of a responsible minister'.

The permanent under-secretary, Sir Eyre Crowe, was a traditional conservative-nationalist-establishment figure, who found his Labour Party ministers only slightly less disagreeable than the Bolsheviks. He was opposed to recognition of the Soviet Union and supported the court in their opposition to a Bolshevik Ambassador and, almost immediately, had a tart verbal exchange with Ponsonby when it was discovered that the Russians proposed to include in their delegation Theodore Rothstein, who, as part of the Russian trade delegation of 1920, had tried to subvert the crew of the destroyer that was bringing him to England. Ponsonby's refusal to be browbeaten on this issue was to stand him in good stead in the later stages of the negotiation. Ponsonby developed a much more satisfactory relationship with J.D. Gregory, the head of the Northern Department, which dealt with the Soviet Union, and, with the exception of Crowe, who made several attempts to disrupt the negotiation by getting at Ramsay MacDonald, found his officials, in spite of their conservative bias, both professional and loyal.

The Russian team was headed by Christian Rakovsky, with whom Ponsonby soon established good relations.

> I also have private conversations with Rakovsky of long duration and with numerous other people. Rakovsky is a Bulgarian by birth. He is pleasant to deal with, astute but tied up by fear of Moscow and by prospects of dealing with France next. We talk in bad French together. His is much better than mine. He sits in a chair very close to my table and gazes out across the horseguards parade while he discourses volubly dividing his statements up into headings which vary and become confused. The irises of his eyes which are small have a pale ring round them. His mouth is very expressive with good irregular teeth and a curl in the lip which shows he has a sense of humour.[45]

Among the more curious social events of the first summer of a Labour government was a Russian reception at Claridges. The Bolsheviks behaved impeccably, but in the far corner of the reception room sat a group of bearded, pipe-smoking Red Russians, who turned out to be English communists, who, while smoking, spat on the floor all evening, so that Claridges informed Rakovsky the next day that they would not let their rooms to Bolsheviks again. On another occasion, the behaviour of the

Russian secretary Berzin was less than impeccable. He turned up to lunch at Shulbrede, lounging in the back of a Rolls-Royce and puffing smoke all over Dolly.

It should not pass without notice that in spite of the cloth cap jibes of the right, Ponsonby, who was in a position to know, was able to give Ramsay MacDonald full marks for the way he handled official occasions, noting that the reception for the King's birthday, was 'done with a tact and dignity which I . . . have never seen equalled'.

Back in Whitehall, the non-contentious areas of the negotiation, relating to the regularising of treaty arrangements and the conclusion of a commercial treaty to replace the 1921 trade agreement, proceeded smoothly towards settlement, but the problem of a loan, given the set positions of both sides, soon threatened a breakdown.

The Russian position was that they were prepared to pay compensation in principle, but were insistent upon a loan from the City as a precondition of settlement. The connection between the compensation and the loan became apparent at a fairly early stage in the negotiations when the Russians, afraid of their reception in the City, began to insist that a clause on a loan should be inserted in the treaty. For the moment, the British maintained that the Soviets should negotiate directly with individual creditors, with arbitration settling the most difficult claims without regard to the question of a loan. For the Russians, this method was most unsatisfactory and, in an effort to clarify the situation, Rakovsky went to see MacDonald on 9 May. He found the Prime Minister uncompromising and the conference seemed headed for an early breakdown. Ponsonby and Rakovsky, who personally were on good terms, then settled down to address the real issues at stake. The deadlock was broken by Ponsonby on 20 May, when he promised the government's moral support for the Russians, if they would go directly to the bankers in the City. He wrote to Dolly after the conclusion of the sixth plenary session:

> All the time I have to consider:
> how far my experts are taking an unnecessarily hard official line
> how far their warnings are just
> how far Rakovsky is trying to be accommodating
> how far he is just trying it on
> what would be Labour policy
> how we can justify to the whole country each step we make[46]

This temporary reprieve only lasted a week, for, at the next plenary session on 27 May, the British shocked the Russians by proposing full compensation for both bondholders and property owners. This was an attempt to widen the basis of the negotiation to avoid a conflict of principle. At a private meeting with Rakovsky on 2 June, Ponsonby was finally convinced that the conference would break down unless the Russians somehow or other got a loan.

Over the Whitsun recess, Ponsonby had time to reflect on the state of the negotiations. He wrote in his diary: 'We have now reached a stage where in a word everything depends on the Russians getting a loan.' He very much doubted his ability to persuade the government to give a guarantee for a loan and talked of coming a cropper and contemplated the possibility of resignation 'If I do not carry it after satisfying myself that it is possible and advisable, I daresay it will be best for me to go as the breakdown of the Conference will be a terrible blow to the Government.' Two days after this was written, he received an enigmatic letter from Lossiemouth. MacDonald told him he was unhappy about the Russian business and wanted a settlement one way or the other before the end of June. 'It cannot continue. If any of our people stand in the way they should be told that they have to turn over a new leaf.'[47] This did not amount to anything and Ponsonby doubted whether he would be able to convince the government that it should give a guarantee.

After Whitsun, Litvinoff, the Deputy Commissar for Foreign Affairs, arrived in London. He was unable to get the Prime Minister to agree to a guarantee and promptly retreated to Berlin. The negotiations, far from being concluded by the end of the month, dragged on into July amidst a mounting chorus of adverse publicity. Some progress on the British side was made when the Prime Minister supported Ponsonby and over-ruled Crowe's objection to the proposition that the bondholders would not be allowed to stand in the way of an agreement. Ponsonby held talks with the Governor of the Bank of England, Montague Norman, and with Snowden, the Chancellor of the Exchequer. Neither offered any solution and so Ponsonby prepared a memorandum for the consideration of the Cabinet. This was not circulated until later in July. In the meantime, Ponsonby heard from his friend Charles Trevelyan that he could expect trouble from the Chancellor of the Exchequer. No sooner had he received this news than he accidentally met Snowden in the House.

> I cannot say how intensely disagreeable he was – I found the greatest difficulty in keeping my temper. But I had to remember I was an underling. So now everything is in the melting pot. If I am turned down I cannot possibly defend the Govt's refusal to grant a guarantee and they will have to get someone else.[48]

The next day, the minute was only mentioned in the Cabinet. His position was supported by Parmoor and Henderson, but Haldane was only lukewarm and Snowden hostile. Everything was left in suspense until the Cabinet meeting of 30 July. In the interval, Snowden had a meeting with Rakovsky, which turned out to be more satisfactory than Ponsonby had feared. Ponsonby was not at all sure that the Prime Minister would come up to scratch – 'he is not at all in a satisfactory mood over-tired and worried by the Inter-allied conference and uncommunicative'. However, Snowden had over-reached himself and at the Cabinet meeting Ponsonby carried the day. Although he was not to know it, this was the only time he was to participate in a Cabinet meeting. He sat between Thomson and Sidney Webb and had to follow Snowden, who attacked the guarantee proposal venomously. In the ensuing debate, Ponsonby found support from Wheatley, Henderson and Webb, so that in the end only four voted against, Snowden, Wedgwood, Walsh and Haldane. What really disappointed Ponsonby was MacDonald's attitude. After the meeting, he told Ponsonby that he hoped the 'Bolshies' would reject it. He had 'no enthusiasm . . . no idealism, no broad vision'.[49]

The negotiation was now free to proceed. However, Rakovsky was in the Soviet Union and the 'Sphinx Joffre remained inarticulate in the Legation with an expressionless face and mask of incomprehension'. Rakovsky returned on 2 August and Ponsonby found, not the friendly Rakovsky he remembered, who had recently told a journalist that he was 'a complete Ponsonbist', but a truculent and hostile opponent, who now demanded further concessions. Rakovsky had led Ponsonby to believe that, once the loan had been guaranteed, the rest of the treaty would fall naturally into place. Now, it appeared that the Russians would refuse to compensate the owners of nationalised properties in the Soviet Union. If this claim were put in with the other claims, it would compromise the principles of their revolution. They were only prepared to consider 'claims' not 'losses'. This was not the only difficulty Ponsonby had to deal with. All along, the view of the British side had been that it was necessary to conclude an agreement before the end of the session, which was due on 8 August. When the Whips put forward the adjournment to 6 August, he found himself with an almost impossible agenda, but it was agreed that he could make his statement on the afternoon of the 5th.

These difficulties led to a breakoff in the early morning of 5 August after twenty hard, continuous and frustrating hours of negotiation. Ponsonby concluded that Rakovsky must have had orders from Moscow to fight every line of the agreement and that Scheinmann, the banker in the Russian negotiating team, and the trade unionist, Tomsky, wanted, for reasons that were not clear, simply to wreck the whole thing. Ponsonby had never been a conventional diplomat and, knowing full well that the Russians had been talking to the Labour backbenchers, had kept in touch with them himself and had already asked E.D. Morel and George Lansbury on 31 July to use their influence on the Russians. Bringing E.D. Morel into the negotiations was bound to be attended by publicity and the myth that the backbenchers had saved the Russian Treaty which was assiduously cultivated almost immediately after the conclusion of the negotiation had unfortunate consequences for Ponsonby's future career and reputation. Morel published his account of what happened in *Foreign Affairs* under the title 'How the Anglo-Russian Treaty was Saved: The True History of the Crisis and its Solution'. In his papers, he gave an even more melodramatic title to a memorandum dealing with his role, 'How the Anglo-Russian Conference was saved by the Labour Back Benchers: Secret History of the Events of August 5, 6, 7, 1924'.[50] However, historians and biographers can unravel secret histories and the true story of what happened is just as dramatic as Morel said it was, although the hero is no longer Morel.

The breakoff on the 5th came only hours before Ponsonby was to make his statement in the Commons. Actually, the Whips had taken another look at the parliamentary timetable and, without telling Ponsonby, had put back his statement until 6 August. So he had another day. All that remained of the negotiation was one point, the demand for compensation for property owners, which in any case Ponsonby was not going to allow to wreck the negotiation completely. The Russians were proposing to pick and choose who would get compensation, which amounted to arbitrary discrimination which the British were not going to admit to in a Treaty. As Ponsonby put it, 'we had to stand up for the whole lot or none'. A formula had eluded the experts for three months. Now a last desperate attempt to find a formula was made in the extra day that the Whips had so unthinkingly provided.

The Labour backbenchers now entered the scene. They had heard Rakovsky's side of the argument in the morning and in the afternoon they met with Ponsonby. He described the meeting as very hostile. They then went back to Rakovsky, who gave them what was purported to be a new formula, but was not, to take back to Ponsonby. On the morning of 6 August, the Foreign Office devised yet another formula and Gregory was sent with it to Rakovsky. He could not accept it and devised yet another formula. In the meantime, Sir S. Chapman, the Board of Trade official, independently devised his own formula which Ponsonby thought might work. Ponsonby

> tore over to Downing Street. By a miracle met Snowden in the lobby, got him in a waiting room with a Treasury expert, a moment of hesitation but he accepted it, tore upstairs, found J.R.M. discussing holidays with Ishbel and knew him well enough to be sure that he must not be interrupted; mutton and apple tart almost stuck in my throat but I was rewarded for not bursting in. He turned to me, I explained the position, got his consent to the new formula and munching pie crust ran down to the House and made up my mind on the way to use the MPs and not the officials.[51]

The new formula was taken round to Rakovsky by Purcell and Morel and accepted. Snowden was right in describing Chapman's work 'as a mere face saving device'. It became Article 11 of the Treaty and called for 'an agreed settlement of property claims other than those directly settled by the Government of the Soviet Socialist Republics'.

When he got up in the House that afternoon, Ponsonby was woolly headed and dead tired. To make matters worse, members did not have the text before them, and Ponsonby felt that he had inadequately explained the Treaty to the House. On the following day, Ponsonby found MacDonald and Clynes casually talking of not signing the Treaty. MacDonald was persuaded to support the Treaty, but he did so in a very back-handed way. MacDonald's biographer has described his speech as being 'the reverse of robust'.[52] MacDonald's half-hearted support of the Treaty was almost certainly produced by his resentment of the role played by the backbenchers during the last stages of the negotiation. The exaggerated claims of the backbenchers were taken up by the press in a partisan manner to create the impression of a weak leader being led by the nose. If 'Money for Murderers' headlines were not bad enough, on 5 August charges were laid against a Communist journalist, John Campbell, for preaching sedition to the armed forces. When these charges were withdrawn on 13 August, the charge of weak leadership seemed to be amply confirmed.

The Treaty, which under the Ponsonby Rule was to lie on the table for twenty-one parliamentary days before ratification to allow a debate after the summer recess, immediately became a peg for the Tories to attack Bolshevism. In itself, the Treaty was unexceptional. The Treaty only provided for a further Treaty which would secure a loan. The final Treaty would only be signed if further negotiations settled the outstanding differences on compensation for bondholders and other claims. As Marquand rightly says, it was only 'a diplomatic signpost pointing vaguely in the direction of a treaty which might or might not be signed at some stage in the future'.[53] This notwithstanding, the negotiation was a personal triumph for Ponsonby. He brought off the negotiation in the face of considerable difficulties. They are listed in his diary. He lacked authority, being only an under-secretary. He was the only politician in the British delegation. The officials seemed determined to force concessions on the Russians. Crowe and others in the Foreign Office did not want any agreement at all. The Prime Minister was, at times, indifferent and showed fear of Tory opposition. Snowden was openly and violently hostile. The Cabinet was ignorant and did not seem to care as they were all immersed in their own jobs. The Labour Party in the House was taken in by the Russians. The timetable in the House was hopelessly mismanaged by the Whips. The Bolsheviks, at times, seemed prepared to wreck the negotiation. Ponsonby was always painfully modest about his own accomplishments, yet here he rightly concluded that nobody else could have done it.

Back at Shulbrede, Ponsonby heard from the Prime Minister. He wanted the Treaty sent up to Lossiemouth so that he could study it in detail. He predicted a great fight to get it through the Commons and they should defy them to turn it down. 'The great thing is – keep your fighting spirit up and no surrender.'[54] The scene was now set for a confrontation in the autumn. Over the summer, Ponsonby followed the growing chorus of opposition to the Russian Treaties in the Tory-dominated press. He was quite sanguine about the future, writing 'the way to treat the Liberals is to stamp on them', for the Russian Treaty was, he believed, a good fighting ground. The government expected to be defeated on the Russian Treaties, but unfortunately the Campbell case intervened and MacDonald lost the vote in the House on 8 October on a Liberal amendment for a select committee. The next day MacDonald asked the King for a dissolution. The mishandling of the Campbell case – this 'miserable affair' – caught out MacDonald, who ended up lying to the House rather than risk being found out by a select committee enquiry. The linkage between the Russian Treaties and the Campbell case was exploited for all its worth during the election campaign, to the detriment of the truth, for, as has been shown, the Labour backbenchers had not played the decisive role claimed for them by Morel in the Russian negotiation, and ultimately to the detriment of Ponsonby's career as a front line Labour politician.

The Zinoviev Letter

The election campaign in Sheffield, the third in three years, was by now almost routine. He always stayed in the Victoria Hotel, which was large enough for him to be inconspicuous, and kept a sitting-room at the Angel. He spoke in a number of other constituencies, and both MacDonald and Snowden spoke in Sheffield. MacDonald's visit was the highlight of the campaign. On the way into Sheffield from Worksop, there were crowds and cheers all the way – 'most touching to see men working in the fields or on the road drop their tools and come running with both their arms extended'. At the Hippodrome, 4,000 squeezed in and 10,000 more waited outside. In Sheffield, the Tory opposition was reduced to vague cries of 'Yah Bolshey'. Across the country, Ponsonby was predicting a considerable increase for Labour, when, on 25 October, four days before voting, the *Daily Mail* published the notorious Zinoviev letter, lending further credence to the red plot bogey, which had been assiduously cultivated in connection with the Russian Treaties and the Campbell case. The Zinoviev letter should, more correctly, be in the plural. Zinoviev, the head of the Comintern, apparently convinced that the

British revolution was imminent, instructed the British Communist Party not only to work for the ratification of the Russian Treaty, but also to continue the good work of Campbell by intensifying 'agitation-propaganda work in the armed forces'. The Foreign Office had come into possession of Zinoviev's letter written on 15 September on 10 October. As only copies of this version of the letter remain in the Public Record Office, no one can say whether this was the original letter. However, other copies were in existence, and two were brought to the attention of the editor of the *Daily Mail*. One came through the medium of the former head of the Directorate of Naval Intelligence 'Blinker' Hall, at this time a Conservative MP, and the other through a minor intelligence official, Donald Im Thurn, apparently acting on behalf of the 'Ace of Spies' Sidney Reilly. Both contacts had made use of the Conservative Central Office. The *Daily Mail* decided to publish the letter immediately.

Whitehall hardly needed any warnings about the subversive activities of the Comintern, and the Prime Minister had, with the assistance of J.D. Gregory, prepared a protest, which, however, he had not initialled when news reached Crowe that the *Daily Mail* intended to publish the letter. Acting on his own initiative, Crowe decided that the protest should also be published to protect the government from a charge of suppressing information.

On the morning of 25 October, Jimmy Thomas woke up Snowden with the cry 'Get up you lazy devil, we're lumbered!' (Thomas, well-known for his salty language, probably said something more alliteratively earthy.) Ponsonby, like almost every other politician, was isolated in his constituency on the 25th, and had gone over to Lincoln from Sheffield. His immediate reaction was to believe that the Zinoviev letter was a forgery. Back in Sheffield, he found Trevelyan in a towering rage at what he thought had been a stab in the back by the Foreign Office. His own opinion was that if he had seen the letter he would have warned MacDonald not to have accepted Scotland Yard's discoveries without great caution as they were always unreliable.[55]

Telegrams flooded in from everyone concerned. MacDonald told Ponsonby that he was dumbfounded when he saw what had happened, and Crowe and Rakovsky, naturally enough, presented opposite opinions as to the letter's authenticity. Crowe's telegram said 'authority of document undoubted', while Rakovsky's dwelt on the letter's internal inconsistencies

Document bears in itself proof of forgery.

No circular of Communist International bears heading 'Third Communist International'

Zinoviev never signs as 'President of Presidium of Executive Committee' but simply as 'President of Executive Committee'

Also text itself is tissue of absurdities from communist point of view . . .[56]

Ponsonby, who was apparently excluded by reason of his status from seeing secret service intercepts, was never given any proof that the letter was authentic, and so came to believe Rakovsky's 'proofs' that it had been forged. If Ponsonby had a sinking feeling at this time, it was not so much about the Zinoviev letter as about another, more private, matter about which all sorts of damaging insinuations could have been made against the Prime Minister. On 28 October Hamilton Fyfe, the editor of the *Daily Herald*, rang him up with the news that the *Daily Mail* had got hold of Markwald's will and were about to fire another broadside into the floundering campaign. Henry Markwald, an extremely rich supporter of the UDC, had died in July 1924 leaving a complicated will. He had, during his lifetime, given money to Ponsonby, MacDonald, Morel and a prize of £1,000 to Fenner Brockway for being the bravest opponent of the first World War. Now, although Markwald was an Australian, his parents were German, and the *Daily Mail*, had it got hold of the story, would certainly have tried to embarrass the Prime Minister with another exposure on tainted money, with even more damaging implications than the McVitie and Price biscuit fund for Ramsay MacDonald's motor car.[57] As Ponsonby told Dolly, 'It would have been only too easy to ·distort it with something shady.' However, the Markwald story never appeared and the electorate had only the red scare to deter them from voting Labour.

The election, which swept the Tories into office with an impregnable majority, was a disaster, not so much for Labour, but for the Liberals, who were virtually wiped out. Ponsonby held his seat with a majority of 3,345 over a combined Liberal/Conservative vote. Labour now held 151 seats, a loss of 40 seats over the 1923 election, but with an increased popular vote, which now amounted to nearly 5½ million. When Ponsonby went to lunch at Downing Street after the election, he found the leadership undismayed and sure from the party point of view that they had done the right thing to contest the election on the issue of the Soviet Treaties. As for the Zinoviev letter, Ponsonby, after explanations from both Gregory and Crowe, concluded that the accusation against the Foreign Office of deliberate mischief was not true. There had been a bungling all along the line.

> The paper ought to have been marked for me.
> J.R.M. ought to have consulted me or one of the Cabinet.
> He ought never to have drafted the letter.
> The draft was not initialled and ought never to have been sent.
> Nothing ought to have been published.
> Each person, Gregory, Crowe, and J.R.M. who touched the thing made a hopeless hash of it.
> As it has served its purpose I don't suppose much more will be heard of it.[58]

It would have been best if Ponsonby's last prediction in his catalogue of mistakes, that not much more would be heard of the Zinoviev letter, had been true. Unfortunately, the letter preoccupied the Labour Party for years. A section of the party, led by Parmoor and Trevelyan, were convinced that they had been betrayed by the Foreign Office and launched a new campaign against them. Ponsonby refused to take part; he dismissed the Zinoviev letter as a forgery and backed the Foreign Office against these attacks. Privately he blamed the fiasco on MacDonald as he had discovered that MacDonald had been telling people in the Foreign Office that he was hostile to the Treaties.[59] This had placed Ponsonby in an embarrassing and false position. In thinking about MacDonald's attitude, he recalled a conversation with a Scots MP who helped analyse MacDonald's character by referring Ponsonby to the study of another highland product, the collie dog, 'Brilliant, vain, jealous, loyal and untrustworthy'.

Recriminations over the Zinoviev letter continued in an atmosphere of complaint, grousing, and backbiting. On 26 May he was barely able to contain himself at a party meeting at the foolish and ignorant discussion of the Zinoviev letter. Two years later in the Commons debate after the Arcos Raid in 1927, on the Conservative government's decision to break diplomatic relations with the Soviet Union, Ponsonby, in a speech attacking the Secret Service, referred to the fact that he had not been told about the Zinoviev letter, 'I was never allowed to come in and I am glad it was so.'

Early in 1928, the Zinoviev letter surfaced again in the most unusual circumstances. Gregory, still the head of the Foreign Office's Northern Department, was implicated in a fraudulent currency operation, the 'French francs' case'. He was suspended from the Foreign Office and after a Civil Service Enquiry was dismissed. Sir Warren Fisher's enquiry almost accidentally drifted into the uncharted and treacherous area of Gregory's involvement in a conspiracy to defeat the Labour government. The Fisher Report led to a House of Commons debate on 19 March 1928.

Ponsonby, while admitting to himself that he had never quite trusted Gregory, decided that he would not join in the hue and cry against him. At luncheon on the opening day of Parliament, he was sitting with Morgan Jones and Sidney Webb

AP: It is curious to think that during those months of Russian negotiations in 1924 I sat between Rakovski and Gregory. Rakovski has been sent to the depths of Siberia and Gregory will be sacked from the Foreign Office.

Morgan Jones: Are you beginning to feel uncomfortable?

Sidney Webb: Why should he? To be between two thieves is not a bad position.[60]

The Labour leadership prepared their case in a meeting in MacDonald's room on 15 March. Fortunately, Ponsonby's scepticism about some Russian forgers in Paris who claimed to have written the Zinoviev letter was shared by others and Tom Shaw was prevented from going back to Paris to buy up the forgers. So on the question of authenticity the party was saved from making a complete fool of itself as Baldwin was able to produce in the debate a written statement from the man who supplied the letter to the *Daily Mail* swearing to its authenticity.[61] Ponsonby's position on the handling of the letter had always been that Ramsay MacDonald should never have allowed himself to become involved at all in drafting a protest, so that any defence he was likely to offer would sound, as it did, like special pleading. The leakage problem, that of how the *Daily Mail* had come by its copy of Zinoviev's letter, has always been the most important unresolved issue in the whole affair. Baldwin's man, Donald Im Thurn, claimed to have got the letter through Sidney Reilly, although this was not revealed to the House, where Baldwin played up Im Thurn's respectable city background, thereby disposing of the Labour claim that somehow either the Secret Service or the Foreign Office had deliberately leaked the letter. The letter, Baldwin told the House, had come from Communist circles. So ended the Zinoviev letter affair, at least in Ponsonby's lifetime. If MacDonald had been outmanoeuvred, it was not Baldwin's but Ponsonby's career that was to suffer in consequence. Guilt by association is not an uncommon fate for politicians.

After the government's resignation, Ponsonby had time to reflect on his work at the Foreign Office, and, both privately and in public, he defended his Russian Treaties – 'I don't care what anyone says I think they are sound and the right way to set to work.' In his defence of the Treaties,[62] Ponsonby admitted that the mistakes had been made on the occasion of the Treaties' presentation to Parliament. There should have been a day set aside to suit the conference, with the text of the Treaties properly laid before the House. The debate should not have been sandwiched in at the tail end of another discussion. This was as far as Ponsonby would go. In view of the subsequent strain in Ponsonby's relationship with MacDonald which led to his exclusion from high office in the second Labour government, the issue of Ponsonby's handling of the Russian Treaty negotiations needs further analysis. The Treaties themselves were a solid achievement, in spite of the somewhat complex nature of the arrangement. The benefits to Great Britain were substantial. The non-controversial Commercial Treaty was badly needed; the fisheries question was settled in favour of Britain, the Soviets agreed to refrain from propaganda, and on the question of debts, the Soviets had been induced to acknowledge their responsibility to compensate both bondholders and the owners of expropriated property. None of these was dependent on the loan, which would not come up until the debt question had been satisfactorily resolved. Where then had Ponsonby failed? By his own admission, his defence of the negotiations had hardly been one of his best parliamentary speeches, but he had kept his end up and MacDonald's intervention in the debate on the following day had hardly been an inspiring performance. The failure in MacDonald's eyes had been the intrusion of the backbenchers. MacDonald craved respectability and had set out to show the country that Labour could be trusted with office. He could hardly avoid the Soviet Union in view of the party's previous commitment on the subject, and, to give him his due, gave Ponsonby his support, although, as has been noted, at least twice he expressed reservations, even going so far as to say that he hoped the negotiations would fail. The intervention of the backbenchers had been given immediate and unfavourable publicity by both the Tories, who were offended by the propriety of the exercise and who suggested that a reluctant government had been forced to kow tow to a threatened revolt, and by E.D. Morel, against whom MacDonald remained childishly jealous, who was, as ever, anxious to gain credit for himself out of the enterprise. It was Ponsonby who invited the backbenchers into the negotiation and it was upon him that MacDonald placed the blame for such unseemly behaviour. Ponsonby felt so at the time and subsequently when he wrote his memoir of MacDonald.

> So it ended. The Government fell and the Treaties were repudiated. Although I tried to defend him in the party, my estimate of him fell very low and equally so his estimate of me. With a bad faltering speech, I had succeeded. He had much rather that with deft eloquence I had failed.

Ponsonby's year end review was not unnaturally despondent. At last, after long weary years of opposition, he had been given the opportunity to exercise power. He had to face the fact that his Russian Treaties had only succeeded in raising a storm of controversy and a climate of opinion in the country that had swept the Conservatives back into power. It is not difficult to see why this happened. The Anglo-Russian Treaties were a tall order for the undivided attention of a full Secretary of State. The Bolsheviks had replaced the Prussians as public enemies and, at any given moment, irrational fear was liable to overtake public opinion. The negotiations were allowed to drag on in their early stages, even though the Russians had made it apparent that they would never be able to close without a loan. After three months of inconclusive talks, the Cabinet agreed to the principle of a loan guarantee and the negotiations were rushed to a conclusion in a little over a week with all-night sittings and the indecent spectacle of backbenchers apparently finding, in a matter of moments, formulae that had totally eluded the experts. Although this was not the way it happened, it was made to appear that way and the opposition was able to portray an effective picture of bungling which was reinforced by one of Ponsonby's less satisfactory performances at the dispatch box. Yet, when all this has been said, the government was only a minority government, not expected to hold office under any circumstances for much longer than a few months. If its achievements were minimal, the Labour Party had demonstrated its ability and fitness to govern.

Before the year was out, Ponsonby suffered two personal losses in the unexpected deaths of Massingham and E.D. Morel. Ponsonby paid a graceful tribute to Massingham 'he was a man whom it was always a pleasure to meet. I never found myself avoiding Massingham, but always going out of my way to meet him.' On Morel, he wrote at length both in his diary and in a subsequent memoir. 'It was almost a profession knowing him. I admired him enormously and was very fond of him.'

Ponsonby, now in his early fifties, remained an enigma to both the public at large and many closer acquaintances. The sketch portrait of Ponsonby by the noted artist, William Rothenstein, reveals an open, sensitive countenance, scarcely concealing an essentially uncombative nature. When allied to the extraordinary gentility of his bearing and manner, the total effect was of refinement not wholly suited to the rough and tumble of politics. As has been noted, the style of his speeches often masked their content. In the House of Commons, his most successful speeches seemed to have been reserved for less important occasions. When he felt passionately about an issue, his voice was liable to rise and break, and when he spoke without notes, he was often overtaken by a woolly-headed feeling that reduced his effectiveness. 'I cannot argue in words, I become confused when heated, a pretty bad handicap for a politician.' Ponsonby recognised that he would never be a combative speaker in the style of Lloyd George or Churchill. He was always conscious of the other man's point of view and erred on the side of giving others the benefit of the doubt – as he rather ruefully put it – he had made a defect of a quality. The air of self-disparagement, which will have been noted in Ponsonby's year end reviews, was also present in his dealings with Labour politicians. He admitted to being mortally afraid of being thought an aristocrat, giving himself airs and asserting himself because of his social superiority. His biggest drawback as a Labour politician was his courtier background. Although he had rejected society, he never failed to attend social functions such as the annual Eton reunion of Cornishes' House, where he saw no contradiction in singing the Eton Boating Song, and at Labour Party rallies in singing The Red Flag.

The Bright Young People

If 1924 was the year of the first Labour government, it was also the year in which the newspapers invented the Bright Young People. The *Daily Mail* ran a headline on 26 July 'The Prince in a Treasure Hunt. Midnight Chase in London, 50 Motorcars. The Bright Young People.' Over the next few years, the Bright Young People were taken up by Fleet Street's society columnists and gossip writers, who chronicled their madcap antics for the benefit of the general public. When it was all over, Viola Tree in the *Sunday Dispatch* wrote 'once when bright young people *were* bright young people, it meant these four: Miss Elizabeth Ponsonby, Mrs. Babe Plunket Greene, Mr. Brian Howard, Mr. Eddie Gathorne-Hardy'. That Elizabeth Ponsonby should blossom as a leader of the bright young people at the same time as her father achieved prominence in the political sphere was hardly coincidental. The Ponsonbys were news. For Arthur, it meant the inconvenience of popularity. Walking down Downing Street to the House with MacDonald usually attracted 20 photographers in addition to the large cheering crowds in Parliament Square.

But for Elizabeth, who was a more than acceptable substitute for Dolly at social functions, the publicity opened up West End opportunities, and soon she had a job in a revue, as a mannequin and then as a walk-on 'super' covered in brown grease paint with shaved off eyebrows for £5 a week. 'It seems to satisfy her as owing to her being my daughter she has received an inordinate amount of publicity. I think she is made for better things but I am helpless.' For Dolly and Arthur, however, Elizabeth's social notoriety was not the only burden they had to bear, for Dolly's sister Gwen, who has only made a fleeting appearance in these pages, was the wife of Harry Plunket Greene. Their younger son, David, married in 1925 Marguerite McGusty – Babe Plunket Greene in Viola Tree's list.

The two Greene cousins, Richard and David, and Matthew were all up at Oxford in 1924, Matthew hugely enjoying himself, but finding the examiners constantly conspiring to trip him up, while the Greene boys effortlessly and wastefully indulged their musicianship, inherited from Sir Hubert Parry, in the blues, jazz and beer.

Gwen Plunket Greene was now devoting herself completely to her children, not so much to the boys, but to her daughter Olivia, whose naive perversity Dolly found even more exasperating than Elizabeth's frivolity. In 1924 Olivia was just 17 and already impossible. Dolly was particularly irked by Gwen's determination to take the part of the young, in spite of Richard's drunken and eccentric life in living in squalor and devoting himself to a rat that haunted his room and David's snobbish affectations.

Poor G. Perhaps some day she will return to her old allegiances. When I think of her young, with her fierce detestation of frivolity, her powers of work, 4 hours practice on the viola every day in the box-room and her love of reading. it is as A says tragic, her determination to be one with her children, because she has no one else, so that she sweeps away everything she used to hold good. She is now frivolous minded and religious, when she used to be seriously minded and agnostic.[63]

If Gwen's solution aroused Dolly's ire, they themselves were helpless over Elizabeth. Arthur could only record the predicament. 'If I were to do the heavy father and reprove, rebuke, and correct she would simply leave us. Slender as it is becoming the link between us and her is still of some value.' So Dolly sat up at night patching up an old discarded coat, so that Elizabeth might have her new fur coat.

E took it as a matter of course and sailed away at Waterloo in a large low noiseless car. And D took it also as a matter of course and walked about in the old worn garment without the shadow of consciousness of martyrdom or sacrifice. The whole incident was eloquent in the extreme.[64]

When they went out, the conversation seemed inevitably to turn to the problem of the young. Logan Pearsall Smith regaled an astonished returning Indian missionary with stories of the young men at Oxford painting the inside of their noses red! while Charles Masterman announced that he did not like his children, as he had no parental instinct, unlike Noel Buxton who had developed 'senile decay' to be with his children. Dolly's laughter at Pearsall Smith's exaggerations must have sounded very hollow when Matthew brought a new Oxford friend, Patrick Balfour, over to Shulbrede for the day.

like a satyr to look at with Chinese eyes and hair only beginning to grow from the centre back of his head with a great piece of bare head in front. Appears to me heartless and rootless, a freak with a touch of the chien de poche, though not particularly amusing. He is one of the clan that hates parents and avoids going home.[65]

If Elizabeth 'recklessly charged at life, creating chaos around her', it was poor Matthew who was the first to land in the soup. Fortunately, Matthew's run in with the law occurred after the Labour government had left office, not that that was any consolation to his distraught parents. One of the Greenes' Oxford friends was Evelyn Waugh. Waugh had gone down in 1924, and had found temporary employment as an usher in a boys' school in North Wales. During the Easter holidays, he had come up to London and, to mark his return to civilisation, had organised a number of drinking parties with the Greenes. Matthew was also in London and in possession of his father's car. Needless to say, the car's erratic course around London eventually attracted the attention of the police and Matthew and Evelyn Waugh were locked up at Bow Street.

So far as I can gather Waugh was distinctly drunk and therefore drew suspicion on M who was not sober. He cut round the wrong side of a refuge which made the police stop him. Waugh – a regular pink trousered, jersey Oxford type got off with a 5/-fine this morning, but of course the charge against M is much more serious and magistrates are treating it with imprisonment without the option of a fine.[66]

Waugh's fine was actually, according to his biographer, 15/6d. and, in his version of events, Waugh naturally concentrated more upon his own predicament than that of Matthew.

I had to sit for about 4 hours in an awful little cell just like an urinal while the police confused about six telephone messages with the result that Olivia thought it would be no good to try and bail us out. Arthur Ponsonby rescued Matthew but rather ill-naturedly, I thought, refused to do anything for me.[67]

According to Christopher Sykes, inaccurate rumours about what had happened soon began to circulate in society, and the Duchess of Abercorn, confusing father for son, became especially distressed over the plight of the Ponsonby children, whose father 'was not only a shameless revolutionary but was now proved to be a drunkard as well'.[68]

Matthew escaped prison, his parents having to pay a heavy fine. What was particularly disturbing to both Arthur and Dolly was that Matthew's good-natured weakness had been exploited by the Richard Greene set 'who regard drunkenness as something amusing and fine'. Family recriminations then began in earnest. An attempt by Waugh to mend the broken fence between the Greenes and the Ponsonbys was rejected outright and, to make matters worse, Lady Maud decided to lend a hand.

Perhaps the last word on these unfortunate events which left Waugh with as heavy a heart as the Ponsonbys can be left to Matthew, who innocently footnoted a letter to his friend Michael Gilmour after it was all over 'I did not know E. Waugh was quite so famous. Of course he has a very large proportion of the so-called modern vices.'

In the House of Commons dining room the day after the case had been tried, a very self-conscious Ponsonby was relieved when nobody mentioned the case to him.

we parents of today are having a poorish time. We have no control whatever. Many others are like us. It is a case of 'The sins of the children shall be on the fathers until the third and fourth conviction.'[69]

Notes

1. *The Labour Leader*, Feb 1919.
2. *Shulbrede MSS.*, A. Ponsonby Diary, IX, 10 May 1919.
3. Cline (1980), pp. 122–5.
4. *Shulbrede MSS.*, A. Ponsonby to D. Ponsonby, n.d. [but June 1920].

5. *Shulbrede MSS.*, A. Ponsonby to D. Ponsonby, n.d. [but June 1920].
6. Gilbert Murray (1915).
7. *The Nation*, 20 Sept 1919.
8. *The Nation*, 27 Sept 1919.
9. *Ponsonby MSS.*, C.667, f.172, Murray to A. Ponsonby, 7 Oct 1919.
10. *Murray MSS.*, Vol. 40, f.40, Ponsonby to Murray, 10 Oct 1919.
11. *Morel MSS.*, file 723, f.16, Ponsonby to Morel, 6 Dec 1919.
12. *Shulbrede MSS.*, Memoir of Campbell-Bannerman.
13. Robbins' careful statement 'The suspicion cannot be avoided that those at the time, who did not know, did not especially wish to know' does not exonerate Grey. Robbins (1971), p. 149.
14. *Labour Party*: Advisory Committee on International Questions (hereafter ACIQ). Preliminary Memorandum, p. 2.
15. Swartz (1971), Appendix A, pp. 223–4; *Ponsonby MSS.*, C.677, A Foreign Affairs Committee.
16. *Hansard*, V, 104, 848–61.
17. *B. Webb Diary*, 30 Jan 1920.
18. 'Control of Foreign Policy, Labour's Programme', Labour Party (1921).
19. Sir George Young, 'Memorandum on the Reform of the Foreign Service', ACIQ, July 1918, and 'Reform of Diplomacy, a Practical Programme', ACIQ, May 1921.
20. Steiner and Dockrill (1974), pp. 131–56.
21. Craig (1953); Nicholson (1939) and (1954); Sharp (1976).
22. Gordon (1969), pp. 31–7.
23. *Daily Herald*, 7 Nov 1920.
24. *Shulbrede MSS.*, A. Ponsonby Diary, X, 27 Nov 1921.
25. Taylor (1969), p. 132.
26. *Shulbrede MSS.*, A. Ponsonby Diary, X, 25 Dec 1919.
27. Arthur Ponsonby, 'Religion in Politics' (London, 1921) and 'A Conflict of Opinion' (London, 1919).
28. Arthur Ponsonby, *English Diaries* (London, 1923).
29. *Shulbrede MSS.*, A. Ponsonby Diary, X, 23 Dec 1921.
30. *Shulbrede MSS.*, A. Ponsonby Diary, X, 10 June 1922.
31. *Hansard*, V, 163, 2166–70.
32. *Hansard*, V, 163, 107–12.
33. After the fall of Lloyd George there were three elections in two years, November 1922, December 1923 and October 1924. The election of 1922 followed the collapse of the Lloyd George coalition. Bonar Law, the new Prime Minister, gave way to Baldwin in May 1923 when he was found to have cancer. Baldwin was forced to go to the electorate when he raised the question of tariff protection to fight unemployment, which Law had pledged not to do in the previous year.
34. UDC MSS 410. Correspondence with Lord Ponsonby, 1916–1939.
35. The early draft of Ponsonby's essay on MacDonald is at Shulbrede. The final version is in *Ponsonby MSS.*, C.684; *Shulbrede MSS.*, A. Ponsonby Diary, XI, 11 Dec 1923.
36. *Ponsonby MSS.*, C.668, f.123, C. Trevelyan to A. Ponsonby, 13 Dec 1923.
37. Marquand (1977), p. 300.
38. *Shulbrede MSS.*, A. Ponsonby Diary, XI, 19 Jan 1924.

39. *Shulbrede* MSS., A. Ponsonby Diary, XI, 27 Jan 1924.
40. *Shulbrede* MSS., A. Ponsonby to D. Ponsonby, 1 Feb 1924.
41. *Shulbrede* MSS., A. Ponsonby to J.R. MacDonald, 22 Mar 1924; *Hansard*, V, 171, 2000.
42. *Shulbrede* MSS., A. Ponsonby to D. Ponsonby, 1 Apr 1924.
43. Eyck (1982), pp. 329–42.
44. Gooch and Temperley (1926–1938).
45. *Shulbrede* MSS., A. Ponsonby Diary, XI, 7 June 1924.
46. *Shulbrede* MSS., A. Ponsonby to D. Ponsonby, 20 May 1924.
47. *Shulbrede* MSS., J.R. MacDonald to A. Ponsonby, 9 June 1924.
48. *Shulbrede* MSS., A. Ponsonby to D. Ponsonby, 21 July 1924.
49. *Shulbrede* MSS., A. Ponsonby to D. Ponsonby, 30 July 1924.
50. *Morel* MSS., F2, 3/1.
51. *Shulbrede* MSS., A. Ponsonby Diary, XI, 18 Aug 1924.
52. Marquand (1977), p. 363.
53. Ibid.
54. *Shulbrede* MSS., J.R. MacDonald to A. Ponsonby, 13 Aug 1924.
55. *Shulbrede* MSS., A. Ponsonby to D. Ponsonby, 26 Oct 1924.
56. *Shulbrede* MSS., Rakovsky to A. Ponsonby, 25 Oct 1924.
57. In order to help meet the expenses of office, a wealthy friend of MacDonald provided the Prime Minister with a Daimler car and £30,000 worth of McVitie and Price shares. Shortly after the friend received a Baronetcy, the newspapers revealed a supposed honours scandal connecting the two events. Insolent youths naturally flung the Biscuits epithet at all Labour people in the 1924 election.
58. *Shulbrede* MSS., A. Ponsonby Diary, XI, 31 Oct 1924.
59. *Shulbrede* MSS., A. Ponsonby Diary, XI, 21 Apr 1924.
60. *Shulbrede* MSS., A. Ponsonby Diary, XII, 7 Feb 1928.
61. The latest research suggests that the Zinoviev letter was genuine. See Andrew (1986), pp. 301–16.
62. 'The Case for the Russian Treaties', *Contemporary Review*, Dec 1924.
63. *Shulbrede* MSS., D. Ponsonby Diary, 29 July 1924.
64. *Shulbrede* MSS., A. Ponsonby Diary, XI, 20 Sept 1923.
65. *Shulbrede* MSS., D. Ponsonby Diary, 17 July 1924.
66. *Shulbrede* MSS., A. Ponsonby to D. Ponsonby, 7 Apr 1925.
67. Davie (1976), p. 206.
68. Sykes (1975), pp. 96–7.
69. *Shulbrede* MSS., A. Ponsonby Diary, XI, 22 Apr 1925.

CHAPTER FIVE

Pacifist Individualism, 1925–1931

Now Is The Time

In keeping with his undeviating pursuit of 'occupations', Ponsonby was soon hard at work on a long-projected new book on pacifism. 'I feel it ought to be done, it wants to be done and I ought to do it.'[1] Ponsonby's decision to write a book on pacifism and, after its publication, to mount the Peace Letter campaign to abolish war, arose out of his conviction that the search for a new international order had taken a left turn in creating a League of Nations whose authority rested on its use of force. He had argued against sanctions in the Bryce Committee during the war, and continued to do so at the end of the war in a vain attempt to influence opinion. A typical example is a piece he wrote in September 1918.[2] Peace, he declared, depended on a state of mind and the growth of enlightened ideas, and force could never assist in promoting its growth. 'The idea that peace is to be maintained in the world by the ultimate use of modern engines of war such as shells, bombs, tanks, gas, mines, etc. would appear to be fatally wrong.' All his fears were realised when the Covenant of the League was published in the Peace Treaty with Germany. The League not only relied on force, but had become 'a committee of victorious powers tied up to the iniquitous peace treaties'. Ponsonby undertook to write a criticism of the Covenant of the League for the Union of Democratic Control.[3] While welcoming the provisions of the Covenant that related to the peaceful settlement of disputes by resort to arbitration, Ponsonby expressed absolute opposition to the use of force as a final authority. He was also extremely sceptical about the disarmament provisions of the Covenant in Article 8. He saw in it the ultimate expression of futility with cant phrases about 'national safety' and 'enforcement by common action'.

> The whole article shows up the futility of attempting to nibble at the question of armaments. It cannot be done. It never will be done. Reduction and limitation are just words. There is only one solution to this problem and that is *disarmament . . .*

Late in 1922, in an interesting exchange with Gilbert Murray, who had become the moving spirit behind the League of Nations Union, Ponsonby told Murray about his involvement in the Bryce Group, 'a little bit of private history', to show him that he wholeheartedly supported the idea of a League and had preached it 'in days when an egg or a fist closed my mouth'. The fact was that such a League could never be a real League of Nations.

In its early years, the League spent much time trying to resolve the problem of how to get nations to disarm in an insecure world. Attempts were made to make the Covenant of the League stronger so that member nations would trust in it rather than in their own armaments for defence. These formulae eventually produced MacDonald and Parmoor's Geneva Protocol for the Pacific Settlement of International Disputes. This was an ingenuous formula for reconciling the French demand for security before disarmament by adding compulsory arbitration to the Covenant. Not surprisingly, the formula was opposed by the service chiefs in the United Kingdom and in the Dominions who were all isolationist in their attitude to European commitments. The Geneva Protocol raised the fundamental problem for Ponsonby of the use of force by the League. The Protocol was, after all, only a device to appease France so that the General Disarmament Conference could proceed. Ponsonby took the simple view that it lay within the power of Great Britain to break the disarmament deadlock by making a unilateral move, without the necessity of prior agreements on security through arbitration. The Peace Letter campaign was designed to be more than an alternative to the League; it was going to be a working demonstration of democratic control. He saw the Peace Letter as the idealist's way of being practical. 'Temperamentally,' he wrote, 'I am an idealist and I approve of pressing what for the moment may seem impractical but having been in office I am expected to take the so called statesmanlike attitude.'

By the autumn of 1925, he was ready. The Peace Letter was printed and ready for distribution. All the peace societies had given financial support and *Now Is The Time* was ready for sale.

Why have I embarked on all this? I could not help it. The war has remained in my memory and the fraud of it all ought to be exposed. I suppose too I had an inclination to be up and doing as I cannot be active in the Trade Union movements where there is most life and in the H of C very little can be done, not enough to make me feel I am pulling my weight politically.[4]

The campaign was opened, appropriately enough, in Sheffield, where his meeting was addressed by the saintly George Lansbury, who became an enthusiastic supporter, and Jimmy Hudson, like Ponsonby a pugilistic pacifist. *Now Is The Time* was in its third edition before the end of October and the Peace Letter was beginning to be quite widely distributed. An office was set up in 40 Smith Street, staffed by Mina Wallis from the wartime UDC office. Over £700 was spent on distributing initially 35,000 Peace Letters. The Trade Union movement took up the campaign and was largely responsible for circulating the letters. The Transport Workers' Union, in addition, bought 500 copies of *Now Is The Time*. Just before the start of the session, Ponsonby addressed a series of meetings at Bristol, Liverpool, Huddersfield, Sheffield and Mexborough, mostly organised through local branches of the UDC. By the end of December, Ponsonby was thinking that his original estimate of one million signatures was not, after all, so far fetched. The Peace Letter to the Prime Minister stated:

> We, the undersigned, convinced that all disputes between nations are capable of settlement either by diplomatic negotiations or by some form of International arbitration, hereby solemnly declare that we shall refuse to support or render war service to any Government which resorts to arms.

It should be made clear that the intent behind this direct appeal to the people was political. A million signatures attached to the letter would certainly have given any government pause for thought. The problem was that, for one man assisted by one secretary and a few volunteers, this was an organisational impossibility, even with a favourable climate of opinion. While 1925 was certainly an opportune moment to launch the Letter, 1926, with its prolonged coal strike and short-lived but damaging General Strike, was a bad year and the campaign was barely sustained. And, in any case, the international climate, which had been so uncertain early in 1925, was immeasurably improved by the successful negotiation of the Locarno Treaties. With the new atmosphere of reconciliation between France and Germany, which was characterised as the Locarno Honeymoon, the original impetus behind the Peace Letter evaporated into thin air.

If 1925 proved to be in retrospect the wrong time for the Peace Letter campaign, the peace appeal in *Now Is The Time* repays careful examination for the insight it provides into the rise of the peace movement from pre-war insignificance to what was to become in the 1930s the most intellectually distinguished pressure group ever assembled.[5] In many discussions of pacifism, a distinction is drawn between pacifist and pacificist attitudes. A.J.P. Taylor tells us that a pacifist holds to the doctrine of non-resistance, while a pacificist advocates a peaceful policy.[6] This taken up by Martin Ceadel becomes pacifism, the belief that all war is always wrong and pacificism, the assumption that although war is irrational and inhumane, it is sometimes necessary.[7] The Oxford Dictionary refuses to admit the distinction and defines pacifism simply as war resistance. This seems to meet the character of the peace movement more closely and pacifism is used here to mean all types of war resistance.[8]

Ponsonby's pacifist appeal in *Now Is The Time* is rooted in the massive assault of the First World War on liberal sensibility. His political beliefs incorporated a belief in progress through enlightenment towards a more perfect world. The activities of the radical group which have been described in Chapter 2 were the practical embodiment of this belief. The sudden eruption of war with its undertones of irrationality and violence could only be reconciled to his progressive beliefs by the existence of conspiracy. Hence Grey's great betrayal in appearing to be working the principles of the concert, when in fact he had committed his country to secret diplomacy and the balance of power as far back as 1906. Democratic control was seen as the necessary step forward in defeating the 'conspiracy' of the Foreign Office and in ensuring that the execution of foreign policy would reflect the true interest of nations in peace.

For many people, the nation's war effort was only justified by the elaboration of the new idealistic war aims of 1917. The gap between the promise of a new world order and the actuality of an imperialist peace with its vindictive Versailles Diktat was obscured from many by the creation of the League of Nations. Not for Ponsonby, who had already worked out to his own satisfaction that the sanction of force behind the League would have the effect of internationalising violence. Ponsonby had been content to work within politics and still continued to do so, but in the context of Labour's commitment to internationalism and the League as expressed in the Geneva Protocol Debate he took the first step that eventually propelled him out of politics altogether.

The pacifist movement after the war was small and weak. The UDC had never been pacifist in the first place and the No Conscription Fellowship that had been so active in the war was wound up in 1919 and became part of the No More War Movement. It had perhaps 3,000 members in the mid-twenties, the same number as the Christian Fellowship of Reconciliation. This did not deter Ponsonby; rather it encouraged him, as he believed the pacifist case would never be listened to when war was in sight or being waged.

The argument in *Now Is The Time* is simple and straightforward. He presents the utilitarian argument for pacifism that first appeared in his 'Ideas and Impressions' during the war. The Balance of Reason had shown that the war had failed to achieve a single desirable object. The scales of the balance of reason revealed on the loss side, hard facts, and, on the gain side, empty words. The list on the loss side is much as expected, dealing in human and material losses, but also adds an insight into the nature of war on international life. Wars, Ponsonby asserted, fail to solve old problems and create in addition many new ones. 'War is always the direct parent of future wars.' On the other side of the balance, Ponsonby attacked the idea that war could be justified as a defence against aggression. The idea that a nation must fight for its independence and honour runs directly into the modern problem of a definition of aggression. Germany was forced to admit in the Peace Treaty that she alone was the aggressor, but the Allies 'never pointed to this case of aggression either because they no longer believed it was true or because they know that a definition based on this example would not hold water before an impartial tribunal'. After examining other less formidable justifications for war, Ponsonby challenged anyone to controvert his arguments.

> I dispute that there is a shred of evidence to show that any conceivable form of international dispute need be a cause of war; and I maintain that there is no possible cause of quarrel between nations which cannot be settled by diplomatic negotiations or international arbitration.[9]

A discussion of security as a legitimate ambition of the nation state leads to the conclusion that neither armaments nor alliances can provide adequate security. The demand for security is met by preparations for war which inevitably produce the next war and security is thereby destroyed. The way out of this vicious circle can never be war or preparations for war. Ponsonby's depiction of international war 'in which people are organized in cold blood to use force and violence with the sanction, approval, help, and encouragement of their governments for causes of which they are ignorant' was to be met by an uncompromising rejection, 'I want to develop the instinct which will make a man when he hears rumours of wars say NO without knowing the facts.'[10] His concentration on the people rather than their governments is deliberate, for he believed that the mistake of earlier peace schemes had been the attempt to impose solutions from above. Ponsonby implicitly believed in the pacifist inclinations of people and the warlike tendencies of governments.

The follow up to *Now Is The Time* was to expose the propaganda lies of governments and press during the war. This book, *Falsehood in Wartime*, was published in 1928. It became an instant best seller, and set the tone for public reaction against the Great War that culminated in the publication shortly thereafter of the great series of anti-war memoirs, *Undertones of War* (1928), *Goodbye to All That* (1929) and *Memoirs of An Infantry Officer* (1930). The new book was well in hand in April 1927 and the laborious process of compiling the entries and checking references which was done with the assistance of a number of helpers, including Lord Tavistock (later the Duke of Bedford), was completed by the end of the year. It was published early in 1928 and found such a response that it went immediately into a second edition. The American edition went into a second edition in 1930. The German edition, published under the title

Lügen im Kriegszeiten, appeared in 1930, with a second edition in 1931. The French edition, *Les Faussaires a l'oeuvre en temps de Guerre* followed a similar pattern. By 1940, Allen and Unwin were publishing an eighth edition.

Falsehood in Wartime is an anthology, whose chapter headings speak for themselves, 'The Mutilated Nurse', 'The Crucified Canadian', 'The Corpse Factory' and 'The Belgian Baby without Hands'. All these and many other atrocity stories are shown to have been manufactured lies. Falsehood is depicted as the deliberate policy of governments concerned to maintain public support for the war effort. The most famous exposure in the book is that of the supposed German Corpse Factory. *The Times* seized on a report in a German newspaper, in which it appeared that the German reporter was describing a *Kadaververwertungamstalt*, a Corpse Exploitation factory, where corpses were being boiled down into soap. When the matter was aired in Parliament, a radical MP correctly pointed out that the word Kadaver referred not to human corpses but to those of animals. However, the government evaded the questions and the Foreign Secretary, Balfour, instructed a reluctant Masterman, who was in charge of the War Propaganda, to prepare propaganda material which resulted in the publication of a pamphlet entitled 'A Corpse-Conversion Factory'. The story was spread in Europe and the East and only discredited in 1925 when Sir A. Chamberlain finally admitted that there never had been any foundation for the story.[11]

In typical fashion, Ponsonby concluded *Falsehood in Wartime* by asking

Is further proof needed that international war is a monster, born of hypocrisy, fed on falsehood, fattened on humbug, kept alive by superstition, directed to the death and torture of millions, succeeding to no high purpose, degrading to humanity, endangering civilization and bringing forth in its travail a hideous brood of strife, conflict and war.[12]

By the end of the decade, this spate of anti-war literature was reinforced by the academic work of revisionist historians both in the United States and in Great Britain on the origins of the war.[13] Gooch and Temperley's volumes were used to add significantly to the Foreign Office conspiracy theory by the German historian Hermann Lutz, first in 1928 against Grey and subsequently against Crowe.[14] In this way, the 'war guilt lie' exposed the futility of the war, reinforcing pacifist opinion that, as the politicians had failed the country, they should work out their own destiny.

Disarmament by Example

In the three years between the initiation of the Peace Letter campaign and the general election of 1929, Ponsonby's involvement in politics was largely limited to foreign policy and the associated question of disarmament. He was in an invidious position within the leadership of the party, a front bench speaker with no position in the party other than as a member of the Independent Labour Party. Twice he failed to get elected to the executive of the parliamentary Labour Party (the Shadow Cabinet), both times by the narrowest of margins, his first defeat after a tied vote settled by the spin of a coin with Hugh Dalton, and his second to Sidney Webb, again after a tied vote by the arrival of a late ballot. If he remained throughout these years in the party but not of it, his detachment provides just the necessary edge to his insights on his colleagues.

> Meals in the House of Commons. I often go out as one gets tired of H of C atmosphere and wants a breather. But as I am a pretty regular attendant I am also often in. There is the ex government table curiously stiff and formal. MacDonald making an effort sometimes to unbend. Philip Snowden very charming and entertaining if you get him with just a few or alone. Arthur Henderson pompous with heavy unamusing jokes. Clynes very quiet and friendly but rather inaccessible unless you get him alone. Sidney Webb always there with his quarter-bottle of claret full of erudition if the table is full, much more human if you get him alone. Thomas very seldom there and when he is monopolizes the whole conversation which becomes concentrated on him. Then the ex under secretaries. Charlie Ammon who is unpopular and unattractive but I like him. Attlee longing for jokes but suppressing them. Rhys Davies with good stories but too often repeated. Morgan Jones by nature an agitator but has schooled himself into an official and so spoilt himself. Alexander an aggressive expert. Margaret Bondfield always refreshingly delightful, Willie Graham talking shop and only daring to be frivolous if the big wigs are absent and I myself making an effort to suppress and adapt myself. The truth is these Labour leaders awe me like no other company. The conversation if political as it generally is becomes much too right wingish for my liking. Although individually I get on with them all, collectively they produce a heavy atmosphere of formality and as the session advances I go to the table far more from duty than from pleasure. It is curious because in no other sphere I have been in have I been in the least bit intimidated by the presence of my chiefs and superiors. So I frequently go off to the other room where with Dalton Charleton, Walter Baker, Gillett and any others I feel infinitely more at my ease and have much more amusing meals.[5]

Ramsay MacDonald's attitude towards the Peace Letter campaign can at best be said to have been cool. MacDonald privately expressed general agreement with the ideas of *Now Is The Time*, with one exception. This was his belief that pledges not to go to war were valueless. 'The only way to get peace is to establish it by a development of the policy which we were pursuing when in office.'[16]

In the autumn of 1926, the Peace Letter campaign, which had been scheduled to be completed in May, got back into stride after the interruptions caused by the General Strike, and was brought to a climax at the Albert Hall in December. Ponsonby was supported on the platform by Morrison, Lansbury, Fenner Brockway, Hudson and Margaret Bondfield. Early in the new year, he took his campaign to America, arriving in New York at the end of January 1927 with speaking engagements in New York, Boston, Syracuse, Chicago, Washington and Philadelphia. Not surprisingly he found America altogether too much. Ponsonby, used to the frigid air of Shulbrede, found New York central heating suffocating and his New York hotel considered his demand for a po bad form. In private houses, the absence of interior doors was noted, but it did not take him too long to adapt to American eating habits, and he was soon adept at eating one handed: 'You cut your meat, put the knife aside, use only a fork, and keep your left hand under the table – most important.'

On his return from America, Ponsonby was 'driven at once into the breathless rush of political life'. He went up to Cambridge to participate in a Union debate and found the pacifist resolution, much to his surprise, supported by 213 votes against 138. The motion was 'That lasting peace can only be secured by the people of England adopting an uncompromising attitude of pacifism'. Ponsonby's argument was that all disputes could be settled by diplomatic negotiation. Back in London, he began to prepare for a parliamentary initiative in advancing the pacifist cause in the House by moving a disarmament amendment to the Air Estimates. The Cambridge Union pacifist debate had nothing like the public impact of the similar debate in Oxford several years later, but the RAF debate was very widely reported and not without adverse repercussions for Ponsonby's position within the party, which always revolved around his personal relationship with Ramsay MacDonald. Although Ponsonby never committed himself specifically to unilateral disarmament, in either *Now Is The Time* or in his campaign for disarmament by example, the press, not unnaturally, seized on his asking for the abolition of the RAF as a unilateral move.

Ponsonby proposed disarmament by example as a means of breaking the technical deadlock which surrounded the preparatory commission to the League of Nations Disarmament Conference. Disarmament by example would be the prelude to general disarmament. Great Britain was in a position to make a bold move in the required direction and if she did, Ponsonby assured a largely incredulous audience, she would be safer and more secure than if she remained armed to the teeth. No one would dare attack an unarmed nation he reasoned because in that case the aggressor would be clearly identified. This second line of argument, it must be admitted, confused the issue, for it now appeared that he was advocating a simple unilateral move. When in 1929 he was challenged by the Sheffield branch of the ILP to vote against all war credits, he explained that, although he was in favour of the personal pledge against war and in favour

171

of the policy of disarmament by example, he wanted to be free to promote the best procurable policy of peace. He appreciated that his was a minority position and, although he had supported resolutions of a drastic kind, he was not prepared to vote against a Labour government because they were not going to abolish the war services at once. He admitted this attitude did not involve the smallest qualification of his belief on war resistance and disarmament, all he wanted to do was to help rather than hinder the government so long as it showed a disposition to advance some way along the right line.[17] The official position of the party on the Armed Services Estimates was that they should abstain and the Air Force question should go before the preparatory commission of the Disarmament Conference. Ponsonby spoke well and was pleased with his performance, but did not convince the party and only 23 MPs followed him into the division lobby.

Shortly thereafter he was reproved by MacDonald, who wrote:

> What I personally felt about the matter was that as you had been with me at the F.O. you might have communicated with me before you did anything, as a Front Bench man is in a different position from a back bencher. Generally I wish you would come and see me oftener and talk things over with me.[18]

Clearly it was imperative for Ponsonby to do more than fire off odd salvoes in the House if his campaign for disarmament by example was to make headway. The party was preparing a platform for the next general election, which was expected some time in 1929. He therefore prepared a memorandum on Peace and Disarmament,[19] which he sent to MacDonald in November 1927 with an offer to talk it over if the leader wished. Ponsonby's case for a Labour declaration of the abandoning of what he called 'the war weapon', followed by gradual disarmament by example, he recognised, would be condemned as too idealistic. Ponsonby suggested a co-ordinated platform that would unite all shades of pacifist opinion from war resisters to the League of Nations Union. This tactic completely failed to move MacDonald, who told Ponsonby bluntly that there were only two opinions about peace and disarmament: those who were willing to accommodate policy to national fears about the need to defend the country against an aggressor, and those who advocated an absolute disarmament policy, as though Great Britain was an isolated nation. He could not see the sense of Ponsonby's proposal and was not prepared to do more than promote the idea of arbitration and peace. Unfortunately, there is no record of Ponsonby's reaction to this rejection, but clearly the writing was on the wall as far as Ponsonby's participation at a high level in the next Labour government was concerned. Gradualism was to apply to foreign policy as well as to domestic policy.

By now, the impetus behind the Peace Letter had run its course and Ponsonby arranged to deliver all the Peace Letters to the Prime Minister at

Downing Street. In the interview, they discussed the unsatisfactoriness of parliamentary life, and Ponsonby told Baldwin that in collecting signatures he had come into contact with people whose indignation about the war was very strong and who seemed to bring him more in contact with reality than the House of Commons. Baldwin agreed to answer the letter after he had time to think it over.[20] His reply was typically astute. His initial emphasis was that Great Britain needed her army and navy to fulfil her obligations to the League and then they also underpinned the Locarno agreements. Baldwin could not conceive of a totally disarmed nation and, although he shared Ponsonby's longing for peace, he told him that he had yet to learn that the cause of peace could not be served by rendering their country impotent.[21] This letter may just as easily have been written by MacDonald.

It was at this time, early in 1928, that the Zinoviev letter reappeared. Whatever the rights or wrongs of the case, there can be no doubt that this constant harping back to the events of the autumn of 1924 could do Ponsonby no good. MacDonald had mishandled the case, but Ponsonby had in effect been responsible for Russia and, given MacDonald's capacity for self-justification and fault finding in others, the result was an inevitable lowering of his estimation of Ponsonby's capacity. Ponsonby only came to appreciate this after the break up of the second Labour government in 1931. He was to write at that time 'As to his attitude to me, I gathered from what he said to friends that he overestimated my capacities.'

With the ever-increasing prospect of office in the near future, the Labour leadership came under increasing scrutiny. Ponsonby had no time for those who still thought in terms of the desirability of a minority government, but at the same time he disliked the heavy, formal, right-wing atmosphere created by the leadership. The left wing of the party had a tendency to self-destruct and their demands for socialism now and a head-on attack on capitalism if adopted as a national policy would have led to inevitable defeat at the polls. Maxton and Wheatley, the two ILP leaders, were both out of court with the right wing, which itself was rent with personal dissension. MacDonald was aloof and unapproachable. Neither Snowden nor Henderson could get on with him. Clynes kept himself in the background and Thomas pushed himself forward and was trusted only by MacDonald. So concerned was Ponsonby about the prospect of office, that he had a passing thought that somehow the party should attempt to control MacDonald in the choice of his Cabinet. More realistically, he started a push to ensure that MacDonald would have more adequate secretarial support than had been the case in 1924. His candidate for the post was King-Hall. Ponsonby should have given more thought to his own position. If it occurred to him that it was not at all clear where he would come in, he was not at all prepared to be excluded.

Minor Office

As the general election of 1929 drew closer, Ponsonby had no qualms about his seat, which was as safe as a rock. The election results confirmed this fact, and, after the votes had been counted, he had a 10,000 majority over his Conservative opponent, and nearly 4,000 over the combined opposition. Nationally, the Labour Party emerged for the first time as the leading party in the Commons, with 288 seats to 260 for the Conservatives. Unfortunately, the Labour Party did not have an overall majority, for, although the Liberals were decimated, returning only 59 members, this was enough to force the Labour Party, as in 1924, into a minority position. Even before the election, Ponsonby had begun to hear on the grapevine speculations about the next Labour government. In March, he had lunch with the Egyptian politician Hamed Mahmud, who told him that MacDonald was planning to solve the difficulty of rival claimants for the Foreign Office by taking it himself. Ponsonby was certain that whatever his fate, and he could not see how he could get into the Cabinet, he would not go back to the Foreign Office as under-secretary. Then, at the end of April, just after he had heard from Mahmud that he was one of three being considered for Foreign Secretary – the other two being J.H. Thomas and Noel Buxton – he met MacDonald, who quite spontaneously told him that Arthur Henderson had sent in an ultimatum that he must be Foreign Secretary.[22] MacDonald's preference was again, as in 1924, for Thomas, but Henderson's refusal to serve at all unless he was given the Foreign Office bullied MacDonald into changing his mind. Ponsonby was not considered at all. Thomas's and Henderson's struggle for the Foreign Office did not escape his attention. 'I suppose one of them will undoubtedly get it. This is most disappointing, not only for me personally, but from the point of view of a real move forward. I cannot see where I can fit in and if I am not even in the Cabinet, I should very much prefer to be free on the back benches.'[23] His worst fears were realised when he heard that the Cabinet was being constructed on the principle of the representation of interests. As he represented no one but himself, he was automatically ruled out of the Cabinet.

The most that could be expected was a minor office, and a suggestion was made that he accept the post of Chairman of Committees. When he was finally called in to see MacDonald on 8 June, he found himself having to refuse the position of Deputy Chairman of Committees, which MacDonald apparently thought Ponsonby coveted. 'He was looking very well and genuinely friendly about having to drop a *friend*.' He was not, then, prepared to consider Ponsonby for the under-secretaryship of the Colonial and Dominions Office, a good minor job as the Minister, Webb, was in the Lords. The meeting closed with MacDonald promising to do his

best. Once home at Shulbrede, Ponsonby wrote to the Prime Minister that
he had decided to remain on the back benches:

> There are many ways still open to me to serve the cause of Socialism and Peace
> and in the great opportunity now open to them your new government will
> require voices from the rank and file to help them to interpret the wishes of the
> vast electorate who have returned them to power.[24]

MacDonald, after second thoughts, found, after all, that the under-
secretary for the Dominions was open. The offer was made over the
phone, which Ponsonby received in the Fernhurst village post office. He
agreed to go up to London on the morrow to talk it over. That evening, he
wrote in his diary that he was still inclined to opt for freedom. There were
two objections to such a course of action. If he dropped out, he would
never be asked to drop in again, and he did not fancy becoming a martyr or
the man with a grievance. So he went up to London and accepted the last
post in the new government.

Not a few people wondered why Ponsonby was left out of the Cabinet in
1929. No satisfactory answer was given. The most that MacDonald ever
said on the subject was to Fritz Ponsonby at Windsor. Fritz gathered that
he had relied upon Thomas and Henderson in making his appointments
and then 'went on in a confidential whisper telling me nothing and talking
vague nonsense'. Beatrice Webb admitted in her diary that Ponsonby,
very naturally, expected to be promoted to the Cabinet, but offered no
explanations of why the event did not take place, and went on to
disparage both Arthur and Dolly, Arthur as being a sentimentalist without
horse, an amateur and a dilettante in politics and Dolly as being sickly,
critical and somewhat rude.[25] There can be no doubt that the reason for
his exclusion was that, although he was an aristocrat, he was also a
socialist and the five right-wing working class leaders of the party,
MacDonald, Henderson, Thomas, Snowden and Clynes, were determined
to exclude all the left-wing members of the party from the government.
Henderson, who considered himself to be the expert in foreign affairs, had
never gone out of his way for Ponsonby, and had been particularly upset by
Ponsonby's Peace Letter and disarmament by example campaigns.

When Ponsonby first heard of his exclusion, he could not help feeling
depressed

> Why should the peace letter tell against me? Is war resistance contrary to
> Socialist doctrine? These people do not realize the receptions and commenda-
> tions I get all over the country just because of my attitude on war. I did my best
> in 1924. I got through the Russian Treaties. But I am not sure that this does not
> tell against me too with these right wingers.[26]

He was not a man who continued to bear grudges, and was soon making
the most of his new job as Dominions' under-secretary. On 26 June, he

saw Uncle A (as Henderson was always referred to) behind the Speaker's Chair:

> He saw me coming, looked very sheepish, and pretended to talk to Lansbury. I went straight up to him and, in a clarion voice, said 'I must congratulate you three times over on your family success, on your office and on the start you have made.' I have never seen anyone so surprised and he did not know what to say as he gave me his flabby hand.[27]

Work as the Dominions' under-secretary had only peripheral interest for Ponsonby. Personal relations with Sidney Webb, Lord Passfield, were good. He soon discovered that there was no work for him, as the post had only been created after the passage of the Statute of Westminster to satisfy Dominion sensitivity. The only opportunity was in the area of Overseas settlement. The committee that looked after this was in an unsatisfactory and chaotic condition, and he thought of recasting it. It was such a dead weight to move that nothing substantive was achieved before he was moved to the Ministry of Transport. As for the House, as emigration was of no consequence, a little piffling Bill, as he described it, was passed through with virtually no debate and Ponsonby more than ever regretted his unnoticed quiet shelf, especially as foreign affairs had become intensely interesting with the discussions at The Hague producing the Young Plan for German reparations. At Shulbrede, during August, Ponsonby was so put out by being asked to comment upon the vexed question as to whether High Commissioners should or should not 'pass the Presence' at courts with their wives, that he went ahead and prepared a memorandum on his own initiative on a question of real importance. The Dominions Office had never really bothered to take a serious interest in the Dominions and foreign affairs. As he put it in his diary, the 'officials were drifting and rather enjoying the complications as they arise'. Ponsonby's memorandum primarily addressed the problem of consultation with the Dominions on foreign policy. He noticed how far the situation had changed since 1924 when the Labour government had never thought of consulting the Dominions about the recognition of the Soviet Union. Now, when the government was simply thinking of resuming diplomatic relations with the Soviet Union, they were consulting them closely. He felt that there was a tendency for London to be over-cautious of the susceptibilities of the Dominions, because the government was not clear which of four courses it ought to pursue, according to the nature and importance of the question at issue. To simply inform, to consult, to await their approval, or not to consult them at all. When the government had a fixed policy it never for a moment contemplated departing from it, even if the Dominions objected, so that the practice of consultation really amounted to a sham.[28]

The particular issue that was exercising the government's mind in 1929 was the League of Nations' Optional Clause, whereby the British government and the Dominions agreed to accept compulsory arbitration of all justiciable disputes. The Optional Clause was a lesser commitment to the League than the Geneva Protocol, which had been abandoned after Labour left office in 1924. Ponsonby went to a Downing Street conference on the question at the end of August. He did not speak, but had prepared Passfield's brief. The Prime Minister, ever reluctant to rock the boat, had bowed before Australian objections, and went so far as to suggest that, if Great Britain could not carry the Dominions with her, she should not sign the Optional Clause, and had to be reminded that the Dominions could not be allowed a constitutional veto on British policy. Eventually, the Dominions and British Government signed the Optional Clause, although with reservations. This peripheral involvement, for the time being, was sufficient to keep Ponsonby reasonably content – 'I must knuckle to and *act* gratitude.' How long the mood would last was difficult to tell.

In the autumn, Ponsonby found himself travelling about the country a good deal, inspecting girls' hostels for emigration in Glasgow, and the Middlemore Homes in Birmingham. There were political meetings in his constituency, and various other functions all of a routine nature. This apparently brought things to a head with Dolly. For the first time in many years, they had a blazing row. They went out for a country drive to Harting Hill and Dolly launched into a tirade, criticising Arthur's absorption in politics, his absence from home and his inferior job at the Dominions Office. The row lasted for an hour and a half, with tears from Dolly and shouting from Arthur, before they lapsed into silence. After a reconciliation outside Shulbrede, Arthur retreated to his diary and mused over the situation. He accepted Dolly's argument that he had landed a dog's job that was not worth it, but felt that to have refused would have been political suicide, and he still had hopes of doing something in the future. However, the argument went deeper than this immediate problem. 'She hates politics, despises politicians, loathes party and thinks the best work is done outside.' Dolly quoted the Hammonds against Arthur, but his view was that politics was his life's work.

My view is not career. I consider myself petty for minding I did not get a better post. I want to give service and cooperate with those who are devoting their lives to a great endeavour to lift their fellow men who are by the million suffering and condemned to ignorance and degradation. These people many of them of humble origin have actually risen to the highest posts in the land by their efforts. I want to help them. It is so easy to criticise them and get some cudos and fame for doing it. I did it with the Liberal govt in 1908 to 1918. It is much more difficult to go in and help in the very responsible and often disappointing work of government.[29]

Ponsonby had heard from Dalton, the new Foreign under-secretary, that the appointment to the Moscow Embassy was shortly to be made, and, taking the bull by the horns, he went to see him. 'Now I said "I am going to throw a bomb at you." In a flash, clapping his hands, he answered, "You want to go to Moscow."' Although Dalton approved, the appointment rested with the Cabinet, and Henderson was known to be in favour of a professional. At lunch before the Cabinet meeting to decide the appointment, Ponsonby broached the matter with Henderson. He was very unsympathetic and, when the matter came up in the Cabinet, Henderson declared in favour of a professional and, backed by Snowden, with no further discussion or even mention of Ponsonby, the appointment was given to Sir E. Ovey. MacDonald wrote afterwards that he had concluded that the Moscow appointment should be made from inside, as the appointment of a politician would only encourage certain Bolshevik methods of diplomacy and not necessarily make them more amenable to fair and friendly dealing. Ponsonby admitted the force of the argument.

Where this personal initiative failed, the unforeseen consequences of the discovery by a country clergyman that the government were breaking the law by having seven under-secretaries in the Commons was to provide Ponsonby with the escape longed for by Dolly. Ponsonby first heard the news of the illegality of seven under-secretaries from a passage in the *Sheffield Telegraph*. The newspaper suggested that the solution to the difficulty was for Ponsonby to go to the Lords. This he indignantly rejected, calling it a humiliation. He could only hope that Labour's opposition to creating hereditary peerages would protect him from being kicked upstairs. The Prime Minister called a meeting of the under-secretaries on 25 November, where the situation was explained. Characteristically, MacDonald avoided making any suggestion.

Two solutions to the problem were open, one under-secretary would become a Peer, or one must take an inferior post with reduced salary. After Lunn's suggestion of his dropping out of Parliament was refused by MacDonald, Ponsonby suggested he would be prepared to become parliamentary secretary at the Ministry of Transport at a reduced salary; this proposal was jumped at by the Prime Minister. The very next day, MacDonald, afraid of a scene in the House, set in motion the changes involved in shuffling the under-secretaries, and Ponsonby came under great pressure from his friend Arnold to consider the advantages of his taking a peerage. Because of MacDonald's move, the decision had to be taken almost immediately. Arnold argued that, as the Minister of Transport was in the Commons, he would be more on the shelf than ever. It was further argued that his prospects of ever getting a good position would always be frustrated by the Trade Unions. On the other hand, his presence in the Lords would be a real help to the party and as Lord Parmoor was 77, he would soon find himself spokesman there on foreign affairs. It was also argued that far from his becoming a Peer being ridiculous, his style was particularly suited to the Lords, which, Arnold added, in the event of a war cloud emerging in the future, would give him an excellent platform. Arnold also saw Dolly, and Ponsonby allowed himself to be persuaded. The next day, Ponsonby went to see MacDonald, who said he would like Ponsonby to go to the Lords, but not as part of the under-secretary mix up. So early in December, without anyone knowing about the move to the Lords, Ponsonby took the step down as parliamentary secretary to the Ministry of Transport. His Peerage was announced in the New Years Honours List and gazetted on 21 January 1930. He took his seat the following day. His title had caused some problems; he had hoped to be simply Lord Ponsonby, but Vere Bessborough objected, as this was one of his subsidiary titles. Ria, Fritz's wife, also objected as she hoped Fritz would be made Lord Ponsonby one day. Fritz was, in fact, created a Peer in 1935 and took the title Lord Sysonby. So Arthur had to include the 'of Shulbrede' in his title.

There can be little doubt that Dolly was the reason Arthur allowed himself to be convinced that he should go to the Lords. Only a few friends were informed of the move before it was announced. Among them was Lawrence Hammond. He thought that it had been the right decision to make in the light of Ponsonby's career.

> Your position in politics is peculiar. Noel Buxton and Trevelyan are the type of politician whose career demands office. Your weight is much more individual. You have made your position by your own methods. You have pushed ideas and methods of your own and gained your influence in that way. Your reputation does not depend on office nor your usefulness.[30]

This was very true and he was astute enough to realise that, as there were always two or three cabinet ministers in the Lords, his chance of high office had probably improved.

Just before Christmas, Ponsonby paid a last visit to his constituents in Sheffield.

> My last visit here as M.P. gives me an odd feeling. I suppose my contact with Brightside people has been the most real thing in my political life in these last ten years. Their humanness, their simplicity, their touching affection and trust. Full of faults, but without any shamness, so valiant and cheerful in their poverty, petty, no doubt, like others in their jealousies and social grades, but wonderfully responsive to any glimmer they may catch of better and finer things. Real people. I am certain that if weighed in the balance with a section of our class, the recording angel would pronounce them superior because their degradation and vice is due to environment and conditions and seldom, as with others, due to deliberate choice. Well, I am sorry to leave them – very.[31]

On Christmas Eve, he went to the House and, as usual, went to a seat in the corner of the last bench under the gallery. As he was surveying the scene with gloomy reflections about his eighteen years in the House, he felt a tap on his shoulder and found Ramsay MacDonald sitting by his side. He seemed to realise what Ponsonby was thinking and said 'I think I shall have to follow you up there', describing how uncomfortable he felt speaking from the box. In his memoir of MacDonald, Ponsonby realised that it had cost MacDonald an effort to make such a gesture and he only wished that 'it had been the end of their meeting on the road'.

The Bright Young People

After his release from the Foreign Office at the end of 1924, Ponsonby had taken up once again his political journalism, notably a weekly commentary on Parliament for the *New Leader*, and, in addition, began to write small pieces and commentaries on contemporary social problems and issues. His most successful contribution in this field was his regular Saturday column, 'Casual Observations', which began to appear in the *Manchester Guardian* at the end of 1927, and which continued until he took office in the second Labour government in June 1929. He also began an equally distinguished broadcasting career during this period, with a broadcast on Diaries in January 1928 from Savoy Hill, at that time still the headquarters of the BBC. Whatever critical success he achieved in these two endeavours, nothing he did quite matched the popularity of an individual piece that he put together at odd moments during the time he was writing his pacifist book, and which appeared under the extraordinary title 'A Plea for Bushy Whiskers' in February 1925. This article on the problem of the sex dislocation of the 1920s which had effeminate men with plucked eyebrows and painted faces dominated by 'flat chested, short haired, cocktail drinking, cigarette smoking, vivacious and enterprising girls' was sensationalised, both in England and in America, from where came offers of large sums of money to create a book on the same theme. Even if he had had the time, he did not have the inclination, for he was already planning to embark on his Peace Letter campaign.[32]

After the Evelyn Waugh débâcle in April 1925, the Ponsonbys' relations with their children settled down on a much more even keel, Elizabeth in regular work in 'Spring Cleaning' and Matthew, at home once again with a tutor, assisting in further Shulbrede excavations. Ponsonby always found Matthew more receptive than Elizabeth. After writing an immense letter on life to Matthew, he noted in his diary 'I should like to get on these same terms with E but that is more difficult.' One day, he heard her say that she had no interests beyond 'social gadding about'. In 1926, because of the pressure of the Peace Letter campaign, Ponsonby abandoned his regular diary and instead made predictions at the beginning of the year and comments upon the predictions at the end of the year. On Elizabeth he wrote 'E will go on as she is going. She will not marry yet but it is conceivable that some different step may be taken.' At year's end 'E – quite correct.'

Elizabeth proved most companionable during the two months' Peace Letter campaign in America early in 1927. This interlude proved to be, however, only a lull before the storm. Exactly what happened in June 1927 remains a mystery. His diary entry for 16 June tells its own story. 'The darkest day of the deepest humiliation I have ever had' and Dolly scrawled on the fly of this volume 'This vol. contains much that is painful and would upset any near relative.' In thinking over his 'failure', Ponsonby rightly concluded that as far as Elizabeth was concerned, even if they had attempted to enforce exterior discipline, the temperament of the child was what mattered. They had not sufficiently taken in 'the luxurious aristocratic heredity' on both sides of their family, which naturally erupted against the austere asceticism of their Shulbrede life. They could not avoid recalling Arthur's great-aunt, Lady Caroline Lamb, and Caroline's famous line on Byron 'mad, bad, and dangerous to know', which, although applied to several of the Bright Young People, probably characterised Elizabeth more than anyone else in the set.

If Elizabeth deliberately courted danger and excitement, Matthew only managed to get into scrapes. He left Balliol and began to prepare for a career in architecture. Many of the parties of the Bright Young People in 1927 had featured female impersonations and, not to be outdone, Matthew made the mistake of attempting to introduce one of his friends dressed as a girl into a formal and highly respectable fancy dress ball. The deception was uncovered, and the resulting scandal nearly cost Matthew his place. Matthew had met and fallen in love with Bess Bigham, the daughter of Clive Bigham, who succeeded to the title of Viscount Mersey on the death of his father, the distinguished judge, in 1929. Matthew, of course, had only prospects and his parents only limited financial resources, so a marriage was out of the question. For the time being, it was agreed that they would wait. Both Arthur and Dolly liked Bess. Although she moved in the Bright Young People set, they thankfully found her different to the modern girl.

The Ponsonbys' experience of the Bright Young People had been, so far, mercifully second-hand. Their initiation came on the first weekend of January 1929. Elizabeth's Shulbrede party consisted of Babe Greene, recently divorced from David Greene, Eddie Gathorne-Hardy 'a young pervert with rather pretentious literary leanings, an innocent young American, and a heavily painted very common dissipated girl'. On Sunday, a further contingent arrived 'a girl picked up off a Piccadilly Street, a shiny cinema actor, a bogus Sicilian Duke and two other undistinguished looking young men'. The bogus Duke, who was probably Count Bosdari, eventually Babe Greene's second husband, amused Ponsonby at dinner and Arthur thought him to be a retired waiter. They proceeded to drink the house dry, and when Matthew brought in four more bottles of brandy, his father's patience ran out and he carried off three of the bottles to the toolshed. This altercation only caused a momentary lull in the proceedings, and when it was all over, it was calculated that they had drunk '1 doz. bottles of Brandy, Sherry and Whisky, several bottles of beer, and a good deal of wine. The Piccadilly prostitute carried off half a bottle of brandy with her in the car to help her through the night.'[33]

As the newspapers continued to convey disagreeable details of Elizabeth's pranks in the following months, which were largely occupied with arranging a marriage settlement for Matthew and Bess, it came as something of a bombshell for Arthur and Dolly to be casually told by Matthew that Elizabeth had become engaged. Matthew had only met the man once and Elizabeth had known him two weeks. Denis Pelly, who worked as an assistant in a gramophone shop, had no money and no prospects. Arthur found him good looking and decent, but doubted 'if he has enough grit for the adventure'. Elizabeth's whirlwind romance created a circus atmosphere, before which the Ponsonbys were helpless. The wedding was fixed for July and, with the general election set for May 1929, Ponsonby hardly had time to reflect on the impossibility of the match. Family opposition was partly overcome by Arthur's finding Denis Pelly a job through his old friend Vaughan Nash. Above all, he allowed his relief that marriage would remove Elizabeth from the 'drift towards the mud' to silence his doubts.

The wedding took place at St Margaret's, Westminster, and the reception was held at Crosby Hall. Arthur recorded his impressions of the reception 'the older people enjoyed it as much as the younger who towards the end got uproarious and broke into song and dance'. The *Tatler*'s description read 'Finally, Mrs Denis Pelly . . . sprang into the arms of Mr Brian Howard whose white velvet tie needs no further advertisement, and opened the ball.'

Not the least difficult part of Ponsonby's arrangements for Elizabeth concerned Dolly's mother, Lady Maud Parry, who, by 1929, was quite mad, although otherwise in good health. Lady Maud had always liked Elizabeth, and intended to give her some money on her marriage. As Ponsonby was her Receiver, and an interview with the Master in Lunacy proved unavailing, a solution seemed impossible. Eventually, a way was found, but it did nothing for the Ponsonbys' financial security. Elizabeth proved to be a greater drain on her parents after her marriage than before, and Clive Bigham continued to be tiresome about a marriage settlement for Bess and Matthew. He finally gave in when Matthew secured a position with the Office of Works, and the marriage took place at the end of the year.

At the end of the year, Ponsonby wrote:

> Well 1929 has been the most astonishing year in my life. Never can I forget it. The mere list of events is enough to show it.

> Record frosts
> Record drought
> Record storms
> Record floods

> That was nature's exaggerated obligato.

> General Election
> Appointment Under Sec. for Dominions
> Elizabeth's engagement and marriage
> Matthew's engagement and marriage
> Transfer to Ministry of Transport
> Peerage

> But the result of it all has yet to come beginning with the peerage which will be published tomorrow morning.

The Duchy of Lancaster

After his Peerage was announced in the 1930 New Year's Honours List, Ponsonby suffered a natural reaction against the avalanche of letters and telegrams of congratulations that descended on Shulbrede. Most of his good friends had the common sense to be fairly muted. MacDonald sent a postcard from Lossiemouth, 'My Dear A. I have this minute signed with a sad heart your new baptismal certificate. Bless you in all your doings.' It was all too much, and he sought the safety of his diary.

> It is pretty difficult for me to escape from my surroundings. I start with a courtier brother, my daughter becomes famous for her extravagant pranks in a wastrel society, my son marries the daughter of a viscount, my niece marries a Duke, my other brother accompanies the Prince of Wales to Africa, and I become a peer. Proper labour people may well say what the devil is the use of a man with those connections. I tried to go left as a radical thought I had made a further move left in joining the Labour Party only to find it was tamely liberal, married to tradition and put me in the Lords. A difficult future.[34]

He took his seat on 22 January, and found it not at all strange. He wrote to Dolly.

> I am still rubbing my eyes – it was a dream which took me back to prewar or perhaps pre 1918 days. There was Banbury with his hat, his little preliminary

stammer and the little pressure of his finger on his upper lip raising little points and telling little stories, there was Bob Cecil casting about for his words, twitching his nose and smiling delightfully, there was Jack Pease lisping rather more toothless and as ineffective as ever, there was Curzon, now Howe, talking away with a rather sham breezy geniality about motorcars and there was Butcher who in spite of calling himself Dansforth was as boring, evil looking, and odious as ever, and of course other House of Commons people to look at. So I was taken back – and felt plus ça change plus c'est la meme chose.[35]

The Tory atmosphere of the Lords soon provoked Ponsonby's combative spirit. He was all for confrontation and not a little disturbed by Parmoor's woolly and conciliatory attitude. His first opportunity to make a fighting speech came in a debate on Russian propaganda. Speaking after Lord Birkenhead, another old adversary, who had, as usual, been clever but bogus, Ponsonby attacked and ruffled more than a few feathers.

He agreed with Virginia Woolf that the atmosphere of the Lords, its urbanity, geniality and dignity, the offspring of luxury and privacy and space, needed disturbing. His radicalism, which had always been hidden only slightly below the surface, seems to have had a new lease of life. Not a few left wingers were upset by the apparent easy absorption of the Labour Party by the establishment. In February, he went to a Foreign Office party where Ramsay MacDonald, who looked well and made a fuss of Dolly, was contrasted with 'Baldwin's undistinguished appearance, increased by Mrs. Baldwin's amazing vulgarity', and Lloyd George, who looked like a pantomime figure.

> But, but there it is – what I have often thought and feared has happened so exactly even to the extent of my being swept along in the stream myself. Here is the Labour and socialist party not breaking a single thread with tradition but carrying on the traditions of authority undistinguishable socially from the other parties, proud and flattered at being in the saddle, and behaving just as the others do accepting honours and pomp and traditions of moderation – not so radical as the Liberal Government of 1906 and me as a 'Lord' sliding along in the line of least resistance making all the dear old excuses and allowing all the fire of enthusiasm to be quenched – all of us taken in – conscientiously doing our jobs deprecating any disturbance or criticism arising from our past professions. I suppose it is inevitable but how authority (if it could be personified) must be holding its sides with laughter. I think some of the Tories do chuckle. but just now they are too much occupied with their own splits and troubles to be anything but rather nervous about the purely political or parliamentary future.[36]

Work as parliamentary secretary to the Ministry of Transport was a different field than the Dominions, but just as depressing, for there was little to do beyond approving the size of vehicle licence plates on motor cycles and similar mundane tasks. However, he was determined to make the most of it and to restrict his grumbling to his diary. He had a beautiful office and a good staff and gradually developed an interest in by-pass construction, which was just beginning on a large scale, to accommodate the ever-increasing number of motor cars on the road. While in Liverpool for a Safety First Conference in May, he could not avoid the conclusion that his job was a dead end and that, if he was never going to get a real job in politics, he might as well go and do something else. He knew that his exclusion had been the consequence of the right-wing orientation of the party, which had become more Tory than Liberal. In taking the line of least resistance and tamely conforming to convention, the last person they wished to see in office was a radical aristocrat.

The most pressing domestic problem of 1930 was the dramatic impact of the Great Depression on the level of unemployment. Throughout the 1920s, the level of unemployment had never fallen below one million. Now, in 1930, it doubled to two million. Nobody, with perhaps the exception of Oswald Mosley, knew how to deal with the problem and, as his plans for a managed economy were manifestly before their time, his efforts to force them on the party only resulted in his own expulsion. Ponsonby was only an interested spectator to these events. His opinion of Mosley was that, although his ability and brilliance were unquestionable, there was something flashy and vulgar in his personality. The shuffle in the government, consequent upon Mosley's removal, did not affect Ponsonby. He was thankful that he had left the Dominions, as he could never have worked under Thomas and supposed that the party hierarchy thought he was well provided for and comfortable. This he certainly was not, and through the summer he continued to reflect on the chain of circumstances that had landed him in the Lords and on the very lowest rung of the government ladder. The thought that it was his two left-wing actions, the Russian Treaties and the Peace Letter, which had been his undoing with the party leadership continually jarred. Now the passive and supine attitude of the leadership in the face of the Depression made things far worse. They no longer seemed interested in embarking on a new cause, content 'to make the old machine, which is pointing in the wrong direction, perform inadequately the outer fringe of Labour policy'.

The crash of the R101 in October, which killed Lord Thomson, opened the possibility of considerable changes for the small team of Labour Peers, who, like Ponsonby, had been passed over for high office. Ponsonby promoted the cause of Lord Arnold for the Duchy of Lancaster with a Cabinet seat, with Attlee, coming up to the Lords and taking over the Air Ministry. As Ponsonby predicted, the Prime Minister paid not the slightest attention to his views, and the Air Ministry was given to Lord Amulree, a 70-year-old unknown. The Labour team in the Lords needed rejuvenating, for Parmoor was now very frail and Passfield was also looking forward to an early release from the Colonial Office. Early in the New

Year, Ponsonby had to talk Arnold out of a threatened resignation. Passfield was informed, but as he had no influence with MacDonald, he was only able to sympathise, advising neither to resign, as he did not think that the government would last much beyond March in any case. However, rather than March bringing the end of the government, it brought the government reshuffle that finally brought Ponsonby his own office.

The March shuffle was caused by the resignation of Sir Charles Trevelyan, the death of Earl Russell, Bertrand's brother, and the resignation of Sydney Arnold. Ponsonby went straight to the Prime Minister and refused his offer of under-secretary of India, telling MacDonald that he could not go on being subordinate to one minister after another, and that he was prepared to take the Duchy of Lancaster and when Parmoor finally went, he wanted also to take over the lead in the Lords. MacDonald would make no immediate commitment and Ponsonby had to wait a week before he was offered the Duchy, unfortunately without the Cabinet.

The Duchy of Lancaster was really only a useful post if it went with the Cabinet, for there was no real departmental work attached to the position and so the occupant was free to help out as and when needed. Outside the Cabinet, the position was purely titular. Of more importance was the lead in the Lords and that was still being handled by Parmoor, or, in his absence, by Passfield. Parmoor was persuaded by MacDonald to stay on to the end of the session. 'Perhaps,' Ponsonby wrote to Dolly, 'this is because Ramsay no more contemplates making me leader in the Lords than making the man who cleans out the closets at Waterloo.' One immediate ordeal had to be faced, and that was to receive the seals of his office from the King. George had reacted with his usual antipathy to Arthur on the announcement of his Peerage, quoting to Fritz Arthur's view on the Lords and declaring that no one could ever place reliance on what Labour politicians said when both Arthur and Sidney Webb had to eat their words and tamely become Peers. Now, face to face, he was more cordial. 'He said, "Fritz is on your council." I said, "Yes, Sir, I believe he pays my salary." He gave a chuckle and I retired.'[37]

Work at the Duchy involved even more remote questions from Ponsonby's interests than ever. The Chancellor was involved in such historic customs as 'pricking' the Lancashire sheriff and mining in the High Peak of Derbyshire. He was also required to interview parsons for livings under the Duchy's patronage. On one occasion, expecting doctrinal or parish matters to come up for discussion, he was amused and relieved to find that his parsons were all more concerned about the absence of a bathroom in the vicarage than about the 39 Articles. He set about a scheme to collect pictures of all his 151 predecessors at the Duchy.

Before the collection was complete, the August 1931 economic crisis broke up the government, and Ponsonby found himself once again sitting on the Opposition side. Before the break-up of the government, Ponsonby managed to bring forward the constitutional question of the Lords. He sent up to the Prime Minister a memorandum on the Labour Party and the House of Lords. In the memorandum, Ponsonby put forward several considerations. Conflict between the Lords and a Labour government was inevitable; the Lords were aware of this, and realised that their present constitution of 400 Conservative, 80 Liberal and 17 Labour peers was indefensible. The delaying veto of the 1911 Parliament Act had become an absolute veto in the case of short-lived parliaments. Labour needed to prepare the ground for an eventual policy to deal with the imbalance and, also, they should take a hard look at their attitude towards the creation of Labour Peers. Ponsonby was himself in favour of some sort of revising second chamber with an injection of six to twelve younger Labour Peers created from among the Laski-Tawney-Cole type, as a means of utilising the Labour pool of talent outside Parliament. Discussions were started with Lees-Smith, the Labour expert on the second chamber, and it was agreed that a reform scheme should be made part of Labour's election policy. MacDonald did not create any Labour Peers in 1931, and, for the rest of the session, Ponsonby found himself shouldering most of the Lords' work, which made up for the lack of work in the Duchy, and the refusal of more senior ministers to use him at all, in spite of the Prime Minister's request given, when he first took office, that they use him.

The collapse of the Labour government in August was not unexpected. Ponsonby was predicting it in July, feeling that the only thing that could keep the government in was the disinclination of the other parties to take responsibility for the drastic measures that were necessary to revive a faltering economy. He heard talk about an 'economic 1914', but, like many others, his utter lack of understanding of economics left him feeling altogether out of his depth. That summer, Arthur and Dolly took motor car expeditions for their holidays, and he was back at Shulbrede, hedging his meadow when a telegram from 10 Downing Street summoned him to London for a meeting on 23 August. When he arrived, he found that he had been invited to a meeting of ministers outside the government. MacDonald spoke to them for forty minutes, telling of the drain of gold from the Bank, which was in danger of collapse, and of the Cabinet having split, of proposals to deal with the situation. He said that his proposal for an *ad hoc* national government, purely for the purpose of passing his scheme, had been agreed to by the King and the Opposition, and that, when they had finished their work, there would be an election and a return to party government. Could he, or anyone else, have imagined that party government was not to return until 1945?

Apparently, MacDonald expected some ministers to stand beside him. Ponsonby was not among them, for, in his opinion, whether or not there had been wild over-reaction on the part of the bankers, the cuts in Unemployment Insurance were a betrayal of trust, and he would not be a party to betraying the unemployed. Earlier in the year, Ponsonby had addressed the question of 'a national government' to meet a national emergency and had rejected it outright. 'The grinding out of legislation and administration between the upper and nether millstone of conflicting opinions is, in the long run, the best form of government. Coalitions have always been a hopeless failure.'[38] As he put it in his diary, when reflecting on the betrayal of the party by MacDonald, 'It is not a matter of country before party, but of strengthening party, which is the proper instrument to put the country in a sound position.' So he resigned, and delivered up the seals of his office. He wrote to the Prime Minister.

> Thank you for your letter. For personal reasons, I deeply regret breaking so long an association with you and, with all the ups and downs, I have been proud to serve the party under your leadership. This panic has broken up everything and must remain rather inexplicable to most of us. For my own part, I have striven to escape from the insinuating and charming influences of the old order, in which I was brought up and the extraordinary cleverness of whose methods I had learned to understand, but again and again, circumstances have made me compromise. I feel now I have definitely come to the parting of the ways. I cannot take the path of so called 'patriotism' so greatly belauded by the opposition press (very reminiscent of the outbreak of war) and I must stick to whatever section of the party will pursue the principles in which I believe and the pursuit of which can be my only excuse for remaining in political life.[39]

The Labour Party in the Lords decided for the moment to carry on as before, with Parmoor and Passfield. Ponsonby told Henderson, who had been elected leader in the Commons, that he expected to take over after the general election. The election reduced the party in the Commons to fifty-two members, with eight in the Lords, not an enviable position for any of them. Following Henderson's defeat in the election, Lansbury became leader in the Commons and Ponsonby in the Lords.

Notes

1. *Shulbrede MSS.*, A. Ponsonby Diary, XI, 26 Jan 1925.
2. 'The Sanction Behind a League of Nations', *War and Peace*.
3. UDC pamphlet 41a, 'The Covenant of the League of Nations: An Analysis with Full Text' (1920).
4. *Shulbrede MSS.*, A. Ponsonby Diary, XII, 11 Sept 1925.
5. Ceadel (1980), p. 223.
6. Taylor (1969), footnote p. 47.

7. Ceadel (1980), p. 3.
8. Nigel Young in reviewing *Pacifism in Britain* (1980).
9. *Now Is The Time*, p. 129.
10. Ibid., p. 20.
11. Sanders and Taylor (1982), p. 147.
12. *Falsehood in Wartime*, p. 192.
13. Fay (1928); Barnes (1926); Gooch (1927); Dickinson (1926).
14. Lutz (1928) and (1931).
15. *Shulbrede MSS.*, A. Ponsonby Diary, XII, 21 July 1928.
16. *MacDonald MSS.*, PRO 30/69/1170/Part 2. f.531–2, J.R. MacDonald to A. Ponsonby, 21 Sept 1925.
17. *Ponsonby MSS.*, C.671, f.59–60, draft to Sheffield branch of the ILP, Aug 1929.
18. *Ponsonby MSS.*, C.670, f.16, J.R. MacDonald to A. Ponsonby, 22 Mar 1927.
19. *MacDonald MSS.*, PRO 30/69/1172, Part 2, f.410–18, Memorandum on Peace and Disarmament.
20. *Shulbrede MSS.*, A. Ponsonby to D. Ponsonby, 8 Dec 1927.
21. *Ponsonby MSS.*, C.670, f.56–60, S. Baldwin to A. Ponsonby, 16 Dec 1927.
22. *Shulbrede MSS.*, A. Ponsonby Diary, XII, 30 Apr 1929.
23. *Shulbrede MSS.*, A. Ponsonby Diary, XII, 4 June 1929.
24. *MacDonald MSS.*, PRO 30/69/672, Part 1, f.101–2, A. Ponsonby to J.R. MacDonald, 8 June 1929.
25. *B. Webb Diary*, 4738–9, 9 June 1929.
26. *Shulbrede MSS.*, A. Ponsonby Diary, XII, 4 June 1929.
27. *Shulbrede MSS.*, A. Ponsonby to D. Ponsonby, 26 June 1929.
28. *Ponsonby MSS.*, C.671, f.20–33, draft memorandum 'The Dominions and Foreign Affairs'.
29. *Shulbrede MSS.*, A. Ponsonby Diary, XII, 27 Oct 1929.
30. *Ponsonby MSS.*, C.671, f.110–11, J.L. Hammond to A. Ponsonby, 9 Dec 1929.
31. *Shulbrede MSS.*, A. Ponsonby to D. Ponsonby, 21 Dec 1929.
32. 'A Plea for Bushy Whiskers', *The Empire Review*, Feb 1925.
33. *Shulbrede MSS.*, A. Ponsonby Diary, XII, 7 Jan 1929.
34. *Shulbrede MSS.*, A. Ponsonby Diary, XIII, 3 Jan 1930.
35. *Shulbrede MSS.*, A. Ponsonby to D. Ponsonby, 24 Jan 1930.
36. *Shulbrede MSS.*, A. Ponsonby Diary, XIII, 24 Feb 1930.
37. *Shulbrede MSS.*, A. Ponsonby Diary, XIII, 21 Mar 1931.
38. *Ponsonby MSS.*, C.672, f.22.
39. *Ponsonby MSS.*, C.672, A. Ponsonby to J.R. MacDonald, 27 Aug 1931.

CHAPTER SIX

Life Here and Now, 1931–1939

Disarmament

These upheavals in domestic politics did not deflect Ponsonby from his continuing interest in international affairs. One day, late in September 1931, he went over to see Dick Sheppard and found there Maud Royden and Herbert Grey. They talked over the whole question of disarmament, and Ponsonby explained to them disarmament by example. He expected to see an early breakdown in the World Disarmament Conference, which was due to meet in February 1932, and persuaded the others to join him, in that event, in stamping the country. After receiving a pessimistic account of conditions in Germany from General Montgelas, he wrote that the return of a deliberate policy of unco-operative and provocative nationalism was likely to encourage both Communists and Fascists. For his part, he told Montgelas:

> Do not blame me, therefore, if I go back to my policy of extreme pacifism – disarmament by example accompanied by refusal on the part of the individual to participate in another orgy of massacre. I am absolutely justified in thinking that there is no other way, no halfway house, no possibility of agreement on the part of the government to discard the war weapon. At the same time, my only hope comes from contact with the common people, who, whenever I address them on the subject, are in enthusiastic agreement with me.[1]

He made his first Disarmament speech for some time at Stockport on 30 November, and, after an enthusiastic meeting, concluded that this really was his line of activity rather than the almost ceaseless round of meaningless meetings and consultations of current politics. So, early in December, when he received an invitation to become Chairman of the War Resisters' International, with Albert Einstein as President, after talking the matter over with George Lansbury, he decided to accept. If Henderson disapproved, then he was prepared to resign the leadership of the Opposition in the Lords.

The War Resisters' International had been founded in 1921 to co-ordinate socialist pacifism. It was run on a shoestring by its secretary,

H. Runham Brown, from a suburban Enfield house. The British section of the WRI was the No More War Movement (NMWM), the successor to Fenner Brockway's No Conscription Fellowship, which had been wound up at the end of the Great War. This organisation was, like most pacifist societies, extremely small, with only a few thousand members distributed in something like 100 branches throughout the country. Ponsonby, who after his Peace Letter campaign, was the only national figure in the peace movement, was undoubtedly a great catch for the WRI. His appointment also presaged a much more active future for the WRI, for Ponsonby would not be content to let the organisation carry on simply as a referral service for conscientious objectors.

The long-awaited opening of the World Disarmament Conference in Geneva had brought the question once more to the forefront of public interest. The committee of the WRI decided that the opportunity was too good to miss, approved of Ponsonby's initiative in raising disarmament in the Lords, and agreed to send the two leaders to Geneva. Over tea in the Runham Browns' suburban sitting room, Ponsonby found Einstein's simplicity and directness most appealing. 'He always understood exactly what one meant and (a very rare thing in a great man) he *listened*.' Ponsonby's motion on disarmament was debated shortly before the trip to Geneva. In a long, three-quarters of an hour speech, which was, as usual reduced by *The Times* to just one small paragraph, Ponsonby attacked the Geneva approach to disarmament. Qualitative disarmament was condemned root and branch as a half-way house that would only lead to trouble. Ponsonby argued that there were two logical opinions on the question of armaments. At one end of the scale, there was the man who, believing that war was inevitable, wanted to be possessed of the best weapons available, and, at the other end of the scale was his position, which was also logical and intelligible. It was that

> war settles nothing; that victors and vanquished alike suffer and nobody really wins; that the loss which is inflicted on nations by the destruction of their youth is so irreparable, a loss that no nation ever really recovers from it, but for generations that loss is suffered. I believe that modern warfare has reached a pitch of destruction where civilisation is in danger.

Ponsonby then asked the Lords to consider Great Britain renouncing war. The declaration was to be followed by gradual disarmament. He was prepared to run the risk that in this stage of partial disarmament, an aggressor might attack, but he discounted the idea as public opinion would never tolerate an aggressive move.

> If a country has declared that it is disarming and has disarmed and intends not to use the war weapon, then if any other country attacks that country it is a self confessed aggressor and at this stage in the world's history it would not get its people to support it.[2]

If this was impractical idealism, he preferred it to the positive futility of Geneva. In his peroration at the end, he said 'We have decorated our capital with the statues of great Generals and Admirals, but I do not think in the future we are going to put up a statue to the man who successfully presses the buttons . . .'

Ponsonby and Einstein left for Geneva on 22 May. Einstein's poor English and Ponsonby's less-than-perfect German produced an uneasy flow of conversation. They travelled overnight, Einstein chuckling in his sleeper over the German edition of *Falsehood in Wartime*, 'I had to suppress my laughter as I looked down from my upper berth at Einstein's ebouriffe [tousled] head under me at the curious position I was in.' Their programme had been arranged before they left London, but the unexpected happened and Madariaga, the chairman of the Air Commission, spotted them in the gallery and invited them to luncheon.

> I rather expected he would defend the League proceedings, instead of which he ridiculed them in a way I should never have dared to and Einstein and I felt very much reinforced in our view. The conversation turned, towards the end, to space time. M. kept his end up well and I listened all ears and was able to follow though, of course, I wasn't such a fool as to venture any remark.[3]

Ponsonby also saw Henderson, the chairman of the Conference, who was ill, and angry with Ponsonby for his Lords' speech. He was told off. His methods would not work and the only approach that offered any chance of success was that of the League. 'So I came away scolded by my master and the little incident will probably send me off on my own tack.' The press meeting followed in the afternoon in the foyer of the hotel, for want of funds to hire a room. They each spoke for about 10 minutes, and then answered a fusillade of questions from about 60 to 70 reporters. Ponsonby called for a programme, similar to that proposed by the Russians, of complete disarmament within five years, including the abolition of conscription, the cessation of recruiting and the manufacture of munitions and weapons. If this was impractical idealism, it had the massive support of popular opinion, which would, in the long run, be more influential than the barren discussions taking place at Geneva. Einstein said that it was absurd to think that one could abolish war or lay down how war should be waged by rules. There is no technical method to avoid war. The only thing that counts is the will in no case to take part in war.

Einstein and Ponsonby parted after the press conference, Einstein to go to Berlin and Ponsonby back to London. On reflection, he wrote in his diary:

> As to what publicity all this will have, I don't know. But I think it will have its use in showing them that the simple direct aim is really what is in peoples'

minds and the tangle of technical obscurities is regarded outside with extreme impatience.[4]

As to his own future in the Labour Party, he came to the conclusion that Henderson was unfit to lead; his long recital of his symptoms of ill health with which he regaled Ponsonby at Geneva had sounded like 'an old man in a workhouse ward', and he had become constitutionally orthodox and conservative. With such unimaginative leadership and lack of drive, he more than ever meditated upon the necessity of getting free from the trammels of the party, in order to press his views on disarmament. He drafted a letter of resignation for the consideration of Lansbury, carefully pointing out that he needed freedom to speak on disarmament, both inside and outside the House, and coupled with this was a protest against Henderson retaining the chairmanship of the Labour Party while he was chairman of the Disarmament Conference. The Executive of the parliamentary Labour Party, however, refused Ponsonby's resignation, and he wrote only privately to Henderson informing him of his attempted resignation.

His energies were all concentrated on disarmament. In addition to his House of Lords' speech and his trip to Geneva, he prepared a radio talk in the BBC's Conversations in the Train series on disarmament and then prepared a dialogue which was published in the autumn.[5] In all these pieces, Ponsonby put the case for disarmament by example. If his earlier advocacy of unilateralism had been qualified, his writings in 1932 were much more definite in appealing for a unilateral move on the part of Great Britain, as a last chance to break the Geneva deadlock. If *The Times* continued to give him short shrift, he had no reason to complain of his reception at the Fabian summer school on 4 August, the anniversary of the declaration of war in 1914, when his appeal for disarmament by example was enthusiastically endorsed.

Family Affairs

As usual, the Ponsonbys spent their summers at Shulbrede. Occasionally, they took extended motor journeys, once making a tour of the West Country, and, on another occasion, motoring through Suffolk, they visited Matthew and Bess and the grandchildren. They also visited Johnnie in Cumberland who, after he had retired from the army had, in 1929, bought back the original family home, Haile Hall. Mostly, they restricted themselves to day trips to favourite places in Sussex. They liked the barren seascapes of Selsey Bill, even more in winter than in summer, and had got into the habit of making an excursion to the coast on Dolly's birthday. On one famous occasion in 1927, they were enchanted by a flock of terns:

> We went off via Chichester to Thorny Island and sat down in the shelter of the shore just by the church and had our sandwiches. The water was low in dark blue streaks cutting into the brown green mud in the distance the spire of Chichester the hills and landscape red and grey with bands of pale yellow dead grass – wonderfully beautiful infinitely more beautiful than it would be in summer. A gull or two attracted our attention and then we were given one of the most lovely sights I have ever seen – small birds white breasted flew up the water from the sea in a long broad ribbon which waved and curled and as they rippled the sun caught their white breasts and they sparkled like diamonds. It was almost like fireworks and the beauty of the motion of their flight was wonderful. At one time a small flock of 50 or so of them came quite close to us and they walked on the mud in quest of their food. One of them seemed to give the signal that there was a better catch a few yards on and the whole flock immediately gave the most marvelously graceful little whirl in the air and alighted again. All the time little showers of sparkling diamonds caught our eye far off sometimes rising up like a broad glittering veil sometimes waving along ribbonlike out of sight. D got her feet deep in the soft muddy sand walking along a narrow path out towards the water . . . On the way home we lingered by the Wren house in Chichester. A most perfect day.[6]

In the summer of 1932, the attractions of nature suddenly palled, when the local Shulbrede wildlife attacked Dolly's garden.

> <u>Rats</u> were troublesome.
> <u>Mice</u> finished off the peas and bulbs.
> <u>Slugs</u> in armies owing to the wet have finished off several beds.
> <u>Moles</u> destroyed both the lawns.
> <u>Rabbits</u> in spite of the wire have finished off all the phloxes, some Michaelmas daisies and other things.
> <u>Sheep</u> came in and strolled about the garden.
> and the latest is the worst of all <u>a deer</u> gets in eats apple trees and devours a number of plants.[7]

September 21, 1932, marked the 100th anniversary of his mother's birth, and, to commemorate the day, Arthur cut out some of her sketches from a scrapbook, framed them, sent them to all the family, and also to their old family friend, Freda Biddulph, and Lord Halifax, who at 94 was probably the last surviving contemporary of Lady Ponsonby. He had the most charming letters in reply, including one from Halifax, who wrote, 'to my thinking, she was just the cleverest, most attractive and delightful person I have ever known'. Arthur also reflected on how his mother would have reacted to the 1930s. 'Her method of not condemning but simply ignoring the vulgar, the coarse, and the stupid was so right. But I wonder today if she would have been able to do it when these three, in their most acute forms, press themselves on one's notice day in, day out'.

These remarks are in marked contrast to the feelings of optimism and well-being that had attended the double wedding year of 1929. They relate specifically to an unsavoury incident connected with a young protégé of Dolly's, John Strachey, a cousin of John Evelyn Strachey, who had come to live at Shulbrede in 1930, and also inevitably to Elizabeth. John Strachey was an artist and in his studio at Shulbrede he had painted what Ponsonby considered to be an obscene nude portrait. 'I am no use with the modern generation. What is called their honest frankness seems to me to mean only drunkenness, doping, harlotry . . .' If Ponsonby despaired of the young, Elizabeth's continuing problems fully justified his attitude. Elizabeth's marriage had not altered her lifestyle one whit. Denis Pelly was a weak character, incapable of holding down a job, so that Ponsonby found himself in short order responsible for two rather than one person's debts. The round of extravagant parties and high jinks of the Bright Young People continued unabashed until the onset of the Depression finally put an end to the publicity which had increasingly become the *raison d'être* of the cult. Perhaps the last word on the Bright Young People was said by Evelyn Waugh in 1930 when he published his second satirical novel, *Vile Bodies*, whose heroine, Agatha Runcible, was based partly on Babe Plunket Greene, but mainly on Elizabeth.[8]

There is no evidence that Ponsonby read Waugh's novels. Had he done so, he might have been more understanding, but probably not any more sympathetic. Waugh had finally come to terms with life through a conversion to Roman Catholicism, a conversion inspired at least in part by Gwen Plunket Greene. Gwen's Catholicism only irritated the Ponsonbys. Lady Maud's sister, Mary, had married Baron Friedrich von Hügel, the Catholic theologian. Uncle Freddie had died in 1925. Ponsonby quite liked him, especially when he told him that 'he was not going to be the Almighty's housemaid tidying up things and putting them in a different position to what they were before'. He had converted Gwen, who shortly after his death, was received along with Olivia into the Church of Rome. Gwen, with all the enthusiasm of the newly converted, began to prepare a book from the letters she had received from her uncle. From the secular world of Shulbrede, these activities were viewed with extreme distaste. Arthur had recognised Dolly's uncle as an amiable fraud, who like George Wyndham in politics had achieved an extraordinary, but wholly unwarranted, reputation. The ecstatic, unintelligible mysticism of Gwen's introduction to Von Hügel's letters[9] was noticed in Ponsonby's diary, but his real indignation was reserved for her attempts to convert Lady Maud Parry, who, in 1928, had had the first of a series of strokes, and a further publishing venture in which Gwen proposed to write about Sir Hubert. No wonder he was writing in 1930 that family matters are most trying. Lady M utterly wild but very well, wearing down all who come in contact with her, almost an Edgar Allen Poe story. Gwen unapproachable, soused in her R. Catholicism. M and Bess getting into their house. E and Denis deep in debt, irresponsible and constituting themselves into what will be a leakage for the rest of our lives.[10]

Gwen was only headed off in her attempt to convert Lady Maud. She brought out a book on Sir Hubert Parry, in which she 'used her father as a peg on which to hang mild self disparagement and egotism and washy religious platitudes'. The Elizabeth problem continued unabated, until, quite suddenly, one day Elizabeth came down to Shulbrede and announced, almost as an afterthought, that she was going to divorce Denis Pelly. Ponsonby was astute enough to realise that the divorce would make little change in her habits and outlook. Divorces took a year in those days, but long before it was completed, Elizabeth, quixotic and fey, was swinging along with a new cast of boyfriends. Michael Gilmour, a friend of both Matthew and Elizabeth, understood Elizabeth better than most, when he remarked that 'you expect to find her waiting at the prison gate when you come out'. At the baptism of Matthew's son, Thomas, one of the godparents arrived almost late. 'Elizabeth, prayerbook in hand, was ready to take her place and said it was a case of the fairy godmother coming in and taking the baby from the wicked godmother.'

As part of the economy moves arising from Elizabeth's extravagances, Ponsonby had given up to the Pellys his Smith Street house, taking himself when in London to 17 Kensington Square where he was able to keep an eye on Lady Maud. One day, not long after Lady Ponsonby's 100th anniversary, Ponsonby recorded the following poignant scene:

> Thomas came to Kens. Sq. D was up and E came to luncheon and was too charming with Thomas who adored her. He was in great form rolling apples about and investigating every corner. Poor old Lady M just seemed to see him but no more, she is very vacant now. The little boy of 2 was as yet unable to express himself and also the old lady of 81.[11]

Lady Maud died the following February. She was cremated and the funeral rites were performed at Wilton, where, owing to Dolly's vigilance in having prevented a death-bed conversion to Catholicism, they were able to be 'pleasantly united' with the Greenes. They had as recently as September 1932 been to Wilton for the funeral of the younger son of Mungo and Belle Herbert, whom Arthur had known as a small boy at Constantinople. They found the assembled mass of Pembroke relations almost impossible to untangle. In what turned out to be a winter of funerals, Ponsonby also lost his old Downing Street colleague, Vaughan Nash. He went to the funeral, an altogether different affair to that at Wilton.

It was a marvellous day, the low sun illuminating trees and hills, woods and grey walls with a soft and lovely light and the cows looked on, and there was just enough breeze to prevent me hearing what the clergyman was saying. Just a few: Dick Massingham, the Hammonds and friends from Woodgreen and brother and sister.[12]

The Challenge of Fascism

Not the least of Ponsonby's problems with pacifism was that individual initiative such as he had undertaken in the Peace Letter had failed for want of organisation. He knew that if he was to be effective, it had to be as part of a progressive movement. The trouble was that united action among progressives appeared to be impossible. In the political field, the greatest parliamentary force of modern times, the Liberal Party of 1906, had dwindled to nothing, the Labour Party was split by MacDonald, and the Independent Labour Party rent with internal dissension. If such a thing were possible, the peace movement was even more divided. The pacifist World Anti-War Congress, which met in Amsterdam in August, had been marked by vehement Communist attacks on 'bourgeois pacifism'. The No More War Movement was itself rent by personal squabbles and the appointment of the argumentative Reginald Reynolds as its new general secretary, instead of Ponsonby's friend Stella Retinger, E.D. Morel's daughter, only made things worse, for he was a supporter of Gandhi and one of his first acts had been to send out a circular letter in support of non-resistance. Ponsonby was adamant that Tolstoyan non-resistance was detrimental to the peace movement which, in his opinion, should stick to anti-international war work, and not get mixed up in civil war and revolution. The future for both the peace movement and for Ponsonby was not clear. He stayed above the incessant and protracted bickering in the NMWM, contenting himself with a protest, which he sent to Harold Bing, a sympathetic member of the executive. As for the Labour Party, he decided not to throw over leading the Opposition, although it would have eased his financial situation considerably not to have had to run a London house, for the time being he felt that his own small contribution was still worth while.

In November 1932, Ponsonby went up to Sheffield to preside over the annual conference of the NMWM. He found that the movement was not very easy to manage, being split into at least four sections: Tolstoyans, Communists, socialist revolutionaries and anti-Labour Party men. He spent his time trying to convince them that they should pull together on making positive contributions to a Peace Book, instead of wrangling over whether or not revolution was a necessary prelude to pacifism. Unfortunately, in his speech, he referred, without names and dates to the fact that Great Britain had recently been very near war. This reference to the Ruhr crisis of 1923 was taken up by the press, and given great publicity. Just before going to Sheffield, he had broadcast on the BBC on the thoughtless type of public school boy.[13] This was also sensationalised by the press, so that on his return to Shulbrede, he found himself submerged in explanations, recriminations, and sacks of mail, not only from Britain, but also from North America, as the broadcast had been hooked up to an American network. He heard from Fritz that he was again being criticised at court, and the King said that now that Arthur was in the Lords, he should stop waving the red flag. 'I suppose he thinks I do it just to be peculiar, he doesn't understand that I believe what I say.'[14] At the Webbs, he met a vastly amused Bernard Shaw and his political friends thought the speech a great success. McNeil Weir and his wife, after listening to the broadcast, got up and shook hands in their delight at the end. Even more hilarity followed, after the BBC engaged Lord Peel to 'answer' Ponsonby. It was all inconsequential, and characteristic of the quirky side of the English character.

Further amused embarrassment came close on the heels of his broadcast. He was asked to give away the prizes at Midhurst Grammar School, and, unrecognised in his battered car, parked it away from the school and walked up. He found the boys, the guard of honour, and the headmaster who, waiting for *Lord* Ponsonby, shook hands and sent him straight through, while they continued to wait on the steps for a shiny car and somebody who looked like a Peer. To add further irony to the situation, it should be noted that 1932 was also the centenary of the Great Reform Bill. Arthur had a print of Grey hung outside the Leader of the Opposition's room in the House of Lords, a position Grey had occupied before becoming Prime Minister.

The mood of the pacifist movement in 1933 tended to be more isolationist in the face of the unpromising international outlook created by the Nazi takeover in Germany. Few people, other than the Jewish community, reacted strongly against Hitlerism, rather the mood of the nation was reflected in the King and Country debate of the Oxford Union, when a massive majority voted in favour of the motion 'that this House will in no circumstances fight for King and country'.[15]

The enormous attention paid to this student debate says quite a lot about the undiminished class bias built into English society. Fleet Street and Oxford were part of the establishment and what happened in Oxford, from its sporting activities to its juvenile politics in the Union, were assiduously and faithfully reported by Fleet Street. The new medium of communication, the BBC, was also extremely establishment-minded, and this worked both for and against Ponsonby. As the acknowledged expert on Diaries, he had made his first broadcast on keeping a Diary in December 1927. The power of the new medium was instantly revealed when Shulbrede was deluged with letters and diary manuscripts for evaluation from all over the country. In 1928, he had broadcast an appreciation of Sir Henry Campbell-Bannerman; this was followed by a conversation on the flapper vote with Elizabeth, which his producer called 'the best conversation they ever had'. Women between the ages of 21 and 30 were to be allowed the vote for the first time in the forthcoming general election. The breakthrough into regular broadcasting occurred after his casual observations talk on 31 December 1930, which was taken up by the press and favourably commented upon. After his Conversations in the Train talk on disarmament, he contracted to do a monthly talk, which became hugely successful, especially when, on 15 November 1932, he made his broadcast on the Public Schools. While this talk was controversial, it was not politically sensitive.

Ponsonby was soon to find out that his monthly talk was not going to be allowed to venture into this area. Like everyone else, Ponsonby took note of Hitler's appointment as German Chancellor on 31 January 1933. 'Hitler appointed Chancellor. We have driven Germany to this swing to the Right. It is dangerous . . . the outlook is black' and, throughout the year, he heard from various quarters of disturbing events in Germany. He was most struck by Leger, the Socialist German deputy, who spoke to the Labour Party, who believed that the régime must fall because so many of the leading Nazis were just ordinary criminals. He had been imprisoned by the Nazis for collecting signatures for 'the Ponsonby letter'. Ponsonby listened, but did not comment upon Noel Buxton's view that Britain should not adopt a too hostile anti-German attitude, which would only be used by Hitler to strengthen his hold on the German people. He heard from Roger Fry's sister, Joan, that the German people had no idea of what was going on in their own country, as the stories of the ill-treatment and internment of socialists, Communists, and Jews were only reported abroad. He also heard from many pro-Hitler Fascist sympathisers and was seriously concerned about the spread of Nazi ideas in Britain. He wrote in his diary:

> Although the session is over it is doubtful whether politics will give us a pause for long. There are strong tendencies showing themselves. Although England has not always been influenced by continental movements their repercussions have been felt and in the smaller world of today it is not impossible that they will be felt more strongly.
>
> The Russian revolution and its consequences have certainly influenced thought in this country (the books the Lancing boys were taking out to read were 75% on Russia). Curiously enough it has not strengthened the Communist movement because they went too far and showed they were under Russian dictatorship and that is a thing no one will stand.

But apart from that Mussolini is commanding a good deal of respect from unsuspicious people and although his dictatorship is personal (unlike the russian) the methods are similar. His cleverness lies in managing to conceal from other countries his cruelties and suppressions to a large extent. Hitler denounced with vehemence at first is gaining support here. His stupid mistake with the Jews already shows signs of being forgotten. His treatment of Communists, Socialist and Pacifists greatly approved. So at both extremes the dictatorship idea is being approved and the Communist menace and the Fascist menace are made the excuse for stronger and more expeditious powers. fortunately there is not only no dictator but an inherent mistrust of a dictator in the British people. Much depends on getting back to clear cut party politics.[16]

A small gesture to get back to clear cut party politics on Ponsonby's part was the idea of a radio talk on a possible British dictator. This, the BBC immediately turned down. 'They are so consumed with caution, they cannot accept anything with pepper in it.' Instead, Ponsonby broadcast an excellent little talk on small things and their importance, which brought down on Shulbrede another sack of mail.[17]

Ponsonby's broadcasting popularity and the astonishing success of his biography of Queen Victoria, which had been near the top of the best seller lists in 1933, gave him a more important public platform for his pacifist views than his seat in the House of Lords. Unlike the situation in the mid-1920s, when Ponsonby had been entirely alone, the peace movement had attracted a number of young, brilliant and enthusiastic recruits in Beverley Nichols, Vera Brittain, Storm Jameson and A.A. Milne. These people looked up to Ponsonby. Nichols wrote, in October 1933, that he had often gained hope and inspiration from Ponsonby's example, and, incidentally, told him that *Cry Havoc* was getting into all sorts of places; because of his previous book on gardening, quantities of bloodthirsty old women had eagerly purchased it under the impression it was all about begonias.[18]

Ponsonby was very active, in 1934, in combatting what he saw to be the delusions of the internationalist position. The Disarmament Conference, which Ponsonby and Einstein had failed to wake up in May 1933, as predicted, became bogged down in arid qualitative formulae and the advent of Hitler did nothing to increase its chances of success. The French had used the conference to state their case once more for security before disarmament, and proposed the creation of an international police force. The British government were then faced with the difficulty, given their isolationist stance, of making a real commitment to collective security. While more meaningless formulae were being worked out, Hitler ordered the German delegation out of Geneva. The emphasis of the international-ists now shifted away from disarmament towards collective security through the means of either an international police force, or an international air force, based on pooled security and collective action.

Ponsonby, who had rejected the use of force by an international authority almost twenty years before, in the discussions of the Bryce Group, regarded these efforts as both undesirable and impractical. He spoke in the same sense in the Lords on 15 March 1934.[19] As always, he thought the internationalists had grasped the stick from the wrong end. He continued to advocate disarmament by example. The Labour Party, at its annual conference at Southport, adopted the Henderson line, and passed a resolution supporting collective security. Ponsonby contemptuously described it as 'the League of Nations Union policy wrapped up in socialist platitudes'. He opposed the executive, but to no avail, as the left wing of the party was impotent, and Lansbury kept very quiet, agreeing with Ponsonby's protest in private, but refusing to take a stand. For the time being, Ponsonby accepted the situation as it was. He was able to follow his own line and was prepared to work with all sections of the peace movement. In June, he had appeared on a platform with Gilbert Murray and Bob Cecil under the auspices of the National Peace Council. He noted that war resistance and disarmament by example seemed to go down better than anything else with their audience. This was because of the general apprehension of war that had seized the public's imagination. Far away at the remote and isolated watering hole of Wawal, on the Abyssinia-Italian Somaliland border in Africa, an incident presaged a real war, which would soon destroy the temporary unity of the National Peace Council.

Early in June 1934, Arthur heard that his sister Maggie was ill. She seemed to be making a recovery, when he was summoned by telegram to Hove. An hour after he arrived, his sister was dead. Maggie was, in some ways, as unconventional as Arthur. She never married. After her mother died in 1916, 'despondent and lonely she turned into St Martin's . . . she met Dick Sheppard and it is not too much to say that he made the whole difference to the rest of her life,' and for twenty years, she devoted herself to the poor and needy of the parish. So it was through Maggie that Arthur first met Dick Sheppard.

After hearing that Sheppard had praised him to the St Martin-in-the-Fields' congregation from the pulpit in July 1917, a meeting was arranged, and they soon became good friends, in spite of the fact that Arthur did not believe in any of the supernatural doctrines of the church; but then, Dick Sheppard was no ordinary parson. Arthur even made the unprecedented gesture of going to hear Sheppard preach, and was struck by his simplicity and sincerity. In March 1922, he attended the pageant at St Martin's and noted the remarkable way in which Sheppard inspired enthusiasm. Sheppard signed Ponsonby's Peace Letter, 'saying "I expect you are right, it must be a complete and uncompromising refusal" and added that this certainly ought to be the attitude of the church. As years passed, this seed under his care and attention was destined to develop some growth.'[20] Sheppard's health was never good, he suffered from asthma, and after a breakdown had forced his resignation from the Deanery of Canterbury, he came to live near Shulbrede at Seale. At this time, Sheppard was too ill to be of any use. After a visit one Sunday afternoon in July 1931, Ponsonby wrote that 'he was far from well in looks, but full of life internally and very keen about disarmament. If only he were well when the time comes to go out again he and I might do much together.' Two months later, the idea of Sheppard's addressing a series of meetings was raised, but he was still too ill to go out. Herbert Grey and Maud Royden were both at this meeting. It turned out that 'the lady [Maud Royden] was not as reliable as he [Sheppard] thought she was' and so nothing came of the move. Sheppard recovered his health with the aid of an inhaler. (Ponsonby put it down to his having his teeth out.) Ponsonby took no part in Sheppard's Peace Army, regarding it as simply too fantastic. He did, however, agree to sign Sheppard's peace pledge.

The peace pledge was launched in October 1934 and immediately ran into the same organisational difficulties that had plagued Ponsonby's earlier campaign. The volume of pledges finally convinced Sheppard to launch the Sheppard Peace Movement with a great rally at the Albert Hall in July 1935, attended by over 7,000 mostly young supporters. The peace pledge was also, to a certain extent, in competition with the Peace Ballot of the League of Nations Union, an altogether bigger affair, which collected over 11 million answers and whose results were published on 28 June 1935, shortly before Mussolini's decision to invade Abyssinia finally forced the peace movement to come to terms with collective security.

Through the summer of 1935, efforts were made in the League to arbitrate the Italian-Abyssinian dispute, and it seemed possible, in spite of Italian troop movements to East Africa, that a peaceful solution might be possible. Public attention in Great Britain was concentrated on the political level on the Government's White Paper on Defence, published on 4 March 1935, and at the social level on the Jubilee given to King George V. These two events perfectly illustrate the personal dilemma facing Ponsonby. At the close of the previous year he summed up his position after five years in the House of Lords when he wrote:

> It is a wonderful Tory institution! I can well understand how liberals going there have become Tories, the so called Liberal Party there now are ardent supporters of the present government. Our deserters have practically become Tories. It is done by kindness, by comfort, by ease and by subtle flattery and men fall like ninepins.
>
> I know the atmosphere, not unlike court and government offices and I know many of the men. They regard me with astonishment but as I am 'Eton and Oxford' and have got brothers etc. they know, they are simply amused at my being such a freak.

But how long shall I go on with it? It is an expense involving living in London. It interferes with my writing pursuits and although it is an adjunct of compulsory work that suits me and keeps me in close touch with politics, it leads nowhere. I'll go on till the General Election. The alternatives then will be going on again for another Parliament (1) in opposition (I dont know if I can stand it) or (2) in a government, unlikely, and I should hate it or (3) chuck the whole thing.

My peace propaganda calls me too and I am getting a bit too old to manage violent activity in all directions.[21]

This peculiar position was brought out again in an exchange of letters with Lord Londonderry, who wrote:

I have only felt sad when sometimes your speeches which are always in the best style, informing and, on occasion, very humorous, are tinged with a note of bitterness, which seems so inconsistent with your character, as I know it as you show it to me in a friendship which I value very highly.

Ponsonby wrote in reply, 'What you say about my bitterness is perfectly true. But it is, perhaps regrettably, fundamental from a political point of view.' The King found himself in a similar dilemma in coming to terms with Ponsonby's biography of Queen Victoria; the King and the Queen, he was told by Fritz, had given it surprised approval. As leader of the Opposition, he was called upon to speak about the King. He did it with such felicity and grace, in marked contrast to the speeches of Hailsham and Reading, that he found himself once more, as in 1928 when he had made a notable contribution to the Prayer Book debate, an embarrassing success, receiving letters of congratulations from the likes of Lord Salisbury and the Archbishop of Canterbury. The continued chorus of praise added to, rather than mitigated, Ponsonby's depression, for, while he was prepared to do this sort of thing and to do it well from a political standpoint, it was all irrelevant for what was important was not the celebration of the Jubilee, but peace and disarmament.

The Defence White Paper was produced by Hankey, the secretary to the Cabinet, on behalf of the Defence Requirements Sub-Committee of the Committee of Imperial Defence, which had been meeting almost continuously throughout 1934. The prevailing opinion in the committee was that Great Britain had already amply demonstrated disarmament by example, and, as no other country had been prepared to reciprocate, they should recommend a degree of rearmament to make the country safe, especially in the air. Hitler, who had been none too secretly rearming, took the opportunity to announce that conscription would be introduced in Germany to build an army of 36 divisions.

The Labour Party were divided on the Defence White Paper and held a meeting before the Commons debated defence on 22 May. Ponsonby found the attitude of the party extremely bellicose, some speeches almost reminiscent of 1914 because of the general detestation of Hitler. He agreed to toe the party line, which was to oppose rearmament and support collective security, stifling for the moment his personal doubts. In the Lords, he was violent, describing the government's policy as being reminiscent of the pre-1914 policy of national armaments. 'If we go up, Hitler goes up, and then we go up again, and so it goes on until there is an explosion.' He repeated the widely held view that there was no defence against air attack, so that what the government was in fact saying to Hitler was that if you bomb London, we will bomb Berlin.[22]

He became increasingly uncomfortable at his position in the party, his isolation only relieved by the support of George Lansbury. They were, however, only two in the face of a dominant Trade Union majority, and were prevented from taking any independent action by the Labour Party's need to present a united front with a general election expected at any moment, Ramsay MacDonald having handed over the Premiership to Baldwin shortly after the Jubilee. In private, he continued to assert an independent line. At a meeting in the Russian embassy at the end of July, he crossed swords with both Dalton, the leading exponent of collective security, and Citrine, who took the Trade Unionist line. While the gathering was prepared to listen to Ponsonby's strictures about the impracticability of collective security, they refused to go along with him because they regarded disarmament by example as even more impractical.

As the Abyssinian crisis grew more serious in August, Ponsonby decided to write to *The Times*.[23] The letter provoked a great deal of discussion; uniquely for a time, he found himself the subject of approval at Printing House Square, and his letter was broadcast by the BBC. The gist of his letter was that collective security, when put to the test, would prove to be a broken reed. Collective security would never be unanimous and, if Britain took the lead, she would soon find herself acting alone. The resources of diplomacy had not yet been exhausted and Britain should continue to work with France.

After Ponsonby's public disavowal of collective security he had no option but to go to a co-ordinating meeting of the three sections of the Labour Party held before the Trades Union Congress at Margate to state his case in person. For his pains, he was strongly attacked by Bevin, Dalton, and Citrine. After this defeat, he decided to give up his leadership of the Lords, before the annual conference of the Party, which, that year, was due to meet at Brighton. In a conversation with Lansbury, after the meeting, he found the old gentleman very despondent, trapped by his leadership. 'With me, it is different. I cannot possibly go on voicing majority opinion and I must in fairness give up my very inferior position of leader in the Lords. It is made easier for me now.'[24]

When the resignation was announced, the press made a great fuss, hoping to accentuate the split in the party, especially as Stafford Cripps had also independently decided to resign. The letters he received were almost entirely sympathetic, which buoyed his spirits, as he was rather dreading having to go before the Brighton conference. Cripps came to see him at Shulbrede and, after he left, Ponsonby could not help feeling that Cripps was just as unconvincing when he was on the same side as when he had been an opponent. His fears about Brighton were unfounded, for he was well received, although inevitably the block vote of the Trade Unions carried the day. His speech emphasised the impracticability of economic sanctions as against other speeches, which emphasised Capitalism v. Socialism and conscientious and religious disbelief in force. He asked 'What are you going to do and how do you suppose it can be done?' His feeling was that the small vote against military sanctions in no way represented the feeling of the party at large. Fortunately, he left the conference before Bevin's intemperate attack on Lansbury.[25]

Although Ponsonby found himself in company with some unusual and strange allies over collective security, it should be noted that his position was radically different from that of the right-wing opponents of the League, who wanted an independent foreign policy untrammelled by idealism. His position on the League and the use of force had been made clear in 1916, and he never departed from it. As far as enforcing sanctions against Italy, his argument was unanswerable as is readily apparent from the list of objections that he drew up early in November 1935.

1. As the League of Nations is not all-inclusive (three great nations being outside), as the operation of sanctions could not be unanimous and as *any* sanctions could not be undertaken immediately, I foresaw they would be ineffective and merely aggravate the situation.
2. The line between economic sanctions and military sanctions cannot be drawn. Blockade will probably become necessary.
3. If force of any kind is used, the chief burden will fall on Britain who will be (indeed has already been) pointed to as the chief enemy of Italy.
4. Italian people and Italian children will be the sufferers by sanctions. Those responsible for Italian policy will not feel them.
5. The enforcement of sanctions will *extend* instead of restrict the area of warfare.
6. Italian imperialism is no different from pre-war imperialism of other nations. As the method laid down by the Covenant cannot be carried out (now for the first time) effectively, it will lead to recriminations, quarrels and possibly conflict between the supposed co-operators.
7. The affairs of the world, the jealousy of nations, the claims and demands of governments cannot be regulated by force.
8. The Italo-Abyssinian dispute is not going to be settled either by Mussolini or by the League of Nations by the use of force.
9. The war should be restricted, every opportunity should be taken for mediation and a declaration should be made that a world conference under

the League should be specially called to deal with the African problems, economic claims, grievances of nations, the revision of the unjust Peace Treaties, and the opening up of markets of the world and extension of mandates under the League.

10. The causes of war, not the weapons to be used in war, should engage the immediate attention of the representatives of nations at Geneva.[26]

Ponsonby refused all invitations to speak in the campaign leading up to the general election, in spite of many invitations. His position was that he would be expected to say something about war and peace, which would be impossible without criticising the party. At the one non-political meeting he addressed during the election campaign, he lectured on the parliamentary state. Questions led from one thing to another, and a few words on disarmament by example were greeted with loud and spontaneous applause. So he kept silent. He predicted 100 to 130 Labour gains, which was very close to the result, which gave the party 154 seats against the 432 seats of the National Government. Ramsay MacDonald was crushingly defeated by Manny Shinwell. Ponsonby noted 'he has dished us not for one but for two elections. I can hardly feel sorry for him specially when he whines to the press.'

The fiasco of Baldwin's treatment of his Foreign Secretary, Hoare, had only the consolation of the government's abandonment of sanctions. Ponsonby spoke on the issue in the Lords on 19 December, where he enlivened the proceedings with an absurd but unintentional mixed metaphor. 'Had Mussolini been left to stew in his own juice,' he said 'he would have bitten off more than he could chew.' The imposition of economic sanctions would inevitably lead to military sanctions, which would do incalculable damage to Anglo-Italian relations. Mussolini could not fight a long war, and his defeat by being left dangling, would accomplish more than League policy. Peace, in his view, was more important than punishment, and the former would not be got by the latter.[27] Letters to *The Times* were now published almost at will. His letter of 27 February 1936, headed 'Some Questions and the Answer' provoked Gilbert Murray to such an extent that he scolded Ponsonby for being an absolute pacifist pledged never to resist evil. Ponsonby had, in fact, posed some very reasonable questions in his letter about the efficacy of collective security. He asked 'Should one uphold the Covenant of the League? Are we prepared to take risks for collective security? Should we prevent Mussolini from getting away with it?' etc. and answered 'Yes. Certainly with the sincere and unanimous and active support of all the nations of the world . . . as contemplated by the framers of the covenant. Otherwise. No.'[28]

The irony of being suddenly taken up by *The Times* after years of neglect did not escape Ponsonby. He knew full well that once Abyssinia was out of the way, his new friends would rapidly desert.

Hitler's Rhineland coup of 9 March 1936 sent Ponsonby hurriedly to the newsagents, where he anxiously scanned seven newspapers and was relieved to find that none of them believed the German reoccupation would lead to war. Ponsonby was not to know that the French and British governments had already decided not to make an issue of any German reoccupation of the Rhineland, expecting to be able to use their permission for reoccupation as a bargaining tool to control the pace of German rearmament. Hitler's initiative certainly took them by surprise, but only to the extent that it ruined their negotiating stance. Ponsonby spoke in the Lords about it and his diary deplored the consequent alliance with France. His opinion was that the alienation and isolation of Germany must eventually bring war. 'Of course, Hitler's cruelties are against him. But we are dealing with countries and peoples who last not with dictators who are gone tomorrow.'

As far as Labour Party policy was concerned, Ponsonby was much concerned that the party should not be drawn too tightly into the collective security net being cast by the Russians. 'Russia,' he wrote, 'is playing exactly the same old game as she did in Tsarist days and she is very clever at it. Maisky, the Russian ambassador has got the party and specially the Trade Unions in his pocket.' He went to a party meeting on 25 March and was reassured by the condemnation of the French alliance and warned both Attlee and Dalton of the Russian trap.

The news of the fall of Addis Ababa early in May led to a number of post-mortem debates on the failure of sanctions and collective security. Dalton, the spokesman of the party in the Commons for foreign affairs, talked of continuing sanctions, while Ponsonby, almost at the same time, was taking an entirely opposite position in the Lords. He decided to clear the air by writing to Dalton pointing out that all he had said about the inadequacy of sanctions had been proved true and party policy was now to continue sanctions, a foolish and slightly dishonest policy when everyone knew perfectly well that it was impracticable. The way to deal with the dictators was to remove all outside grievances and then they would have to rely on their internal policy, which in a short time would show them up.[29]

At this juncture, Ponsonby was approached by Dick Sheppard to become a Sponsor of the Peace Pledge Union (PPU), the new name of Dick Sheppard's Peace Movement as from 22 May 1936. Sheppard was anxious to widen the base of his organisation by recruiting non-religious, anti-war people. 'It would help enormously,' he told Ponsonby, 'for people like myself are only where we are by standing on your shoulders.' After receiving assurances that the PPU did not have a specifically religious bias,

Ponsonby agreed to allow his name to be put forward as a Sponsor. The sponsors of the PPU were required to attend monthly meetings. On 5 June 1936, Ponsonby wrote in his diary:

> Once more in dingy committee rooms trying to organize the anti-war movement with all the trump cards on the other side and a feeling that one is doing something wrong illegal disgraceful. This time Dick Sheppard seems to have energy drive and funds. Canon Raven was there Jimmy Hudson, Crozier who is odd and others. Plans good and undoubtedly we have a widespread anti-war feeling in the country to work on.[30]

Not content with this new activity, Ponsonby accepted an invitation to go to the inaugural Conference of the Parliamentary Pacifist Group, composed mainly of disgruntled Labour politicians led by Cecil Wilson. He found nearly 50 people there, 'practically everyone who counts', and they decided to draw up a manifesto to try and reach the tens of thousands who agreed with them.

Ponsonby chaired the drafting committee meetings, working with Henry Carter, H.F. Head, Runham Brown, Sorenson, Salter and Cecil Wilson. Wilson did most of the work and Salter tried everyone's patience with his buoyant, over-positive, self-assertive ways. Ponsonby was more than ever pleased to be associated with the work, when he went to a party meeting in July and found himself almost totally isolated, the field being held by Philip Noel-Baker persuasively advocating collective security, a League war, international air force and the strengthening of the Covenant. This did not prevent his putting down a motion in the Lords on sanctions and arguing very effectively against their continuation, leaving Strabolgi to defend the Labour case.[31]

He was still President of the War Resisters' International and attended its meetings of the British affiliate, the NMWM. He came to the not too difficult conclusion that the whole organisation would collapse without the indefatigable efforts of Runham Brown. The NMWM was in great difficulty over its attitude towards the Spanish Civil War, which had broken out in mid-July 1936. He wrote about the problem to Runham Brown, and also to Bertrand Russell with whom, quite recently, he had resumed relations after drifting apart during the 1920s. Russell asked Ponsonby to read his new manuscript on peace, eventually published as *Which Way to Peace*, telling him that he was out for complete unilateral disarmament and individual refusal to fight in any war between states. Ponsonby, in agreeing to read the manuscript, took the opportunity to put down his views on the problem of the Spanish Civil War telling Russell that the Spanish Revolution was the very devil for the pacifists. He went as far as to admit that if he were a Spaniard, he would help the government even by force of arms![32] The NMWM proved unable to withstand the tensions created by the Spanish Civil War and the defection of Fenner Brockway, who favoured supplying arms to the Republican Government, proved to be the forerunner of its total demise. While Ponsonby had always excluded civil wars from his pacifist position, others were unable to do so, and so, after a winter of acrimonious debate, a decision was made to wind up the affairs of the movement and to amalgamate with the PPU in February 1937.

Ponsonby's rapprochement with *The Times* survived the Abyssinian embroglio long enough for that newspaper to put a letter from Ponsonby on its editorial page on 15 September. Ponsonby was on holiday in Devon when a sympathetic *Times* leader encouraged him to write. Subsequently, he found that the leader had been written by Capt Liddell Hart, who told Ponsonby that he was 'continually reflecting with an ever-growing desire to find convincing arguments for the morally better case you uphold'. Liddell Hart had written what amounted to reflections on how the Democracies could confront the Dictators. If the Democracies had a case, it was a moral one and before adopting the line of Force v. Force, which amounted to accepting the Dictators' view of the world, the believer in defence by arms was obliged to try and understand the intellectual position of the pacifist. Ponsonby's letter asserted an uncompromising pacifism. He opposed Defence because it led to arms races, which always culminated in war. He was prepared to say 'Halt'. 'Someone should refuse to participate directly or indirectly and someone in season and out of season should urge the government to abandon the weapon of violence and take the lead in the world by turning its back on war such as science has now made it.' If he urged complete disarmament as a surer defence for freedom than rearmament, he did so not because he did not understand the realities of power politics, but because he felt the need to state the moral case against war.[33]

General support for the PPU had risen in the autumn to about one hundred pledges a day, which gave considerable satisfaction, and Ponsonby had to start refusing invitations to talk at small meetings in order to save himself for the big occasions. One big occasion he purposely avoided that year was the Labour Party conference at Edinburgh. He vented his frustration at Labour policy, which, before the conference, he had unavailingly tried to influence through Herbert Morrison, in his diary, and in an article in *Forward*. Naturally, the diary entry was more unrestrained.

> The Labour Party is unspeakable. Go Jingo if you like and swallow all you are told, split the party and wave the flag or go definitely against armaments, war, the bunkum of collective security and the hysteria against Hitler and the party would have rallied. But at Edinburgh, the Executive speeches were trimming, vacillating, self contradictory, timid, feeble, forcible and hopeless.[34]

It was not all plain sailing at the PPU, however, for the very success of the movement brought inevitable tensions within the leadership. The PPU was Dick Sheppard. The man's extraordinary charisma brought together an extremely talented, but diverse, group of Sponsors, as has already been noticed. It included, among others, Vera Brittain, Aldous Huxley, Laurence Housmann, Storm Jameson, George Lansbury, Rose Macaulay, Stuart Morris, Max Plowman, Charles Raven, Bertrand Russell, Alfred Salter, Siegfried Sassoon and Donald Soper. For Ponsonby, the main problem was the undoubted predominance of the Christian pacifists in the movement. At an Albert Hall meeting in November 1936, he noted that the audience regarded it more or less as a religious gathering. He felt uncomfortable speaking under the protection of an odour of sanctity, although prepared to concede that Soper could bring the house down with God and Jesus. At the Sponsors' meetings he was greatly impressed by Sheppard.

> In the chair, he drew out members whose advice he valued and by intensely amusing chaff overcame controversy and suppressed bores. I remember him one day in the chair making arrangements for the program of a mass meeting. Should there be a hymn. If so which? etc. He threw back his head and began singing an old favourite with such elan that it was impossible for others not to join in and pass nem con that item on the agenda.[35]

Undoubtedly, the early success of the movement in the 1936 and early 1937 period was due, not only to the ineffectiveness of the League of Nations in the Abyssinian crisis, but also to the widespread belief that the next war would be started by a rain of bombs obliterating London and other great cities all in one day. The way out for many pacifists, now that the League had proven to be a broken reed, was non-violence. Passive resistance derived from Gandhi and his American prophet, Richard B. Gregg, whose book *The Power of Non-Violence* appeared in an English edition in 1935. Non-violent resistance to war was soon labelled Greggism in the movement, and its emphasis on 'Yogi-Bogie' (a phrase of Max Plowman), soon aroused Ponsonby's antipathy towards faddists. He talked over the situation with Bertrand Russell, who told Ponsonby that the reason Aldous Huxley was supporting Gregg was because he was spoilt by having Arnold blood in his veins. Russell told him that 'he was going to invest his money in drink, because the love of drink was just stronger than the love of war and if further strengthened might prevent war'.[36]

The Greggism furore created a shake up in the central administration of the PPU and an executive committee, upon which Ponsonby agreed to serve, was set up in February 1937. Characteristically, nothing more was done about Greggism, other than to withdraw support for Gregg's pamphlet 'The Complete Pacifist', which Sheppard admitted to Ponsonby in an apologetic letter should have been edited more carefully.[37] The movement had really no option but to take a middle road if it was ever to become large enough to exert political influence. Clearly, this was Ponsonby's view, and the further success of the movement had become imperative with Labour's conversion to rearmament. Membership, however, stuck at about the 120,000 mark, almost exactly the number of signatures on the Peace Letter. Talk of a million pledges were to prove hopelessly over-optimistic. With or without faddists, the Peace Pledge Union only occupied a fringe position in the world of practical politics. Ponsonby very early on had noted that the atmosphere at the PPU reminded him of the UDC.

Much the same could be said for the War Resisters International. It had always held a big triennial conference. The 1934 conference had been held in England, the 1937 conference was scheduled for Copenhagen. Ponsonby decided to use the occasion to pass on his office to George Lansbury and went to Copenhagen, partly to help out, but largely because he had been there thirty-nine years before. Ponsonby read a paper in his rusty Danish, which had been vetted before he went out and pronounced to be 'paa fortrefelight Dansk' by the Copenhagen daily. The Conference was wonderfully stage managed by the Danes, with meetings in the Danish Parliament House and the Raadhus. There were 220 delegates from twenty-one countries, mostly, Ponsonby noted, cranks, but with a healthy contingent of Danes. Lansbury, having just returned from visits to Rome and Berlin, was strongly attacked by the left wing at the conference who were, according to Ponsonby, so consumed by their hatred of Fascism that they had forgotten their pacifism. When Lansbury over-reacted, threatening not to take over Ponsonby's chair, he had to use all his powers to persuade Lansbury to carry on. He doubted whether Lansbury's meetings with Hitler and Mussolini had done any good, although he felt he was right to try and extract some good out of the worst quarters. 'But behind all was the dream-like recollection of Copenhagen of nearly 40 years ago.'

Whatever hopes the PPU may have had of becoming an effective political force were dashed by the not-unexpected but nevertheless sudden death of Dick Sheppard on 31 October 1937. Sheppard had been to Shulbrede in September to talk over his tragic private life – Sheppard's wife had left him and his daughter, aged 16, had just been told she had cancer – and the death of General Crozier, who had been one of the most active of the PPU sponsors.

The blow of Sheppard's death could not have come at a worse time for Ponsonby, who had just returned from the annual Labour Party conference held in 1937 at Bournemouth. Before the conference, he had had a long talk with Sydney Arnold about the party's foreign policy. Arnold was contemplating resignation; Ponsonby was not yet ready for that ultimate step. As he put it in his diary, 'the cross-bench idea puts me off. I am more rootedly opposed to Toryism than he is.' At Bournemouth, the executive's support of the government's rearmament policy was criticised by both Lansbury and Ponsonby, who recorded that he was told that his speech was the only one which hit the nail on the head. Although he was buoyed by the conviction that many in the Labour Party had misgivings about the official line, there was no escaping the fact that he was isolated. His strong personal conviction that 'a militarized nation must undermine the foundations of Socialism' was not shared by the new leadership, which, in his opinion, lacked the fundamental drive of the old socialists. The party had 'blundered up the wrong road morally, intellectually, practically and electorally'. He was thankful that they had no chance of getting back into office in the immediate future.

Not surprisingly, it was just at this time that he decided to undertake by far his most ambitious and difficult literary project. After discussions with his brother Johnnie, it was decided that he should tackle Papa's life. Fritz had made a start with sorting the papers, and the other two brothers had expected that he would have written the biography, but Fritz had died rather suddenly towards the end of 1935. So Arthur began the daunting task of looking through 70 large boxes of papers. His estimate of five years' work was very near the truth and increasingly occupied and diverted his attention as the international situation deteriorated in the spring of 1938 after the relative calm of 1937.

Domestic Affairs

After serving as Sidney Webb's under-secretary in 1929, Ponsonby saw an increasing amount of the Webbs at Passfield Corner. Beatrice Webb was an even more prolific diarist than Ponsonby, and quite regularly both diarists wrote about their meetings.

> Ponsonby: 2 Feb 1935: Went over to tea with.Webbs. Horrabins there. Bernard Shaw told Webbs that in old age one either became scatter brained as he was or obsessed (as they were). She very well at 77, but increasingly garrulous. It is always difficult to get more than a couple of consecutive sentences in. Their gigantic Russian book is coming out in the Autumn. Their industry is abnormal, their vision specialised and restricted but there is something touching about them.

> Webb: 4 Feb 1935: Ponsonby dreads a Labour majority at the next election. He has a queer little team in the House of Lords, but is an admirable captain of this tiny force of reputables and disreputables in the citadel of inaction. He is not enthusiastic about Stafford [Cripps], he barely knows him and regards him as immature and rude in his thought and indiscreet in his expression. Ponsonby is first and foremost a pacifist. He accepts socialist economics but is not intellectually interested in socialist questions. On account of his moral refinement, culture, personal disinterestedness and undoubted charm of bearing and manner, reinforced by a long experience of human nature in politics, he is an asset to the parliamentary Labour party.[38]

Ponsonby: 31 Jan 1937: I went to tea with the Webbs. They were marvelously vigorous prompting one another in such a way as to make any intervention on my part difficult. They not only defended and excused but praised the Soviet trials and murders. The chief argument was that this is a necessity for a revolutionary government. The failure in Germany, Austria and Spain has been due to the fact that the left once in power never asserted themselves by polishing off their opponents in the same way! We managed to get on to other subjects and they were reasonable about the Labour Party, Stafford Cripps and his lack of political judgment and in hearty agreement about the Archbishop of Canterbury. On Peace they do not know the elements of the case and do not want to hear it.

It would seem that in Ponsonby's failure to appreciate Fabian socialism and the Webbs' disinterest in Peace, there was little common ground between the two couples. That they found time for each other, was largely due to the publication in the summer of 1936 of Ponsonby's book which he entitled *Life Here and Now; Conclusions Derived from an Examination of a Sense of Duration.* Ponsonby's thinking about time had gradually evolved into a home-spun philosophy of life which he called H & N, Here and Now. More than a few readers have found the book quite impossible, but not Beatrice Webb, who wrote that she found *Life Here and Now* surprisingly superior when compared to H.G. Wells' *Anatomy of Frustration* which was outstandingly inferior.

A sensitive aristocrat by birth and temperament and who has been considering his opportunities a partial failure as a politician. An amateur author and broadcaster, earning a precarious livelihood. A queer nondescript career of little apparent importance. And yet Ponsonby's book has a charm and wisdom and one lingers over its pages because of its refinement of thought and feeling in the delicacy and singular aptness of his style. It is a sort of spiritual autobiography and yields a vivid description of contemporary thought and feeling about home and world affairs in the governing class of Great Britain.[39]

The title of the book is drawn from an article on Tolstoy by H.W. Massingham. In discussing Tolstoy, Massingham had pointed out that 'man can act for his own well being, that he can act here and now and that his enlightened reason, his "rational consciousness" fully reveals to him the law of life in which he stands in need'.[40] The book is only indirectly concerned with pacifism, and as it is not mentioned until its last pages, it is rather hard to accept Ceadel's abrupt dismissal[41] of *Here and Now.* Ceadel's main thesis, that the peace movement had became, by the late 1930s, a faith and not a policy hardly jibes with Ponsonby's activist pacifism. He continued to believe that an individual decision to renounce war was a worthwhile act. If enough individuals spoke out, then individual decisions would have public consequences, so that for Ponsonby, at least, pacifism was both a faith and a policy.

Of much more concern to Ponsonby's life-long friend Jack Talbot was

Ponsonby's rationalist rejection of the Christian doctrine of the immortality of the soul. Their correspondence on the subject was only cut short by Talbot's untimely death in June 1937. In his reply to Talbot's opening letter which put forward the orthodox defence of Christian revelation, Ponsonby summarised his 'spiritual autobiography':

> I have passed through thoughtless childish acquiescence in what I was first taught to a more thoughtful Christian belief in moral values; then on to doubt as to whether these values were strengthened or weakened by the Supernatural background; and so finally to a consciousness that infinitely greater strength came once the supernatural with its very doubtful evidence and confusing and contradictory interpretations was wholly rejected.

Talbot concluded that, like Carlyle and Sterling, they had been 'arguing copiously but except in opinion not disagreeing'. Talbot had quoted Jesus' teaching that 'the Kingdom of God is within you'. 'This' Ponsonby said 'is precisely what I in another language and very lamely am trying to insist on.' He believed that the supernatural detracted from Jesus' precepts, and while recognising that moral standards may have changed, he doubted very much whether they had improved. 'New circumstances keep on arising which baffle us and nothing in man's history is worse than our acceptance of modern warfare.'[42]

All through their relationship, which went back to the auxiliary choir at Eton, the OUDS production of *Frogs* and 'Bebb's trunk', their relationship had been sustained by their extraordinary harmony in being able to leap from the serious to the absurd and back again; this, in spite of their widely different careers, for while Talbot had spent his official life in the obscurity of the Education Office without ambition for place or office, Ponsonby, as he himself admitted, had been infected by the careerism of politics. Their delight in the idiosyncrasies of character was shared with another close friend Charles Strachey, and together they popularised the word 'bogus', creating a Bogus League, with headquarters in Tintagel and a branch office in Stratford-on-Avon (Ann Hathaway's cottage). Membership of its various categories was limited to people 'who had just that trace of rather spurious and often quite successful aptitudes and qualities which gave them reputations and positions they did not really deserve'. The deliberations of the 'Selection Committee' were a source of great amusement. In addition to historical figures – Richard Coeur de Lion was Patron – the Selection Committee took particular relish in looking over *Crockford's Clerical Directory*, where traces of bogusness were found in abundance. One day a postcard arrived at Shulbrede 'Activities of the League' beneath which was pasted a newspaper cutting.

214

The Bishop of London announces that as next Thursday is the day of the Royal Wedding he grants dispensation for this occasion to those of the Churchpeople of his diocese who would otherwise feel bound to fast on the Vigil of St. Andrew.

Another rich field was politics. J. Ramsay MacDonald was Visitor, until displaced by the Emperor Haile Selassie, and Viscountess Snowden, President of the Women's Section. Logan Pearsall Smith assisted the Selection Committee with the artistic and literary world, and championed the case of 'Father' William Rothenstein, when he found his son, Dr John Rothenstein, had risen to Vice-president. Denis Pelly, whose indiscretions with a petty cash box had cost him his job with the Ministry of Works, was Auditor. The badge of the club was to be an obelisk, except that it was discovered that in ancient manuscripts an obelisk used to point out a spurious, corrupt, doubtful or superfluous word or passage was ÷ and not the spit, an Obelus, that they had in mind. It was decided to overlook the difficulty as the NED under 'Obelus' did refer to 'Obelisk'. This sort of thing is much more suitable than ÷ (see page 216).

The Ponsonbys' delight in the absurd and ridiculous also found expression in a book of cuttings put together by Dolly under the title 'The Book of Horrors'. Included among the 1935 mementoes of horror was a Christmas greeting card from Sir Samuel and Lady Maud Hoare (a studio portrait of the Hoares in court dress), a picture of Mrs Stanley Baldwin wonderfully overdressed at the Chelsea Flower Show and a postcard bearing the favourite maxim of King George V 'Teach me neither to proffer nor to receive cheap praise.' He last saw the King at the Jubilee celebrations, where he noticed that he was unwell. Of more immediate concern was the appearance of Fritz who looked at least as ill as the King. Fritz died in October 1935; the King in January 1936. While the brothers were poles apart in politics, Arthur always felt that he had only to ask to be helped and he liked to feel that he was there even if he did not see him very often.

Having paid a public tribute to King George V during the Jubilee celebrations, Ponsonby felt that he had done his duty and did not go to the Windsor funeral. There never had been any sympathy of outlook between the two men; the King had obstinately clung to the impressions left by the Garden Party incident and Ponsonby knew enough of the martinet quarterdeck atmosphere of the court to be concerned for the future of the monarchy. He did not himself know the younger generation of the Royal Family, but the circle of courtly friends of the family had provided enough information for concern. While no one doubted the new king's keenness on social reform, Edward's restlessness, obstinacy and curious friends all raised doubts. Ponsonby heard about Mrs Simpson during the summer of 1936 through Lady Minto and, after he had offered his political services

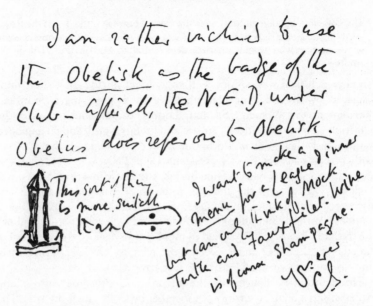

I am rather inclined to use the Obelisk as the badge of the Club — especially, the N.E.D. under Obelus does refer one to Obelisk.

This sort of thing is more suitable than ÷

I want to make a dinner menu for a League dinner but can only think of Mock Turtle and Faustfilet — wine is of course champagne.

Yrs ever W.Ch.

through Lord Hardinge to the King's new Secretary, Alec Hardinge himself broached the subject of the King and Mrs Simpson:

> He is evidently worried to death as the American press is awful, the Dominion and continental press getting worse and he cannot see how our own press can long be controlled. It is certainly extraordinary that the K with his undoubted intelligence, character and charm should flaunt public opinion with this second rate American woman who has now divorced her husband. The American press say: 'Ernest Simpson has laid down his wife for the King.'[43]

His interest was sufficiently aroused to go and see the King at the opening of Parliament. He saw very little except masses of Marchionesses with 'colossal tiaras like nursery fenders'. Then, late in November, he heard that real trouble was brewing for apparently the Cabinet had asked Geoffrey Dawson to write a leader in *The Times* which would open the press floodgates and, while the King was doing his job admirably, 'his obstinacy on the point is adamantine (like Q. Victoria and George III). I am quite sure he won't marry her. But I hope it will not resolve itself into a political question.'[44]

When the public were presented with the constitutional crisis on 3 December, he took the side of the King:

> I am not quite clear as to how far the P.M. and his ministers have a right to veto a King's marriage, because marriage it seems to be. At any rate it has never happened before in our history. If it reaches the stage of a political public

question while no party may support the King quite undoubtedly there will be a fairly large section of the population who will say 'Why shouldn't he marry whom he likes?'[45]

He clarified his own mind on the issues at stake in a long diary entry giving the pros and the cons of the situation for and against, of the King, of Mrs Simpson and of Mr Baldwin. For the King and Mrs Simpson was the fact that they were happily in love, against them that they had played their cards all wrong; for Baldwin the constitutional position was that Parliament must always, in the end, prevail over the King, but while 'no other minister would have done better than he has done . . . he is not the blunt honest man he pretends to be'.

The day after the abdication, he wrote:

It has all passed off on greased wheels, no hitch and the King has left the country! His broadcast last night was moving and pathetic in the extreme. I have so hated the sanctimonious hypocrisy and censoriousness, the rapid switch on of adulation and flattery to the new King and the easy abandonment of a popular and in some ways undoubtedly remarkable figure, that I have been torn in two. Luckily I did not have to speak.[46]

Among his friends, he found John Gore, who had recently completed a biography of George V, virulently anti-Edward, and Lord Rutland also thought him impossible, 'a six cylinder motor with four cylinders functioning perfectly and two completely broken'. His own view was much more sympathetic. He found Edward exactly like Elizabeth, 'remarkable qualities of courage, loyalty, fearlessness and entire inability to humbug, mixed with complete disregard for conventions and preference for dissolute frivolity'.

In May 1938, he had the benefit of a private discussion with Baldwin on the Abdication crisis in the garden at Wilton.

He referred once or twice casually to the Abdication crisis so at last I asked him about it and to my surprise he told me all the details, the anxieties, the possible crises, the personalities, some of them very strange, involved. What stood out was his liking of Edward. He said that there was a side of him which was entirely undeveloped, he acted like a child and major obligations of duty and morality were non-existent. He had no imagination. His infatuation for Mrs S obliterated part of his mind. His more intimate friends were hopeless advisers, he read the signs of opinion in press and party politics all wrong and he was impetuous and obstinate. His careless treatment of secret papers was most dangerous. He would have made a dangerous King although he might have done the functions well. As the crisis developed he said to B 'You don't mind my living with Mrs Simpson but you object to my marrying her. Isn't that rather hypocritical.' B found this rather a poser but got out of it by saying. 'There has always been a leniency regarding the private relations of Kings just because they are the only people subjected to strict regulation with regard to their marriages and wives.'

B dwelt on the possible upheavals which seem to loom on all sides. He was helped by the bad advice given to Edward, the impossibility of Mrs Simpson, the change in public opinion when they got to know about her, and more especially the absolutely frank talks he was always able to have with Edward himself.

He had wanted to abdicate much earlier when George V was ill. But once he became King he liked it but gradually found he was caged and his amazing infatuation gave him the spur to break through. B doubted if it would ever be possible for him to live in England and did not seem to think he wanted to. I said there would be another act to the episode as I thought it would be impossible for any human being to continue to live the life he was leading.

When I said I thought George V, his father, was as much responsible as anyone for Edward's upbringing and reaction towards a dissolute life, B more or less agreed. But of course had to deal with the crisis as it came to him. Undoubtedly he showed skill.

B has wisdom, nice ideas, and high ideals. He is pedestrian, too fond of moral tags and not very profound. His exceptionally friendly attitude towards me rather surprised me. There was much chaff at our pacing the garden for so long. They said we were forming a new party 'the Wilton group'![47]

Strangely enough, that same evening the conversation among the men turned on Elizabeth. David Herbert in particular championed her, saying that her reckless disregard of public opinion was a characteristic inherited from her Herbert grandmother. Ponsonby pointed to his great-aunt Lady Caroline Lamb for mad irresponsibility and penchant for the dissolute life. However, they were all loud on her courage and loyalty.

Elizabeth's peregrinations, which had recently included a 'sugar daddy' in the form of the 73-year-old Prince Henry of Pless, also took her into the world of films and film-makers. Ponsonby's interest in the theatre had changed direction over the years, for he no longer went to the West End theatre as much as in pre-war years, concentrating his attention on private amateur theatricals staged at Shulbrede for which he wrote the scripts with extraordinary felicity in a matter of hours. One day, Elizabeth just happened to mention this to the film producer, Mendes, who was about to make a film starring the famous Polish pianist Paderewski. The film's story was undeveloped and so Mendes approached Ponsonby and, after he had produced a story outline, asked him to join in the production as a literary assistant. Ponsonby's diary records one visit to the film set at Denham in September 1936. He met both Paderewski and Marie Tempest, who confided in Ponsonby that she was desecrating her art by acting in films. The film was released in May 1937, shortly after the coronation of George VI. Ponsonby, who had attended a private showing of the film, had high expectations that *Moonlight Sonata* would be a popular success. When it was released, he took Matthew and Bess, who did not like it, which gave Ponsonby pause for thought. So it turned out. Although an artistic success, the film crashed at the box office, not because of its title or its music, but because Paderewski's name put off the filmgoers. When the books were made up, the film did not make a penny and Ponsonby sadly reflected that it would teach him not to embark on business he did not understand.

Appeasement

In the winter of 1937–38, the new National Government of Neville Chamberlain grappled with Mediterranean issues arising out of the Abyssinian affair and the Spanish Civil War. The burden of work was borne by Anthony Eden, who had succeeded Hoare as Foreign Secretary in the previous Baldwin government. Ponsonby was much taken with Eden, and, in January 1937, he recollected, after hearing Eden speak, that he had seen quite a lot of him in 1924 and had then thought that he 'saw far beyond the superficial aspects'. He thought that Eden's resignation, purportedly over Chamberlain's refusal to act on a tentative American offer of help in Europe, but really over a difference of opinion on the appeasement of Mussolini, was badly handled by the government. He was in the House to hear the speeches and reached the conclusion that Chamberlain was right in attempting a new approach to Mussolini. The new Foreign Secretary was Edward Halifax, in whom Ponsonby also had great confidence. Halifax was a Peer, and also a second cousin, but relations between the two men, although cordial, were never close. He saw Halifax shortly after his appointment and told him that the supposed constitutional convention laid down by Campbell-Bannerman in 1905 that excluded the Foreign Secretary from the Lords was quite incorrect. In the course of the conversation, it was apparent to Ponsonby that Halifax knew nothing about Campbell-Bannerman and had no idea Ponsonby had been his private secretary.

The new team of Halifax and Chamberlain were put almost immediately to the test by Hitler's march into Austria in March 1938. When he heard the news, Ponsonby wrote 'So the fat is in the fire again.' He found the common expression to be 'What can we do?' He thought it unfair for some to blame the Prime Minister for his approaches to the Fascists, and condemned the renewed insistence on collective security on the part of the Labour Party as being more futile than ever. A Labour MP, Tom Johnston, said to him 'it is merely one dictator ousting another and it is no concern of ours'.[48] He had an opportunity to speak in the Lords, but declined, feeling it useless to inveigh against rearmament when he supported the government's diplomatic line. At the end of the month, he did speak against rearmament. The House listened, but no one paid the slightest attention.

After this, he decided not to speak in the Lords on the next foreign affairs debate on the Italian agreement. Instead, he listened and thought Halifax was admirable. He did not speak again, and then only briefly, until the end of July. Most of his time was devoted to sifting the enormous pile of Henry Ponsonby papers that, at times, threatened to engulf him. He attended quite regularly the PPU Sponsors meetings and at the June meeting came out on the side of the younger members, who wanted to be more active.

The Ponsonbys were on holiday in Dorset when the Czech crisis finally broke in September. He put his point of view quite succinctly in one sentence. 'It is hardly credible that we should fight Germany because she wants to protect or even incorporate 3,500,000 Germans into the Reich.' He described Chamberlain's decision to go to Munich as sensible and courageous. The Labour Party, which had become quite militant, was described as being furious at not having a smack at Hitler. He wrote 'I am sure Chamberlain is right.' He wrote a strong letter of support for Chamberlain to *The Times* and his letter was given a prominent position[49] under the heading 'Settlement before Fighting'. He argued that for the first time an attempt was being made to reach a settlement before, rather than after, fighting and deplored the righteous indignation against Munich as coming only from those who had been thwarted from getting at Hitler. He went up to London on 29 September, but failed to get into the Commons and so had to make do with the inadequate transmitter in the Lords Library. All he managed to do was to get some reactions to his letter to *The Times*, which ranged from approval from Londonderry and other appeasers, to offensive rudeness from Strabolgi, who told him that if he made a speech in the same terms, the Germans would name a street in Berlin Ponsonbystrasse.

After Chamberlain's return from Munich, Ponsonby suspected there would be a reaction against the extreme jubilation with which Chamberlain had been greeted.

> War has been averted but what now? In my opinion the first thing was to stop the war. This Chamberlain has done. I should like to say a word in the Lords. But the opportunity seems doubtful.[50]

However, he did speak and urged the government to consider ending rearmament. True to his belief that all international disputes could be settled by negotiation, Ponsonby took the line that even the worst settlement was better by far than a resort to violence.

Before the post-Munich euphoria evaporated in the wake of the Kristal Nacht pogrom of November 1938, Ponsonby had felt sufficiently confident to launch a campaign for the restructuring of the League under a revised Covenant.[51] He argued that the failure of the League now gave an opportunity for its reconstruction, not on the old alliance pattern with its fallacious dependence on force, but as a genuine international organisation committed to deal with the fundamental causes of economic grievance which existed between nations. This was in keeping with Chamberlain's own ideas on economic appeasement. In spite of the ill omens of the pogroms of

November 1938 that Hitler was not to be trusted to live up to his promises, Ponsonby went ahead and presented his arguments in the Lords. He noted in his diary that the pro- and anti-Chamberlain camps were waging furious war with a bitterness of feeling fiercer than any controversy in politics that he had ever known. He recognised that preaching peace had become more difficult, but drew courage from a mostly complimentary mail bag.[52]

At the end of the year, he wrote in his diary that the prospects for 1939 were very uncertain. He believed that there was no reason for war, and that the one danger was the competition in rearming.

> I suppose it would require too much courage to disarm by example because they have debauched public opinion by telling them that defence by armaments means security and peace. Of course, the exact opposite is the truth.

The prominence given to his views by the national press after years of neglect was immediately reflected in his speaking engagements, which now became extraordinarily wide and diverse. He was no longer speaking to peace activists, but to an audience assembled at the Imperial Defence College, to a naval and air force officers group of 400 at Portsmouth, to a group of ladies assembled in Philip Sassoon's flat in Park Lane, and an audience of 700 working men in Hull. He debated with Norman Angell at Birkbeck College, and spoke to the boys at Christ's Hospital. The theme of his talks was that, in spite of impending conscription, the antics of the ARP (Air Raid Precautions force) and rearmament, war was not inevitable.

In February, he wrote to Neville Chamberlain about rearmament, enclosing a leaflet of the PPU, which quoted Edward Grey on the dangers of armaments competition. Chamberlain used it in the Commons and wrote to Ponsonby that he was conscious of the dangers as well as the costs of armaments

> but the stakes are so big, the existence of the British Empire as we have known it, that I dare not gamble them on trust in the pacific intentions of the dictators. Of course I have the idea of a truce to armaments not in the back but in the front of my mind, and I am watching anxiously for any favourable opportunity of reaching it.[53]

Ponsonby had suggested that a simple budgetary reduction of 25 per cent to begin with would suffice and emphasised that he did not wish to press on the Prime Minister his extreme policy – he only preached that line because he believed in the French saying 'on atteint le but qu'apres l'avoir depasser'.

Ponsonby's support of appeasement was based primarily on his long-held belief that war created new problems without solving old ones. This had been his view in 1914, and was so in 1939. He was only in part applying the lessons of the 1914 crisis to 1939. He believed that Europe had drifted into war then and in 1939 he believed that, although Hitler talked a lot of rot, he really wanted peace. He did not condone Fascism, as did a great many of the right wing supporters of appeasement. His attitude towards Fascism was put very clearly in a letter to a correspondent who challenged Ponsonby to deny that force was the only way to oppose the dictators.

> Hitler has been tearing up the Treaty of Versailles – a vindictive abomination for which we were partly responsible. Does anyone really think we shd have fought to preserve it?
>
> Mussolini's adventure in Abyssinia to wipe out the defeat at Adowa is precisely parallel to our conquest of S. Africa to wipe out the defeat of Majuba.
>
> Dictatorships are disturbing phenomena, but they never last and dictators never have successors.
>
> To take up the cudgels for the persecuted and oppressed all over the world is an impossible task and manifestly cannot be done by the exercise of force and violence.
>
> To fight Nazism and Fascism in war so as to overthrow the dictators would be just as successful as fighting to destroy German militarism and make the world safe for democracy (1914–18).
>
> Wrong and evil ideas can only be suppressed by the people of the nation where they exist *not* by intervention of outside nations.
>
> Abuse and condemnation of and threats against Hitler and Mussolini will only strengthen them by enabling them to distract public attention from the ills at home to an enemy outside.
>
> Both Germany and Italy are more rotten financially, economically and commercially than we are allowed to know.
>
> The idea of correcting anything or helping anyone by modern warfare – the massacre of men women and children – can never enter into the calculations of any true pacifist.
>
> Sympathy and compassion are all very well but they are bad as a basis for a foreign policy and they are generally selective according to political creeds and not really humanitarian because that field is too vast all the world over.[54]

From what is now known about the frailty of the Nazi régime, which was only consolidated by the war, Ponsonby was right to emphasise that Hitler could only profit from foreign criticism. What he and, it should be pointed out, many others failed to appreciate was the demonic and crazed lust for violence of the Nazis. Chamberlain has been vilified as a dupe for treating Hitler as a normal person, but what other course of action could he have followed? In retrospect, it has been all too easy to put post-1945 attitudes and feelings towards the Nazi regime into the 1930s. The general expectation of those days was that Fascism had come to stay and would be a permanent feature of European politics for the foreseeable future. It is well to remember that, when Great Britain went to war with Germany in 1939, she did so, not to destroy the Nazis, but to prevent German domination of Europe.

Chamberlain's response to Hitler's absorption of the rump of the Czecho-slovak state was to give a guarantee to Poland which, with Roumania, was seen to be next on the dictator's list. Ponsonby noted that the threat of force seemed to satisfy people. After Mussolini made his move against Albania over the Easter weekend, Ponsonby recognised that neither Hitler's nor Mussolini's word could be relied upon, so it was no good recommending conciliatory talks. He was not sure what course of action to pursue.[55] Roosevelt's message to Hitler of 15 April asking for assurances that no aggression would be committed against thirty-one named nations seemed at first to offer the prospect of a peaceful negotiated settlement of European differences. Ponsonby's view was that Roosevelt's initiative could only embarrass the dictators. He wanted initiatives that would promote conciliation. Hitler's negative response, delivered on 28 April, emphasised German grievances against Poland. Ponsonby was adamant that, although Poland might provoke a crisis, he could see no sort of *casus belli*. It was inconceivable to him that Great Britain should go to war over either the status of Danzig, or the corridor through Posen connecting it with Poland. Anything that he said was liable to be countered by the old tag Force v. Force, and in the Lords, he found it increasingly difficult to get anyone to listen to his point of view. He spoke against the new network of East European commitments in a debate in June, but failed to get Halifax's attention, who, it appeared to Ponsonby, treated him with a 'courteous patience tinged with contempt'.[56] Halifax's speech at Chatham House on 30 June provoked Ponsonby into writing a direct letter of protest urging Halifax not to fall into the trap of exchanging insults with Goebbels, which only inflamed public opinion. He wrote in the same sense to Goebbels, but had the sense, in the time taken to prepare a translation, to stop it. Halifax made no apologies for his strong line and his reply reflected the stronger line that the Chamberlain government had adopted.

> The only thing that will halt the Germans is the belief that they will be met by force. When they are convinced of the simple fact that we have the will and the means to resist further aggression, will they be persuaded to abandon the policy of force for that of negotiation.[57]

After Prague, the Munich bubble, as far as public opinion was concerned, was well and truly burst. The strange alliance between Ponsonby and the Conservative appeasers came to an abrupt end and Ponsonby's speaking engagements tailed off. He made no public appearances at all during June, July and August, and a short speech in the Lords on 3 August was his first there since early June. At the Bessboroughs, he met Brunning, the former Chancellor, who was very depressing, predicting that Hitler would absorb Danzig without force. Hitler would only be stopped by England saying firmly 'we will march'. Ponsonby doubted whether such a last minute threat would deter Hitler. They did agree that Hitler would have no successor, and that his régime was nothing more than a remarkable personal ascendancy. As the Polish crisis worsened in August, Ponsonby's despair at the thought of another war deepened. After a conversation with Baron von Hirsch on 21 August about the violence of the press, he came to the conclusion that while he still disapproved of threats of force, he was ready to accept increased armaments if it would stop Hitler.[58]

Ponsonby spoke in the Lords on 25 August, supporting Arnold, who put the pacifist case. By this time, the Russo-German Pact had sealed the fate of Poland, and Ponsonby, like everyone else, watched helplessly while the partition of Poland was accomplished. The coming of war did not change his conviction that any final settlement could be accomplished by resort to force.

Notes

1. *Ponsonby MSS.*, C.672, f.143, A. Ponsonby to Montgelas, n.d. [late 1931].
2. *Hansard*, V, Lords, 84, 355–84.
3. *Shulbrede MSS.*, A. Ponsonby Diary, XIV, 24 May 1932.
4. Ibid.
5. 'Disarmament: A Discussion', Day to Day Pamphlets No. 14, Hogarth Press (1932).
6. *Shulbrede MSS.*, A. Ponsonby Diary, XII, 13 Jan 1927.
7. *Shulbrede MSS.*, A. Ponsonby Diary, XIV, 8 June 1932.
8. Linck Jr and Davis (1969); Jervis (1967).
9. Greene (1928).
10. *Shulbrede MSS.*, A. Ponsonby Diary, XIII, 29 Jan 1930.
11. *Shulbrede MSS.*, A. Ponsonby Diary, XIV, 1 Dec 1932.
12. *Shulbrede MSS.*, A. Ponsonby Diary, XV, 19 Dec 1932.
13. 'To an Old Public School Friend', *The Listener*, 23 Nov 1932.
14. *Shulbrede MSS.*, A. Ponsonby Diary, XV, 1 Dec 1932.
15. Ceadel (1979).
16. *Shulbrede MSS.*, A. Ponsonby Diary, XVI, 30 July 1933.
17. *Shulbrede MSS.*, A. Ponsonby Diary, XVI, 6 Feb 1934.
18. *Ponsonby MSS.*, C.675, f.46, B. Nichols to A. Ponsonby, 2 Oct 1933.
19. *Hansard*, V, Lords, 91, 511–14.
20. *Shulbrede MSS.*, 'Travellers on the Road', Memoir of Dick Sheppard.
21. *Shulbrede MSS.*, A. Ponsonby Diary, XVI, 31 Dec 1934.
22. *Hansard*, V, Lords, 96, 1019–21.
23. *The Times*, 24 Aug 1935.
24. *Shulbrede MSS.*, A. Ponsonby Diary, XVI, 4 Sept 1935.
25. Bevin answered Lansbury 'with a brutality such as had never been directed against Ramsay MacDonald during the first World War'. Taylor (1965), p. 470.
26. *Ponsonby MSS.*, C.676, f.193–4, 'Why I Resigned', 4 Nov 1935.
27. *Shulbrede MSS.*, A. Ponsonby Diary, XVII, 19 Dec 1935.
28. *The Times*, 27 Feb 1936.

29. *Ponsonby* MSS., C.678, f.4–7, A. Ponsonby to Dalton, 10 May 1936.
30. *Shulbrede* MSS., A. Ponsonby Diary, XVII, 5 June 1936.
31. Ceadel (1980), pp. 274–5; *Shulbrede* MSS., A. Ponsonby Diary, XVII, 1, 14 July 1936.
32. *Ponsonby* MSS., Facs, C.66, f.28, A. Ponsonby to Bertrand Russell, 26 Aug 1936; *Shulbrede* MSS., A. Ponsonby Diary, XVII, 22 Aug 1936.
33. *The Times*, 15 Sept 1936; *Ponsonby* MSS., C.678, f.129, Liddell Hart to A. Ponsonby.
34. *Shulbrede* MSS., A. Ponsonby Diary, XVII, 8 Oct 1936.
35. *Shulbrede* MSS., 'Travellers on the Road', Memoir of Sheppard.
36. *Shulbrede* MSS., A. Ponsonby Diary, XVII, 26 Dec 1936.
37. *Ponsonby* MSS., C.679, f.37–9, Sheppard to A. Ponsonby, 2 Feb 1937.
38. B. *Webb Diary*, 4 Feb 1935, 5915.
39. B. *Webb Diary*, 2 Nov 1936, 6255.
40. Massingham (1900), pp. 809–20.
41. Ceadel (1980), pp. 237–8.
42. *Shulbrede* MSS., Correspondence with Jack Talbot.
43. *Shulbrede* MSS., A. Ponsonby Diary, XVII, 29 Oct 1936.
44. *Shulbrede* MSS., A. Ponsonby Diary, XVII, 21 Nov 1936.
45. *Shulbrede* MSS., A. Ponsonby Diary, XVII, 3 Dec 1936.
46. *Shulbrede* MSS., A. Ponsonby Diary, XVII, 12 Dec 1936.
47. *Shulbrede* MSS., A. Ponsonby Diary, XVIII, 29 May 1938.
48. *Shulbrede* MSS., A. Ponsonby Diary, XVIII, 14 Mar 1938.
49. *The Times*, 24 Sept 1938.
50. *Shulbrede* MSS., A. Ponsonby Diary, XVIII, 2 Oct 1938.
51. *The Times*, 'Planning for Peace', 15 Oct 1938.
52. *Shulbrede* MSS., A. Ponsonby Diary, XVIII, 3 Dec 1938.
53. *Ponsonby* MSS., C.681, f.59–60, A. Ponsonby to N. Chamberlain, draft, 19 Feb 1939; C.681, f.61, N. Chamberlain to A. Ponsonby, 21 Feb 1939.
54. *Ponsonby* MSS., C.681, f.54 undated [Feb 1939].
55. *Shulbrede* MSS., A. Ponsonby Diary, XVIII, 11 Apr 1939.
56. *Shulbrede* MSS., A. Ponsonby Diary, XVIII, 12 June 1939.
57. *Ponsonby* MSS., C.681, f.134, Halifax to A. Ponsonby, 6 July 1939.
58. *Shulbrede* MSS., A. Ponsonby Diary, XIX, 21 Aug 1939.

EPILOGUE, 1939–1946

Throughout his life, Ponsonby had always kept himself busy with his 'occupations' and after war was declared these work habits helped to preserve a sense of equilibrium. Over the years, he had evolved a method of work at Shulbrede of putting together papers and reference materials for each project on separate tables. In September 1939, he had a table for his biography of Sir Henry Ponsonby, which became his main occupation, a table for 'Travellers on the Road', and also a table for his political work, which was concentrated during the winter of 1939–40, not so much on the pacifist cause as on an attempt to bring about a negotiated peace.

The view that during the period of the 'phony war' the country closed ranks behind the government in a united resolve to rid the world of Nazi tyranny completely ignores the extent of public misgiving in going to war to defend Poland, and overlooks altogether the public and private debate in the months before the fall of France on the necessity of avoiding the mistake of 1914–18 when a negotiated peace had been rejected in favour of the knock-out blow with all its disastrous consequences in 1919. Fighting on, while it may have been taken for granted by Churchill, was being seriously questioned, as Ponsonby's post-bag revealed after he began to advance the case for a negotiated peace. He told Lord Stanhope that when he spoke now, instead of receiving abusive letters, blows and rotten eggs as in the last war, the letters that came to Shulbrede were warmly supportive. He attributed this to people not knowing what they were fighting for.

> If against aggression, why not against Russia, Italy and Japan. If to change the German government, we did that last time by removing the Kaiser. If for the restoration of Poland and Czechoslovakia, the P.M. gave an unanswerable argument in his Birmingham speech about Czechoslovakia which applies exactly to Poland.
>
> But this bewilderment which is widespread is further aggravated by Halifax's broadcast which described a perfect Europe, a quite obviously unattainable ideal, and Winston's blatant vulgarities which have deeply offended many people.[1]

Ponsonby's case was that it was an illusion to suppose that this war was

226

going to be a war to end war; a great victory was not going to attain permanent peace now any more than it had ever done in the past.[2] The rebuilding and carving up of Central Europe was an insoluble problem; it was not possible to tidy it up to satisfy all the nationalities and the big powers that surrounded the area. Above all, Ponsonby urged a sense of proportion about the Hitler phenomenon.

> the agonies and the terrible distress, the persecutions and the cruelty which go on in Germany – well we feel for the Germans who have to endure them, but it is their business to alter it. They can alter that . . . But they are going to join with him if we continue to fight him.[3]

His one hope all along had been for a revolution in Germany; his one certainty was that every attempt to try and remove Hitler from outside would strengthen his position. Ponsonby's brother Johnnie was used as a sounding board for these ideas, as he had been in the Great War. General Ponsonby was not at all optimistic on the prospects of Hitler's being removed nor did he think a conference with or without an impartial mediator would do any good. In his opinion, Hitler was not about to give up either his Czech or his Polish conquests. 'Germany and Russia are now led by two ex-lance-corporals, Hitler and Stalin. Napoleon was originally a lance corporal. He also aimed at world conquest – he also could not be trusted.'[4] Helena Swanwick hit the nail on the head in pointing out that Hitler did not seem to be prepared to look at any moderate terms. She predicted that the little 'game of spillikins' that had been played out in 1919 was only a preliminary shake to the tremendous shuffle that was about to take place.[5]

Two peace initiatives were taken in the autumn of 1939, the first by Hitler on 6 October, which was rejected by Chamberlain who demanded some positive proofs of the sincerity of Hitler's peace offer, and the second by the sovereigns of Belgium and Holland, whose mediation proposals were given short shrift by Halifax on the same grounds. Ponsonby hoped to get his mediation idea off the ground by having guarantees as a first item on a mediator's agenda, not as a precondition of talks, but as part of the negotiated agreement. This rather obvious clutching at straws on Ponsonby's part illustrates the predicament of the peace advocates in dealing with the Hitler problem, for if part of their perception was the injustices of the territorial settlement of Versailles, so also did it include Munich. Any negotiation with Hitler without positive proofs would raise the possibility of a second Munich.

When Ponsonby finally took up his pen again to make his first diary entry since the end of September, his predicament is clearly recorded:

> I miss not writing my diary because I have an engrained 'itch to record'. But what should I record? Almost the identical fears, feelings, anger of 1914. The

same attempts to make an occasional speech (in the H of Lords this time) loathing of an even greater outpouring of cheap vulgar senseless 'patriotism' false sentiment carrying away quite decent people, futility of Peace Societies, lies of course rampant, warm approval of the spreading the poison of hate and far more than last time silly petty annoying restrictions and burdens on the individual.

And yet, the thing has not really begun yet, the issue and purpose are by no means clear, the international diplomatic tangle so complicated that there is undoubtedly more misgiving and lack of enthusiasm. While those few of us who are for stopping the war before the great carnage begins have to be denounced publicly, many tell us privately that they entirely agree. The high falluting self righteousness is nauseating. A high principled good man like Edward Halifax repeating all the old tags has a tremendous influence in the wrong direction. These considerations stand out:

We are not fighting aggression as we first said we were because we are making up to Italy and never mention Japan.

We cannot undertake a war against Germany and Russia combined. It would take too long a time to win.

In spite of their blindness they do not believe that a big massacre will be the means of solving the intensely complicated problems of central Europe or of inaugurating a new and better Europe.

Both sides are hesitating to begin it.

The delay may conceivably allow reason to penetrate into the minds of statesmen.[6]

It occurred to Ponsonby early in the new year that there was no sufficiently authoritative voice, party or section to point the nation in any other direction than the continuation of the war. Within the government, Chamberlain was sick and Halifax inadequate; the Labour Party was more and more committed to support the war, and the Peace Pledge Union ill-led and ineffective. Within his more immediate circle of politically active Peers, he corresponded with a Tory Peer, Lord Brocket, about a joint letter to the Prime Minister, but rightly concluded, after much prevarication on the part of the Tory Peers, that they did not intend to act. The letter eventually sent by Lord Arnold was fobbed off by Chamberlain. Through the good offices of Lord Londonderry, Halifax agreed to see Arnold. He assured him that he felt the gigantic responsibility of the war, but could not find any guarantee that Hitler was prepared to keep his word. In these circumstances, Ponsonby proposed to put down a motion in general terms and a question beforehand asking that it should be discussed in secret session.[7]

Before putting down his motion, he heard through Stuart Morris of the PPU of Lord Tavistock's individual peace initiative and went to a meeting in Belgrave Square on 13 February to hear what Tavistock had to say.[8] Tavistock, an old acquaintance of Ponsonby, who had helped with

Falsehood in Wartime in the 1920s, had, during the thirties, developed strong pro-German sympathies and had formed an anti-semitic British Peace Party before joining the PPU. Through the good offices of the German Minister in Dublin and the German Ambassador in Washington, Tavistock had communicated twelve proposals, which Hitler had approved. He had then gone privately to Halifax, who immediately seized on the fact that nowhere among the proposals was there any reference to the removal of the Nazis. Tavistock now proposed to send a deputation to 10 Downing Street. Ponsonby rightly predicted that Tavistock's move was going to leak out and come to nothing, which it subsequently did when the *Daily Express* got hold of the story. In the meantime, Ponsonby's question had been put to Halifax, who delivered a not-unexpected snub, but he kept his motion on the order paper, feeling inclined to move it, speaking out and risking the consequences. Charles Buxton, with whom Ponsonby was in close contact at this time as they had been in 1914, when, as Ponsonby remembered, they had sat together on a bench in St James's Park wondering how they could bring a stop to that war, strongly urged him to withdraw his motion, as an open government rebuff would put paid to all chances of any negotiations taking place. He decided to follow Buxton's advice, but before withdrawing his motion he sought an interview with the Foreign Secretary. This took place on 1 March.

Halifax told him that 'we never said we won't deal with Hitler, but that we cannot trust him or Germany under the Nazi regime'. He also said that people had been so impressed by the failure of Versailles and the knock out blow upon which it had been based, that there was no chance of its being repeated. He did not think the war would last long and expected a break up in Germany. The Germans, he was assured, were not about to make any move on the western front.[9] After his talk with Halifax, Ponsonby felt slightly more optimistic, or, as he put it, less hopeless, about the future than before. All this was to change in May 1940 when Hitler's stunningly successful Western offensives brought an abrupt end to the 'phony war' and all attempts at negotiation. The Labour Party's decision to join the Churchill government led to his resignation from the Labour Party. He was not a little bitter that his opposition to war should result in his being 'considered unworthy for acceptance as a member of any political party of the state'. On the spur of the moment, he decided to go and see another political outcast, Lloyd George. At the meeting he found an extraordinary similarity in Lloyd George's and his own views on the war. After lunch, walking in the garden, he asked George the vital question '"Do you think Winston Churchill is the man to see this thing through?" To my amazement his estimate of Winston was precisely the same as mine, brilliance, unrivalled parliamentary powers and no judgement whatever . . .'[10]

If Bertrand Russell's response to the crisis of the war in May 1940 was to abandon his pacifism in favour of jingoism (Ponsonby noted in his diary 'I am not at all surprised. He has always been adapting his philosophy to his varying emotions and uncontrolled passions'), Ponsonby's reaction remained strongly and unequivocally pacifist. When a correspondent asked if he still held the view expressed in *Now Is The Time* that an individual should be against the next war without knowing what it would be about, he replied

> I need only say that I abide still by the sentence you quote from Now is the Time and I may add: in present circumstances even more emphatically than I thought possible when I wrote that book 15 years ago.[11]

It should be noted, however, that Ponsonby's attention was no longer focused on the Peace Pledge Union. Before the war, he had pointed out that the Union could do useful propaganda work in times of peace and in the time of apprehension when war seemed likely, but that in the event of a war the Union would be 'out of action and can do nothing'.[12] In May 1940 at the beginning of 'Notes in Wartime' which came to be a substitute for his diary, he wrote

> although I joined Dick Sheppard's movement I do not believe that collecting refusals to fight can ever stop war and if the propaganda of such an organization is continued during a war, it will in all probability be suppressed or incapacitated.

This recognition of the limitations of the peace movement led him to ask what then could be done to prevent war in the future? Obviously not by his former arguments:

> I used to think that the diabolical brutality of modern warfare might impress people sufficiently to make them hesitate to support such a method of attempting to settle international disputes, just as I used to think that decent men in high positions would have learnt that this was not the way of establishing peace in the world. But in both cases I was quite wrong.

His faith for the future lay not in individual action but in the common people.

> Nevertheless I am not without hope still just flickering in the midst of the darkness that humanity is not destined to continue to degrade itself by fratricidal massacre and that something will arrest the descent into an abyss where such civilization as we have reached must be shattered.
>
> While I have said no man will appear as a prophet to point to a better way, I believe a nation might; and I do not cast away a faint hope that my own nation might. Gullible, handicapped by ignorance, easily swayed under the present system as they may be, I do not believe that the majority of the common people, who if left to themselves will I am quite sure respond to a moral appeal, are either fatalistic about the recurrence of wars or believe that international

disputes can ever be settled in this way. There I believe is the material in which a faint hope may be realised, if only they can be reached, made articulate, made impervious to the lying appeals of politicians and more especially achieve power. The determined lead of a nation speaking through the people as a nation, with freedom to make its declarations and power to execute its ideals, I think would be responded to by an evergrowing number of other nations. But this promising ground can only be cultivated by so many other concurrent changes that the very idea of hope springing from such a source can be disposed of as Eutopian.[13]

At the practical level, Ponsonby's advice was sought by a number of young pacifists who were about to face the call-up, and not least from his own son. His advice was not to resist Registration and, on being called up, not to refuse to do anything at all at the direction of the government. When it came to being called up for military service, those who were sincerely convinced that warfare was not the way to defeat Naziism and that violence could never settle international disputes had as much right as Christian pacifists to refuse combatant service and other forms of alternative service. They could, however, accept constructive work such as teaching and farming.[14]

If Matthew was to require courage to face the unpopularity of the pacifist label in wartime, Ponsonby was himself to be put to the test in having to face his daughter's unexpected and tragic death as an alcoholic at the end of July 1940. In Evelyn Waugh's satirical novel *Vile Bodies*, the character of Agatha Runcible, loosely based on Elizabeth Ponsonby, was used by Waugh to portray the shallow emptiness of the pursuit of pleasure for its own sake. Agatha's demise at a cocktail party in her hospital room, where she is recovering from a spectacular car crash, is the central act in Waugh's portrayal of the Bright Young People. He has her say 'I had the most awful dreams. I thought we were driving round and round in a motor race and none of us could stop.' Rather less dramatically, but no less inexorably, this was to be Elizabeth's fate.

More than anything else, Ponsonby was kept going by the biography of Sir Henry Ponsonby. Ponsonby quite understood that, even if all the papers that constituted the raw material of his father's biography came from Sir Henry's personal archive, his official position from 1870 to 1895 as private secretary to Queen Victoria made much of the material subject to royal copyright.[15] With this in mind, at an early stage in the preparation of the book, he decided that it would be prudent to let Windsor Castle, where he had a friend at court, into the picture. The friend, who was available through Arthur's sister Betty, who had returned to Windsor to live in a grace and favour residence on Castle Hill, agreed to help. The course of action decided upon was for Ponsonby to go ahead and complete his manuscript before knowledge of it would become official, his friend rightly taking the view that the book should be judged as a whole rather than as the sum of separate parts. Accordingly, the Castle received the typescript of the biography in the summer of 1941. The friend liked what he read, suggesting only minor alterations to protect the Duchess of Teck and Princess Beatrice. He approved the next stage of production, the setting up of galley proofs, which he then proposed to show first to Wigram, the Keeper of the Archives, and then to Queen Elizabeth, who had expressed enthusiasm when told of the book.

When the galley proofs reached the desk of Wigram, he, in turn, found the book a delight, but ominously pointed out that it was exactly for this type of book that the 1933 restrictions had been drafted. They had been specifically put up to forestall the possibly spicy memoirs of Sir Ralph Harwood who, under Fritz, had carried out massive economies in the Household. Clearly, Ponsonby's book was not in the same category as that projected by Harwood, which was reminiscent, while the biography dealt with past history. They had all reckoned without Queen Mary. While events of the last quarter of the nineteenth century were history to some, to that upright and imperious lady they were but yesterday, and she took the strongest exception to the private affairs of the Royal Family being put into print for the benefit of the public, even if these events had occurred more than fifty years previously.

Queen Mary's position was not altogether reactionary. The Royal Family, then, and perhaps even more so today, has suffered from unwelcome publicity in the sense that if their servants were allowed to go public, any private life at all would become impossible. The Royal Family should have the same rights of privacy as everybody else to say and think what they wish at home without fear of Fleet Street 'revelations'. This having been said, it is also true that Sir Henry Ponsonby was not a domestic servant, but the Queen's Private Secretary, a post which, by the late nineteenth century, had a recognised position within the constitutional process. The relationship between the Sovereign and the Private Secretary was political, and therefore clearly a legitimate field of enquiry. Both Ponsonby and his friend appreciated that the real grounds of Queen Mary's opposition was an outraged royal *amour propre* at the 'tone' of Sir Henry's letters to his wife, which revealed not a subservient master/servant relationship but a working relationship between Queen Victoria and the Ponsonbys based on friendship and mutual respect.

In view of Queen Mary's position, King George VI read the book, apparently with great pleasure and went over the whole manuscript with Ponsonby's friend. They agreed upon toning down a number of passages which, in the King's opinion, unduly portrayed Queen Victoria as an old dragon. The King perfectly understood that the only reason they were all reading the manuscript was because Ponsonby wanted to include some things actually written by Queen Victoria, and that Queen Mary's root and branch objection was untenable. The problem of bringing her round to a more reasonable view was settled when Queen Mary went over to Windsor from Badminton for the christening of Prince William of Gloucester. Ponsonby, anxious to know how matters would turn out, went over to Windsor where he waited at Betty's for a phone call from within the Castle. His friend then came, met Ponsonby at 'Betty's Gates' across Castle Hill, to which he had a key, and in his friend's house a relieved Ponsonby received the news that the King was pleased to give his approval to the publication of *Henry Ponsonby*.[16]

The cuts that were made in the manuscript were none of them very important. One that was suggested, but not carried out, inevitably referred to Margot Asquith, whom Queen Victoria had thought unfit to be a Cabinet Minister's wife. Another that was carried out was the preservation of the story that Queen Victoria, when at Balmoral, had been in the habit of reading the Bible to the poor in their cottages.[17]

When the book appeared, it became a best seller, sold out almost immediately, and was reprinted twice in 1943. It was with great pleasure that Ponsonby received the news that the book had been awarded the James Tait Black Prize for the best biography of the year by Edinburgh University. The Black Prize was the 'blue ribband of the literary world in Scotland'.

There was not much else to give Ponsonby pleasure at this time. A new edition of *Falsehood in Wartime* was sought out as avidly as the first edition, but Ponsonby drew no comfort from it for he knew that the new crop of lies being produced by government propaganda outstripped the ones that he had so brilliantly exposed in 1928. He was pressed on all sides to prepare a new edition dealing with current propaganda. This he declined to do, pointing out to Vera Brittain who broached the subject to Ponsonby in December 1942 that the real value of his original publication was that he had been able to repudiate the lies. This was what made the story of the Corpse Factory so good. He went on

> To tell you the honest truth, what has depressed me most in this war has been the shortness of memories of quite intelligent people. Not a single lesson has been retained from the last war although in many ways events have followed precisely the same course and of course it will be just the same when 'Peace' comes which is now referred to in the current jargon as 'the cessation of hostilities'.[18]

He found quite the most objectionable the angry anti-German diatribes of the government's Chief Diplomatic Adviser, Sir Robert Vansittart, broadcast by the BBC on its Overseas Service, now in the war functioning as an arm of the Ministry of Information, in the form of seven broadcasts in November and December 1940. Extracts of the BBC talks were published simultaneously in the *Sunday Times* and then they appeared in pamphlet form as 'The Black Record. Germans Past and Present'. Vansittart's biographer admits that, even today, the 'Black Record' makes strong reading.[19] In 1940, portraying all Germans since the dawn of history as lovers of war, brutal, perfidious, aggressive and arrogant was, in Ponsonby's view, simply repeating the propaganda errors of the First World War that he had so successfully exposed in *Falsehood in Wartime*. Condemning an entire nation from top to bottom was to fall into the totalitarian delusion, for all Germans were not Nazis, and treating Germany as such made the task of both winning the war and securing peace afterwards more difficult. The BBC should have provided an opportunity for a rebuttal of Vansittartism, but its policy of an unofficial censorship excluded not only Ponsonby from the airwaves, but also Donald Soper, unless he was saying prayers, and the musical sounds of the Glasgow Orpheus Choir, because its conductor had pacifist propensities.[20] Ponsonby's broadcasts had tapered off somewhat in the late thirties, and what turned out to be his last broadcast, 'I was page of Honour to Queen Victoria', was given in the Children's Hour series 'When I was Young' in December 1938. Fortunately, the tentacles of the Ministry of Information did not extend into the august precincts of the House of Lords, and Ponsonby countered Vansittart with a particularly effective speech in February 1941.[21] His view was endorsed by *The Times* and an embarrassed government decided to rid itself of Vansittart, who was persuaded to resign. Even in these most trying circumstances, Ponsonby did not lose his sense of humour, for when Vansittart was raised to the Peerage in the Birthday Honours List of 1941, he amused his two old Foreign Office friends, Strachey and Vicars, predicting that Vansittart would now become a greater danger than ever, for, as a Peer, he would be independent, eligible for a government post, and perhaps the next Foreign Secretary.

In addition to his Sponsor's work for the Peace Pledge Union, Ponsonby was still a member of the council of the War Resisters' International, and used his position to intercede with the authorities on behalf of a number of refugees who were ensnared by wartime bureaucracy. In the summer of 1941, Runham Brown attempted to interest Ponsonby in a post-war planning project. His reaction was very different from his active participation in the Bryce Group of the First World War. His experience taught him that these schemes were purely academic, and not the work of the War Resisters', which, in his opinion, should stick to the simple idealism expressed in its title.[22] For Ponsonby there was one basic principle that they should stick to, and this was that organised force could never solve international disputes. Beatrice Webb, who saw an increasing amount of the Ponsonbys at this time, professed to detect in Ponsonby a pacifist-anarchist. Her *'anti*-pure and simple'[23] fails to do justice to Ponsonby's position. If his writing was tinged with a hint of despair, it was occasioned by the futility and horror of the war from the air, with its destructive rain of incendiary devices, which, from both sides, was laying waste the great cities of Europe. As Shulbrede lay along one of the routes of the German bombers making raids on London, his war diary records their coming up from the south in what sounded like a procession. They were spared the direct effects of bombing, although he did not fail to notice that one visitor to Shulbrede's crypt assessed it entirely from its efficacy as an air raid shelter. He saw a bomber crashing in flames on Lynchmere common and noticed that the fearfully burnt pilot was taken off in a lorry and not an ambulance. He received a harrowing account of the two December 1940 blitzes on Sheffield in a letter from his old friend Miss Gillott. It was obvious that the bombing by night from high flying aeroplanes was indiscriminate, and that the objectives were not military, and it was equally obvious that the bombing of Germany was not simply a reprisal for raids on Britain. Ponsonby added his own voice to the rising chorus of indignation over indiscriminate bombing. A number of protest committees were formed; the Committee for the Abolition of Night Bombing, and the Bombing Restriction Committee were two whose literature was received at Shulbrede. It is not clear whether Ponsonby played any more active role in the campaign, although among his papers is preserved a protest sent to Downing Street in April 1941 and early in May he raised the subject in the Lords.[24]

At the beginning of the war, the Home Office had swept up several thousand people whose loyalties were considered suspect under the 18b regulations. While many of these people were properly incarcerated, many more had been put away for dubious reasons. It fell to Ponsonby and the other dissenters with public positions to draw attention to these cases and to act as public watchdogs against excessive zeal on the part of the Home Secretary. In November 1941, Herbert Morrison, in the Commons, made a particularly uncalled for and disparaging attack on the Duke of Bedford, as the Marquis of Tavistock had become on his father's death in August 1940. Ponsonby raised the matter in the Lords, delivering a particularly telling defence of freedom. Unfortunately, carried away by his own eloquence, he suggested that the Home Secretary 'has me under observation and I want to throw out a defence as early as I can before I find myself in Brixton.' Naturally, the cartoonists had a field day.[25]

Just as in the First World War when the authorities had found a reason to lock up E.D. Morel, the Secretary of the UDC, so in the Second World War, with rather more justice, they found occasion to lock up Stuart Morris, the general secretary of the Peace Pledge Union. Morris had foolishly received confidential government documents containing plans

"HE'S GOT *ME* ON THE LIST!"

"I am pretty sure that the Home Secretary has got me under observation."—*Lord Ponsonby.*

for dealing with Gandhi in India.[26] He was tried in camera and no details of either the charge or the sentence were at first revealed. Morris got nine months, a light sentence in Alex Wood's estimation, for he wrote to Ponsonby 'I believe that if you had seen the stuff that was removed from Stuart's files at Endsleigh Street, you would agree.' The PPU leadership was much exercised about its position in relation to Morris' future, Wood, the chairman, wanting a public dissociation with Morris' actions. Ponsonby's position was, as usual, more level-headed than most and he continued to urge a low profile for the PPU. The advice he gave to Vera Brittain, who had taken upon herself Morris' defence, was to be quiet.

I hope the rot won't spread much further. I shall not write another line to add to the burden. But I do not want the Union to be broken up. People in these days lose their sense of proportion very easily.[27]

Ponsonby sought permission from the Home Secretary to visit Morris in Wormwood Scrubs and, with Dr Kathleen Rutherford, met him on his release in July 1943. Over lunch, Morris told of his trial and incarceration. The lunch was at the RAC, which Ponsonby had recently joined, having earlier in his career been dissuaded by the threat of a blackball from applying at either Brooks's or the Oxford & Cambridge Club. He did not fail to record Morris' recognition of one of the cloakroom attendants as a former Scrubs inmate.

Later in September 1943, after a short holiday visit to Matthew and Bess in Suffolk, Ponsonby, who had hitherto been in good health, suffered a stroke. He never recovered from its effects, although he lived until March 1946.

Among the many letters of sympathy that arrived at Shulbrede in March 1946 was one bearing the once-familiar heading of 10 Downing Street, Whitehall. In that letter, the Prime Minister recalled their friendship in the interwar period and Arthur's delightful personality. Attlee's letter concluded. 'His services to the cause of Labour and Peace will not be forgotten.'[28] It is to be hoped that this biography will do something to justify Attlee's prediction, for in the forty years since he died, if he has not been entirely forgotten, he has certainly been neglected. It was well said by Runham Brown that Ponsonby was always in advance of the parties he served; he had to leave them behind. This is still the pacifist dilemma. Shortly before his incapacitating stroke, he wrote in his little volume of *Ideas and Impressions*

Keep on inventing, constructing and creating in however small a way and in so doing *never* think of its possible or even probable futility.

I hate people who begin 'Why don't you . . .?' They are often right.

Notes

1. *Ponsonby MSS.*, C.681, f.218–19, A. Ponsonby to Lord Stanhope, 19 Nov 1939.
2. *Fortnightly Review*, 'War Without End', Nov. 1939, 545–51.
3. *Hansard*, V, Lords, 114, 1319.
4. *Shulbrede MSS.*, J. Ponsonby to A. Ponsonby, 26 Jan 1940.
5. *Ponsonby MSS.*, C.681, H. Swanwick to A. Ponsonby, 19 Sept 1939.
6. *Shulbrede MSS.*, A. Ponsonby Diary, XIX, 25 Dec 1939.
7. *Shulbrede MSS.*, A. Ponsonby Diary, XIX, 5 Feb 1940.
8. Fieldhouse (1971).

9. *Ponsonby MSS.*, C.682, f.42–3, A. Ponsonby's notes of an interview with Lord Halifax.
10. *Shulbrede MSS.*, A. Ponsonby Diary, XIX, 2 June 1940.
11. *Shulbrede MSS.*, on letter from D. Rowland Morgan, 4 June 1940.
12. *Peace Pledge Union MSS.*, A. Ponsonby to S. Morris, 17 June 1939, Minutes of PPU Sponsors' Meetings.
13. *Shulbrede MSS.*, 'Notes in War Time'.
14. *Shulbrede MSS.*, A. Ponsonby to Matthew Ponsonby, 11 May 1940.
15. 'Royal copyright', *The Times*, 20 July 1933.
16. This story has been put together from mouse-eaten scraps and fragments of correspondence found in a Shulbrede outhouse.
17. A. Ponsonby, *Henry Ponsonby*, p. 123.
18. *V. Brittain MSS.*, A. Ponsonby to V. Brittain, 15 Dec 1942.
19. Rose (1978), p. 245.
20. *BBC Written Archives*, Board Minute, 20 Mar 1941; *Shulbrede MSS.*, H. Robertson to A. Ponsonby, 18 Dec 1940.
21. *Hansard*, V, Lords, 118, 388–93.
22. *Ponsonby MSS.*, C.682, f.176–7, A. Ponsonby to Runham Brown, 1 Aug 1941.
23. *B. Webb Diary*, 3 Feb 1942, 7259.
24. *Hansard*, V, Lords, 119, 135–8.
25. *Hansard*, V, Lords, 121, 34–8.
26. Ceadel (1980), p. 312.
27. *V. Brittain MSS.*, A. Ponsonby to V. Brittain, 18 Feb 1943.
28. *Shulbrede MSS*, C. Attlee to D. Ponsonby, 26 Mar 1947.

APPENDIX

PRIVATE Mr. *PONSONBY'S NOTE* on the suggested Amendment to the
PROPOSALS FOR THE AVOIDANCE OF WAR

In order to save time when we meet it will be best for me to put in writing very briefly some of the reasons for my uncompromising opposition to the suggested addition to our draft proposals,

It was with great reluctance that I eventually acceded to the insertion of the word 'forcible' in clause 19. This was not because I did not think force might eventually be used on certain occasions but because I did not want a specific obligation to use force to be a part of any international agreement. After revision in November 1915 our proposals stood primarily for new and effective diplomatic machinery for the settlement of disputes and only admitted incidentally that force in certain circumstances might have to be resorted to. The new suggestion imposing an obligation on the signatory powers to 'declare war' not only emphasises the use of force but makes armaments the basis of the whole project and substitutes fear for moral obligation.

I conclude that the formation of an international force (as recommended by Prof. Eliot in his pamphlet of Dec. 1914 and by Prof. Marburg in Feb. 1915) is not in contemplation as it is obviously impracticable.

Joint action with available armaments is therefore the suggestion. This means:

(1) a perpetuation of high expenditure on armaments generally.
(2) less probability of all Powers consenting to join the league.
(3) a considerable minority being found outside the league, it will be necessary for armaments inside the league to be sufficient to counteract armaments outside: consequently there will be renewed competition and the old evil of the Balance of Power perpetuated.
(4) the most effective sort of armament to enforce obedience anywhere and at any moment will obviously be Naval.

　　　Result　(a) an excuse for Great Britain to keep an all powerful Navy.
　　　　　　　(b) an excuse for U.S.A. to construct one.
　　　(indeed I understand that much support for the League to Enforce Peace comes from those who desire greater expenditure on Naval armaments in America.)

However disinterested the motives of these two nations may appear to us, in the eyes of other nations they are just as likely as any other of the great powers to fail on occasions to fulfil their obligations. Yet they will both be placed in a superior position. Armies will be of secondary importance.

(5) The necessity of a declaration of war will overshadow everything else in the proposals and is the one point war-mongers and armament firms will emphasize.

(6) A serious and dangerous international dispute is now to become the excuse for a world war not possibly but certainly.

(7) The first occasion for a declaration of war as proposed will mean in all probability the end of the Council. Whereas its failure or apparent impotence on any occasion would not interfere with its existence or continued activity.

(8) We are endorsing in a new form the old fallacy '*si vis pacem para bellum.*'

The case of one isolated recalcitrant power need not be considered. Because without this addition to the draft or indeed any mention of force at all, no single power would stand out against the consensus of opinion of all the other powers which might be backed by force even though this were not specially provided for in the agreement.

The case we have to meet is that of one or more powers whose position is so strong that though they refuse to submit the dispute to the Council or to await the period of delay, they know they will have the backing of a considerable minority. In this event the majority are all bound to declare war. With a little stretch of the imagination the present war may be taken as an instance of an operation of the League to Enforce Peace. The righteous and law-abiding majority – Great Britain, France, Russia, Italy, Japan, Belgium, Serbia, Portugal and Montenegro – endeavouring to persuade the recalcitrant and treaty-breaking minority – Germany, Austria-Hungary, Turkey and Bulgaria – of the error of their ways and of their duty to conform to international agreements. Has the use of force proved effective or is it likely to? War, whatever the motive, will always resolve itself into a mere desire on either side for military victory. It has never persuaded any country of the error of its policy.

Without this obligation to declare war it is true that the operation of the International Council might break down. But if it did the war would only be confined to the two or three powers immediately concerned.

The more we drift away from the idea of creating machinery to facilitate co-operation and strengthen moral obligation the less likely are we to succeed even from a practical point of view and the more temptation will there be for breaking up into rival groups once the continued existence of effective armaments has been internationally sanctioned.

Moral obligation may fail at first because the moral sense in nations is either not sufficiently developed or, as in the case of the great powers, cannot express itself under the present system. The gradual abolition of secret diplomacy and the institution of parliamentary control will assist and eventually the International Council will find its authority based on a strong foundation and each country will find the need for maintaining expensive armaments decrease.

By emphasizing the necessity for using force and by imposing a direct obligation to declare war we are laying all the powers who subscribe to such an agreement open to suspicion and we are destroying the real source from which the Council should derive its authority. Its operation will be doomed to failure. There will be no minor cases in which it can prove the success of joint forcible action because, as I have already said, in no minor case will the opportunity arise. The new sanction for the maintenance of armaments will lead very soon to international conflict perhaps on a larger scale than before.

The idea of navies and armies being maintained solely to enforce peace is even more ludicrous than that of their being maintained solely for 'defensive purposes'.

The theory that you can maintain peace by force is in my opinion fundamentally unsound. The desire to maintain peace and the recognition of the sanctity of international agreements cannot be forced upon a nation by fear, it can only grow by the enlightenment of each nation when they are fully informed of what their international commitments consist and when they become aware that their own interests are bound up with the interests of other nations and that war even when successful is disastrous to national life and therefore futile.

This enlightenment of nations is not so far off or Utopian as people suppose. In fact:

(1) if their integrity is safeguarded not by ancient treaties but by living instruments renewed and approved by each succeeding generation,
(2) if their representatives are continuously acting in co-operation with one another in a Council,
(3) if negotiations are concentrated and dealt with in a judicial spirit,
(4) if alliances formed by secret diplomatic intrigue become neither necessary nor desirable,
(5) if the peoples, among whom the international spirit is growing, are allowed to express themselves.

The moral sense of nations will very rapidly develop and supplant the immoral ambitions of governments. This war too will help considerably. The terrific display of force far from making more people believe in the efficacy of war is likely to persuade more people of its utter futility.

Therefore to formulate deliberately a method of continuing and even creating large armaments under the auspices of a Federation for the maintenance of peace – which would really be under the cloak of organised international hypocrisy – will entirely defeat the impulses for peace. It is taking the wrong road and makes the whole scheme worthless.

[Dickinson MSS., C.402, f.112–15]

BIBLIOGRAPHY

1. Arthur Ponsonby: Manuscripts

The book is based on the papers of Arthur Ponsonby, most of which have been deposited in the Bodleian Library, Oxford, but much still remains at Shulbrede. This material includes his main diary and three smaller subsidiary diaries and his almost daily letters to his wife when he was away from Shulbrede. Dorothea Ponsonby also kept a diary, which I have used occasionally to throw light on particular events. As Ponsonby employed a cutting agency, Shulbrede has a virtually complete record of his journalistic writings. It should be noted that Ponsonby's Memoir of Campbell-Bannerman, which has been reported to be lost, is at Shulbrede. Other useful manuscripts include his biographical sketches 'Travellers on the Road' and three small volumes of 'Ideas and Impressions'.

2. Arthur Ponsonby: Books

The Camel and the Needle's Eye (1909)
The Decline of Aristocracy (1912)
Democracy and Diplomacy: A Plea for Popular Control of Foreign Policy (1915)
Wars and Treaties (1918)
The Priory and Manor of Lynchmere and Shulbrede (1920)
English Diaries (1923)
Now Is The Time; An Appeal for Peace (1925)
More English Diaries (1927)
Scottish and Irish Diaries (1927)
Samuel Pepys (1928)
Falsehood in Wartime (1928)
Casual Observations (1930)
John Evelyn (1933)
Queen Victoria (1933)
Life Here and Now; Conclusions Derived from an Examination of the Sense of Duration (1936)
The Little Torch; quotations from diaries for every day of the Year (1938)
Henry Ponsonby, Queen Victoria's Private Secretary. His Life from his Letters (1942)

with Dorothea Ponsonby, Rebels and Reformers: Biographies for Young People (1917)

3. Arthur Ponsonby: Booklets, pamphlets and articles

'Diplomacy as a Profession', by a Diplomatist, National Review (March 1900)
'Tycho Brahe', Nineteenth Century (June 1900)
'Spiritual Perfection: A Discussion' (1908) (under pseudonym Thomas Clune)
'The Two Sovereigns', The Nation (May 1910)
'Our New and Old Nobility', The Nation (September 1910)

242

'Public School Religion' by an old Etonian, *The Nation* (January 1911)

'After the Crisis', *Contemporary Review* (September 1911)

'Unsichten englischer Unterhausmitglieder uber die Beziehungen zwischen Deutschland und England', *Deutsche Revue* (August 1912)

'Social Reform Versus War', National Peace Council, Social Reform Series No. 1 (1912)

'Foreign Policy and the Navy', *Contemporary Review* (September 1912)

'Democracy and the Control of Foreign Affairs' (1912)

'The Future Government of the United Kingdom', *Contemporary Review* (November 1913)

'International Morality', *The International Journal of Ethics* (January 1915)

'The Basis of International Authority', League of Peace and Freedom Pamphlet No. 10 (n.d.)

'Mr. Ponsonby and Mr. Trevelyan in the House of Commons', UDC Leaflet No. 15b (November 1915)

'Parliament and Foreign Policy', UDC Pamphlet No. 5 (1915)

'Why Must the War Go On?', UDC Leaflet No. 29b (1916)

'How to Obtain Popular Control over Foreign Policy', UDC Leaflet No. 46b (1918)

'Mr. Ponsonby's Opinions, 1908–1916',

'The Intellectuals and the War', *The Socialist Review* (January–March 1916)

'The Crank', (1916) reprinted as 'The Crank written in 1916' (1940)

'First Class Lies', *The UDC* (September 1917)

'Changing Opinion', *The UDC* (March 1918)

'The Sanction Behind a League of Nations', *War and Peace* (September 1918)

'A Conflict of Opinion: A Discussion on the Failure of the Church' (1919)

'The Covenant of the League of Nations; An Analysis with Full Text', UDC Pamphlet No. 41a (1920)

'Control of Foreign Policy, Labour's Programme', Labour Party (1921)

'Religion in Politics' (1921)

'The Case for the Russian Treaties', *Contemporary Review* (December 1924)

'A Plea for Bushy Whiskers', *The Empire Review* (February 1925)

'Disarmament by Example', speech by Arthur Ponsonby in the House of Commons, 17 March 1927, No More War Movement (1927)

'Disarmament by Example', *Contemporary Review* (December 1927)

'Disarmament by Example', *R.I.I. Affairs* (July 1928), an address given 22 May 1928

'Any Daughter (Modern) to Any Father', *The Listener* (6 February 1929)

'To an Old Public School Friend', *The Listener* (23 November 1932)

'Disarmament. A Discussion', Day to Day Pamphlets No. 14 (1932)

'Will Parliamentary Government Survive?', *Contemporary Review* (February 1933)

'What shall I do about War?', address at Guildhouse (November 1933)

'Collective Security and Regional Pacts; a Discussion between Wickham Steed and Lord Ponsonby', *The Listener* (16 February 1938)

'The Present Outlook', *The Nineteenth Century and After* (May 1938)

'Peace Service Handbook', PPU (1939) (This PPU production is A.P.'s Peace Book)

'War Without End', *Fortnightly Review* (November 1939)

with E.D. Morel, 'Peace Overtures and their Rejection, Dec 1916–March 1918', UDC Pamphlets no. 27a, 28a (1918)

Ponsonby was a regular contributor to the following papers and journals:
Manchester Guardian, *The Daily Herald*, *Reynolds News*, *The Labour Leader*, *Forward*, *The Nation*, *The UDC* and *Foreign Affairs*, *Common Sense*, *The Friend*, *The Pioneer*, *War and Peace*.

4. Other Manuscript Sources

Bodleian Library. Murray; Denman; Dickinson; Bryce; Harcourt; Asquith; Dawson and Hammond Papers
British Library School of Economics and Political Science (L.S.E.). Lansbury; Webb; Morel; Courtney and Dalton Papers
King's College Library, Cambridge. G.L. Dickinson Papers
Labour Party Headquarters. Joint International Committee Minutes, 1919–23; Advisory Committee on International Questions, Minutes and Agenda
Peace Pledge Union. Annual Reports and Sponsors' Meetings Minute Books
Borthwick Institute, York. Gore and Halifax Papers
Sussex University Library. Woolf Papers
British Museum. Herbert Gladstone; Knollys and Campbell-Bannerman Papers
Newcastle University Library. Trevelyan Papers
Rhodes House Library, Oxford. C.R. Buxton Papers
Redfern Library, McGill University, Montreal. Noel-Buxton Papers
Public Record Office. MacDonald Papers; F.O. 370, 371, 800; Cab 23, 24
Sheffield City Library. Minutes of Sheffield Trades and Labour Council
BBC Written Archives, Cavesham, Reading, Berks.
Hull University Library. Papers of the UDC

I have also been sent Ponsonby items from the Bertrand Russell and Vera Brittain Papers at McMaster University, Hamilton, Ontario; the N. Angell Papers at Ball State University, Muncie, Indiana; the Lady Ottoline Morrell Papers at University of Texas, Irving, Texas; and the Royal Archives, Windsor Castle, Berkshire

5. Other Sources

Titles of particular interest are annotated accordingly.

Andrew, C. (1986) *Her Majesty's Secret Service: The Making of the British Intelligence Community*, New York. Includes the latest developments in the Zinoviev Letter case
Barnes, H.E. (1926) *The Genesis of the World War*, New York
Bennett, Y. (1985) 'Testament of a Minority in Wartime: The Peace Pledge Union and Vera Brittain, 1939–1945', PhD thesis, McMaster University, Hamilton, Ontario. Fills a longstanding gap on the history of the Peace Pledge Union
Brailsford, H.M. (1909) 'The Control of Foreign Affairs: A Proposal', *English Review*, 4 (Dec), pp. 122–31
Brockway, Fenner (1947) *Socialism over Sixty Years: The Life of Jowett of Bradford*, London
Buxton, Noel (1912) 'Diplomacy and Parliament', *The Nineteenth Century and After*, LXXI (Apr), pp. 632–42

Callcott (Dundas), Maria (1835, etc.) *Little Arthur's History of England*, London
Ceadel, M. (1979) 'The "King and Country" Debate', *Historical Journal*, 22, 2
— (1980) *Pacifism in Britain, 1914–1945* (Oxford). Particularly useful on the peace movement
Cline, C.A. (1980) *E.D. Morel, 1873–1924: The Strategies of Protest*, Belfast
Conwell-Evans, T.P. (1932) *Foreign Policy from a Back Bench, 1904–18: A study based on the papers of Lord Noel-Buxton*, Oxford
Craig, Gordon A. (1953) 'The British Foreign Office from Grey to Austen Chamberlain' in G.A. Craig and F. Gilbert (eds.), *The Diplomats, 1919–1939*, Princeton, NJ, pp. 15–48
Davie, Michael (ed.) (1976) *The Diaries of Evelyn Waugh*, London
Dickinson, G.L. (1926) *The International Anarchy 1904–1914*, London
Dubin, M.D. (1970) 'Toward the Concept of Collective Security: The Bryce Group's "Proposals for the Avoidance of War" 1914–1917', *International Organization*, XXIV/2 (Spring), pp. 288–318
Eyck, F. (1982) *G.P. Gooch: A Study in History and Politics*, London
Fay, S.B. (1928) *The Origins of the First World War*, New York
Fieldhouse, H. Noel (1966) 'Noel Buxton and A.J.P. Taylor's "The Trouble Makers"' in M. Gilbert (ed.) *A Century of Conflict 1850–1950: Essays for A.J.P. Taylor*, London, pp. 175–98
— (1971) 'The Anglo German War of 1939–42: Some Movements to End it by a Negotiated Peace', *Proceedings of the Royal Society of Canada*, pp. 285–312.
Gooch, G.P. (1920) *Life of Lord Courtney*, London
— (1927) *Recent Revelations in European Diplomacy*, London
Gooch, G.P. and Temperley, H.W.V. (eds.) (1926–1938) *British Documents on the Origins of the War, 1898–1914*, 11 vols, London.
Gordon, M.R. (1969) *Conflict and Consensus in Labour's Foreign Policy*, Stamford, Calif.
Gorodetsky, G. (1977) *The Precarious Peace*, Cambridge
Greene, Gwendolen (ed.) (1928) *Friedrich von Hügel: Letters to a Niece*, London
Hammond, J.L. and B. (1911) *The Village Labourer, 1760–1832*, London
Hazlehurst, C. (1971) *Politicians at War, July 1914–May 1915*, London
Hazlehurst, C. and Woodland, C. (1974) *A Guide to the Papers of British Cabinet Ministers, 1900–1951*, London
Hirst, F.W. (ed.) (1926) *A.G.C. Harvey, A Memoir*, London
Howard, M. (1978) *War and the Liberal Conscience*, London.
Jefferson, George (1982) *Edward Garnett: A Life in Literature*, London
Jenkins, Roy (1954) *Mr Balfour's Poodle*, London
Jervis, S.A. (1967) 'Evelyn Waugh, Vile Bodies and the Younger Generation', *South Atlantic Quarterly*, pp. 440–8
Jones, Ray (1971) *The Nineteenth Century Foreign Office: An Administrative History*, London
— (1981) 'The Social Structure of the British Diplomatic Service, 1815–1914', *Histoire sociale*, XIV (May), pp. 49–66
Jowett, F.W. (1909) *What is the Use of Parliament*, London
Koss, S. (1970) *Sir John Brunner, Radical Plutocrat*, Cambridge
Leventhal, F.M. (1985) *The Last Dissenter*, Oxford
Linck Jr., C.E. and Davis, R.M. (1969) 'The Bright Young People in Vile Bodies', *Papers in Language and Literature* pp. 80–90

Lloyd George, D. (1933) *War Memoirs*, 6 vols, London

Loreburn, Lord (1919) *How the War Came*, London

Lutz, Hermann (1928) *Lord Grey and the World War*, London

— (1931) *Eyre Crowe der Böse Geist des Foreign Office*, Stuttgart

McKibbon, R. (1974) *The Evolution of the Labour Party, 1910–1924*, Oxford

Marquand, D. (1977) *Ramsay MacDonald*, London

Marrin, A. (1979) *Sir Norman Angell*, Boston

Massingham, H.W. (1900) 'The Philosophy of a Saint', *Contemporary Review*, 78 (Dec), pp. 809–20

Masterman, L.B. (1939) *C.F.G. Masterman*, London

Mayer, Arno J. (1967) 'Domestic Causes of the First World War' in H. Krieger and F. Stern (eds.), *The Responsibility of Power: Historical Essays in Honour of Hajo Holborn*, New York, pp. 286–300

Morrell, Philip (1912) 'The Control of Foreign Affairs: The Need for a Parliamentary Committee', *Contemporary Review* (Nov) pp. 659–67

Morris, A.J.A. (1972), *Radicalism Against War, 1906–1914*, Totowa, NJ

— (1982) *Sir Charles Trevelyan, 1870–1958. Portrait of a Radical*, Belfast

Murray, Gilbert (1915) *The Foreign Policy of Sir Edward Grey, 1906–1915*, London

— (1916) 'Control of Foreign Policy', *Contemporary Review* (Jan), pp. 180–92

Nicholson, H. (1939) *Diplomacy*, London

— (1954) *The Evolution of Diplomatic Method*, London

Nightingale, Robert (1930) 'The Personnel of the British Foreign Office and Diplomatic Service, 1851–1929', *American Political Science Review*, XXIV, pp. 310–31

Pimlott, Ben (1985) *Hugh Dalton*, London. Of importance in dealing, from Ponsonby's perspective, with Labour's apostasy in the 1930s

Robbins, K.G. (1967) 'Lord Bryce and the First World War', *Historical Journal*, X, 2, pp. 255–78

— (1971) *Sir Edward Grey*, London

— (1976) *The Abolition of War: the 'Peace Movement' in Britain, 1914–1919*, Cardiff.

Rose, Norman (1978) *Vansittart: Study of a Diplomat*, London

Sanders, M. and Taylor, P.M. (1982) *British Propaganda During the First World War, 1914–1918*, London

Sharp, A.J. (1976) 'The Foreign Office in Eclipse, 1919–1922', *History*, 61, pp. 198–218

Steiner, Zara S. (1969) *The Foreign Office and Foreign Policy, 1898–1902*, Cambridge

Steiner, Z. and Dockrill, M. (1974) 'The Foreign Office Reforms, 1919–1921', *Historical Journal*, 17, pp. 131–56

Swartz, M. (1971) *The Union of Democratic Control in British Politics during the First World War*, Oxford.

Swift MacNeill, T.G. (1911) 'Foreign Policy and Parliamentary Control', *Fortnightly Review*, 95 (Jan), pp. 209–20

Sykes, Christopher (1975) *Evelyn Waugh*, London

Taylor, A.J.P. (1965) *English History*, Oxford

— (1969 edn; originally pub. 1957) *The Troublemakers: Dissent and Foreign Policy 1792–1939*, London.

Young, Nigel (1980) Review of *Pacifism in Britain*, *New Society* (28 Sept)

INDEX